ON THE PUBLIC AGENDA

To the people of Iraq—and a quick end to their long nightmare.

ON THE PUBLIC AGENDA

Essays for Change

John Spritzler and David Stratman

BLACK
ROSE
BOOKS

Montreal/New York/London

Black Rose Books No. II336

National Library of Canada Cataloguing in Publication Data

Spritzler, John

On the public agenda : essays for change / John Spritzler, David Stratman

Includes bibliographical references and index.

ISBN: 1-55164-271-9 (bound)   ISBN: 1-55164-270-0 (pbk.)

(alternative ISBNs 9781551642710 [bound]   9781551642703 [pbk.])

1. Social action. 2. Social problems. I. Stratman, David G. II. Title

HN65.S67 2005   361.2   C2004-907116-5

Cover design: Associés libres

BLACK ROSE BOOKS

C.P. 1258	2250 Military Road	99 Wallis Road
Succ. Place du Parc	Tonawanda, NY	London, E9 5LN
Montréal, H2X 4A7	14150	England
Canada	USA	UK

To order books:

In Canada: (phone) 1-800-565-9523 (fax) 1-800-221-9985
email: utpbooks@utpress.utoronto.ca

In United States: (phone) 1-800-283-3572 (fax) 1-651-917-6406

In the UK & Europe: (phone) 44 (0)20 8986-4854 (fax) 44 (0)20 8533-5821
email: order@centralbooks.com

Our Web Site address: http://www.web.net/blackrosebooks

Printed in Canada

TABLE of CONTENTS

INTRODUCTION

WITH THE DECLARATION OF THE WAR ON TERROR, the choices open to humanity have considerably narrowed. We must either accept a future of permanent war, or somehow we must dismantle the war-making National Security State and create a very different future.

For much of the 20th century, the world was caught between capitalism and Communism, neither of which offered a promising future to the world's people. The dark presence of Communism seemed to give credibility to Margaret Thatcher's assertion that "There Is No Alternative" ("TINA") to capitalism.

Then Communism collapsed in Eastern Europe and the Soviet Union, leaving the world stage to a triumphant capitalism. Ironically, with the collapse of Communism people started wondering whether capitalism, with its savage laws of profit and loss, competition and inequality, should be forever permitted to govern our lives. If Communism could collapse, perhaps capitalism could also be pushed into its grave.

Soon many millions of people—at demonstrations against the World Trade Organization (WTO) in Seattle in 2000 and later in Genoa and Davos, in uprisings in Argentina and Bolivia and Paraguay, in popular movements in Venezuela and Brazil, in two general strikes in Italy and one in Spain in 2002, in the largest labor upheavals in China since 1949—began openly to question capitalism and to seek a revolutionary alternative. Capitalism, in its unrestrained guise of "neoliberalism" and "globalization," had been on the offensive for thirty years, and for thirty years it had wreaked havoc in the societies in which it had been unleashed. Now it was being challenged by movements no longer under the thumb of Communism.

This book of essays is part of the global quest for a new world. It looks in depth at the War on Terror and other current issues with a relentless commitment to view these issues in terms of the class war and the necessity and possibility of revolution against capitalism.

What distinguishes this book is that it shows the revolutionary transformation of society to be eminently possible. Its starting point is a belief that the source of a new world is already here before our eyes. The source of revolution is not to be found in texts of Marx or Lenin or in inevitable laws beyond human control. It is rather to be found in people's everyday lives. As David Stratman explained in his "Remarks to the Community Church of Boston," his confidence that we can change the world comes from the fact that this is what most people want:

> We know that capitalism is the most dynamic social system in history. The fundamental principle of capitalism is competition, the idea of dog-eat-dog. The logic of capitalism is that this world should be a loveless and savage place; we should each be trying to screw each other all the time. But you can look around and see that this is not so. You can look around and see that most people, in the little piece of the world that they feel they can control—which might just be with their wife or husband or students or colleagues or friends—most people try to create relationships the opposite of capitalism. Most people try to create relations based on love and trust and mutual respect. We may not get very far in creating these relationships, but to the extent that any of us have any fully human relationships in our lives, we have created them in the face of a culture that is profoundly hostile to them.
>
> This means, I think, that most people are already engaged in a struggle against capitalism in their everyday lives. The revolutionary movement already exists. Our job is to make that revolutionary movement more aware of itself, so that it can succeed in its goals.

The following essays take this fundamental insight—that most people are already engaged in a struggle against capitalism and for a better world—and apply it as an analytical tool and a guide to action, to build a revolutionary movement capable of challenging the goals, values, plans, policies, and power of capitalism with the values, goals, aspirations, and power of ordinary working people.

One further note about the historical context in which we present these essays. In our view, capitalism and Communism share fundamental similarities which are themselves no accident. Both these undemocratic systems are based on the same paradigm of human and social development, in which economic development is the basis of human development in a history driven by economic forces beyond human control. In this view of history, ordinary people are merely the passive victims or beneficiaries of the actions of elites. Clearly democracy cannot be based on this model of society.

If it is to succeed, the growing world movement for a new society needs an understanding of the role of ordinary people in society different from the capitalist and Communist views we have inherited, and a new paradigm of social transformation on which revolution can be based.

The essential elements of a new paradigm are that the struggle to change the world is the most human and most pervasive of activities; that most people have goals and values opposed to those of capitalism and Communism; that, far from being passive, most people are already engaged in a struggle to create a new society; that it is the irrepressible struggle of people to humanize the world, rather than the forces of economic or technological development, that drives history; and that ordinary people, rather than intellectuals or a revolutionary party, are the source of the idea of a new society, and of the values that should shape it.

These ideas are not really new, of course: they have underlain every revolutionary movement of the past and are already part of most people's understanding of the world. Our contribution in these essays is simply to articulate and validate what many have already thought, so that we may learn from each other and push the discussion forward.

The worldwide demonstrations against the Iraq war before it began illuminated the conflict between the values of billions of the world's people and the values of the war-making elites who govern in the U.S. and elsewhere. It is our hope that this book may help to clarify this conflict and give confidence to the world's people that it is they rather than the war-makers who can and should rule society.

John Spritzler and Dave Stratman

Part One

WAR, TERROR, *and* SOCIAL CONTROL

by John Spritzler

I.   THE "GOOD WAR" MYTH OF WORLD WAR II

THE "GOOD WAR" STORY OF WORLD WAR II is a Big Lie, used today by the likes of George W. Bush and John F. Kerry to create a mind set in which America's rulers are the good guys who, despite all of their faults and foibles, are saving the world from the really, really bad guys. FDR told Americans that the war was about fighting fascism and tyranny. But FDR lied about his real war objectives, just as Hitler lied to the Germans and Japanese militarists lied to the Japanese people to get them to fight the bloodiest war in history.

War: An Instrument Of Social Control

Franklin Roosevelt, Adolf Hitler and the Japanese militarists all faced the same problem in the years leading up to the war. Their own working class populations were growing increasingly revolutionary. The elite rulers of these nations were terrified that they were losing control. In the United States the governors of numerous states were forced to call out the National Guard and Federal troops, including infantry and machine gun units, to put down enormous strikes (in some cases general strikes) by textile workers, steel workers, auto workers, coal miners, and a host of others.

When a longshoremen's strike in 1934 led to a general strike in San Francisco of 130,000 workers, which spread to Oakland and then up the Pacific Coast, the *Los Angeles Times* wrote: "The situation in San Francisco is not correctly described by the phrase 'general strike.' What is actually in progress there is an insurrection, a Communist-inspired and led revolt against organized government. There is but one thing to be done—put down the revolt with any force necessary." FDR's National Recovery Administration chief, General Hugh S. Johnson, went to San Francisco and declared the general strike a "menace to the government" and a "civil war."[1]

In the same year 325,000 textile workers, many of them women, used "flying squadrons" to spread their strike throughout the South from mill to mill, often battling guards, entering the mills, unbelting machinery and fighting non-strikers. So alarmed was *The New York Times* that it warned, "The grave danger of the situation is that it will get completely out of the hands of the leaders...The growing mass character of the picketing operations is rapidly assuming the appearance of military efficiency and precision and is something entirely new in the history of American labor struggles. Observers...declared that if the mass drive continued to gain momentum at the speed at which it was moving today, it will be well nigh impossible to stop it without a similarly organized opposition with all the implications such an attempt would entail."[2] Declaring martial law, South Carolina's governor said that a "state of insurrection" existed. When the strike spread to New England, Governor Green of Rhode Island declared that, "there is a Communist uprising and not a textile strike in Rhode Island," and then declared a state of insurrection.[3] Georgia Governor Eugene Talmadge declared martial law. National Guardsmen began mass arrests of flying squadrons and held them without charge in a concentration camp where Germans had been held during WWI. "By September 19 the death toll in the South had reached thirteen."[4]

Events like these hit all parts of the nation, and this was just the warm up to the wave of sit-down strikes in 1936-7 during which 10,000 workers occupied GM's Flint, Michigan plant with help from thousands of workers who traveled hundreds of miles to join them. Following that strike, Chrysler faced 6,000 sit-downers with 50,000 picketers outside its plants and the *New York Times* felt obliged to warn business and government leaders, "It is generally feared that an attempt to evict the strikers with special deputies would lead to an inevitable large amount of bloodshed and the state of armed insurrection."[5]

Big business was even afraid that the electoral system, which was supposed to ensure that Americans would forsake mass direct action for reliance on tame and trusted politicians, was about to fail in this purpose. Louisiana's governor, Huey Long, had seven million followers who wanted a dramatic redistribution of wealth and viewed FDR as an obstacle. Most alarmingly, the Democratic Party in California was captured in 1934 by a radical mass movement which wanted the state to seize land and factories so that unemployed people could operate them in a moneyless network of production for need, not profit. Their leader, Upton Sinclair, a long-time socialist, swept away his opponents and won the Democratic Party primary, making him its candidate for Governor. He was only defeated in the gubernatorial election by an unprecedented smear campaign launched jointly by liberal and conservative California newspapers. But the handwriting was on the wall.

FDR tried to control the rebellion with New Deal promises. But it didn't work. His famous Wagner Act of 1935, for example, tried to pacify workers by making unions legal. The Act also locked unions into an elaborate system of government regulations designed to ensure that conservative labor leaders would be able to control their unruly rank-and-file. But workers developed the sit-down tactic in the next two years precisely to keep control in their own hands.

Ruling elites have known for centuries that when revolution threatens at home desperate measures are required, and the most effective one is to go to war. For example, on the eve of the Russo–Japanese War in 1904 the Russian Czar's interior minister, Vyacheslav Plehve, declared, "What this country needs is a short victorious war to stem the tide of revolution."[6] This is the only way to understand the little-known truth about how FDR's advisors reacted to the news of the Japanese attack on Pearl Harbor. Secretary of War Stimson's diary entry at 2 p.m., December 7, written after learning from the President about the attack on Pearl Harbor, reads: "Now the Japs have solved the whole thing by attacking us directly in Hawaii...My first feeling was of relief that the indecision was over and that a crisis had come in a way which would unite all our people."[7] Not shock, but relief. Relief that war would finally force American workers to unite with instead of rebel against America's rulers.

People like FDR and Stimson fully appreciated that the best way to rein in the growing insurrection they faced was to somehow get the United States into a war that would be perceived by Americans as a fight to the death between the entire population of the United States and the entire population of enemy foreign nations driven by satanically evil fanaticism. This way, American workers could be put on the defensive ideologically, by the assertion that it was unpatriotic for them to fight over class grievances or to pursue class aspirations when the country needed to unite (with its capitalist leaders) against the common enemy. For sophisticated upper class politicians like Roosevelt, this was simply Social Control 101.

Pretending To Fight Fascism

Roosevelt needed an enemy and fascism was the logical best choice. FDR certainly had no genuine desire to defeat fascism, however, or else he would have helped the Spanish working class in its fight to defend the Spanish Republic in the Spanish Civil War against the fascist coup attempt by General Franco in 1936. When FDR used a "moral embargo" and then got legislation passed to prevent American arms from getting to the Spanish workers in their fight against fascism, it was as clear as daylight that when the choice was between working class people or fascists coming to power, FDR was on the side of the fascists.

But fascism was an excellent pretend-enemy. Except for one problem. Workers and peasants in Germany and Japan opposed their fascist rulers. A real fight against fascism would have meant an alliance between the American working class and the German and Japanese working classes against all of their upper class rulers. After all, the rulers of all three nations shared the same anti-working class aims even if they didn't all use exactly the same methods of subjugating workers and peasants. (Indeed, many American bankers and industrialists, most famously Henry Ford and Joseph Kennedy, but others as well, were actually pro-Nazi and some even aided the Nazis substantially during the war. Roosevelt placed many of these individuals in high government positions during the war. He made Joseph Kennedy Ambassador to London. And he made GM President William S. Knudsen head of the powerful Office of Production Management (OPM) formed in 1941 even though Knudsen had told reporters that "Germany was the miracle of the twentieth century" when he returned from a meeting in October of 1933 with top Nazi Hermann Göring to establish friendly business ties with the regime which had by then imprisoned all of Germany's labor leaders and political opponents.[8] If fighting fascism had been FDR's real aim this would be paradoxical. But the paradox disappears when we understand that the "Good War" was based on a Big Lie. Since controlling the American working class was the true aim, it was a matter of little account to FDR how somebody like Joseph Kennedy or William Knudsen felt about the Nazis as long as their class loyalty was unquestioned.)

To solve this problem (of so many Germans and Japanese being anti-fascist), FDR made sure that Americans were never informed about the truth of the anti-fascist stance of German and Japanese workers and peasants, or the extreme measures used by their governments to control them, such as the "Thought Police" in Japan and the 165 miniature concentration camps set up next to German factories for workers guilty of "only a minor infraction, a lateness, an unjustified absence or an angry word."[9]

Another problem for FDR was that Americans were overwhelmingly opposed to getting into another war after seeing how horrible the First World War was, and how it mainly enriched arms dealers and war profiteers at the expense of ordinary people. Franklin ("Day of Infamy") Roosevelt's solution to this problem was to secretly scheme to get the Japanese to attack the United States. FDR embargoed U.S. oil for Japan and at the same time made it clear to the Japanese government that if they tried to take oil from the only other source—British or Dutch Asian colonies—the U.S. would consider it an act of war against itself. This had the intended effect of making the Japanese attack the United States. Far from being a shocking surprise, Pearl Harbor was the long awaited and eagerly sought solution to the elite's most pressing problem—the American working class. This is why Secretary of War Stimson felt so much "relief" when Japan finally attacked. Pearl Harbor got the U.S. into the war. But how would FDR fight it?

FDR's wartime strategy was not geared to defeating fascism; it was aimed at 1) ensuring that Americans would believe they faced entire populations of Germans and Japanese who, from the lowliest peasant to the Chancellor or Emperor, were fanatical fascists and 2) making sure that workers and peasants in Asia or Europe would never succeed in overthrowing their upper-class rulers.

FDR's Strange Pacific Strategy

In the Pacific, FDR had to choose between a strategy of fighting the Japanese in China in order to secure China as a staging area for an attack on Japan, or one of abandoning China to the Japanese occupying army and fighting the Japanese in bloody battles for islands like Iwo Jima and Guadalcanal to use them as a staging area instead. FDR's choice of strategy reveals his true war objectives, but at the time it simply perplexed his military advisors who thought the object of the war was to defeat fascism.

Not only was China closer to Japan and more suited as a staging area, but it would have been infinitely easier to defeat the Japanese army in China than on the isolated Pacific Islands. In China there was a full-fledged peasant revolution in progress with Chinese Communist Party leadership. The Japanese army was made up of peasants who hated their viciously anti-peasant Samurai officers. Japanese peasant soldiers felt more sympathy for revolutionary Chinese peasants like themselves than they did for their officers or the Emperor whom they reviled. Many Japanese soldiers after being captured by the Chinese engaged in efforts to persuade their fellows to switch their loyalty. The Japanese government was well aware of this. As reported in the August 13, 2003 issue of *The Japan Times*, "The army's staff headquarters was considering pulling troops out [of China] around this time due to the decline in their will to fight." On the little, isolated Pacific Islands occupied by the Japanese, however, there was no peasant revolution happening and the Japanese soldiers knew that they would be killed by their own officers if they didn't fight to the death against the Americans.

So what did FDR do? In China he backed Chiang Kai-shek, the chief enemy of the peasants. Chiang Kai-shek had an army of horribly mistreated conscripts which he used only to fight the Communists and never the Japanese. U.S. military leaders wanted to back the Communists, who had an army with extremely high morale and popular support that was fighting the Japanese very successfully. But FDR refused. He insisted on fighting the Japanese on islands like Iwo Jima where there would be no chance of international working class solidarity ideas infecting American troops and getting back to the home front, and where the bloodthirsty fighting would give American newspapers and Hollywood all they needed to whip up the flames of racism and nationalism, which (for those very few in the know) was a central purpose of the war. No matter that thousands of Americans would die unnecessarily in this way and that the war would be greatly extended in duration. (The excuse that FDR didn't want to help the peasants because he opposed communist dictatorships doesn't hold water, since FDR allied with and indeed publicly praised Stalin who was by this time well known to be a ruthless dictator. Stalin also backed Chiang Kai-shek and never helped the Chinese Communists for the same reasons that motivated FDR.)

FDR's Strange European Strategy

In Europe FDR did the same thing. An organization of 7,000 people secretly opposed to fascism and still in positions of some responsibility in Germany had made several assassination attempts on Hitler. A high-ranking German intelligence officer, Admiral Canaris, was part of this resistance. He "leaked vital intelligence to the British and Americans, including the German army's order of battle, an invaluable insight into the Wehrmacht's intentions." And he offered "the support of General Rommel for a bloodless conquest of the western front if the Anglo-Americans would give the slightest sign of a disposition for an armistice...The British reply: there was no alternative to unconditional surrender."[10]

Unconditional surrender was FDR's way of ensuring that Americans would perceive the war in Europe as a fight-to-the-death war against the entire German population, and that the war would drag out for a longer time than necessary. American military leaders were as baffled by FDR's unconditional surrender strategy as they were by his Pacific strategy. When Roosevelt made unconditional surrender Allied policy, the reaction of military leaders was universally negative because they knew it was disastrous from a military point of view. General Eisenhower thought it would do nothing but cost American lives, and said, "If you were given two choices, one to mount a scaffold, the other to charge twenty bayonets, you might as well charge twenty bayonets." Major General Ira C. Eaker, commander of the U.S. Eighth Air Force wrote: "Everybody I knew at the time when they heard this [unconditional surrender] said: 'How stupid can you be?' All the soldiers and the airmen who were fighting this war wanted the Germans to quit tomorrow. A child knew once you said this to the Germans, they were going to fight to the last man. There wasn't a man who was actually fighting in the war whom I ever met who didn't think this was about as stupid an operation as you could find."[11]

In all of Europe the Allies's main concern was to prevent the popular Resistance movements of workers and peasants from coming to power. Americans arrested and disarmed the Italian resistance (Partisans) when they took Rome, and even made a radio broadcast for Nazi ears saying that they would not aid the Resistance forces in the north of Italy, who were the only ones directly fighting the Nazis. The result, as expected, was that the Nazis used this information to attack and wipe out the Italian resistance force in the North.

In Greece the same story played out when, in 1944, the Greek Resistance organization, EAM, whose labor organization "controlled the entire [Greek] working class and helped lead strikes in the occupied territories throughout the war,"[12] announced a general strike for December 4th. On December 5, Churchill sent General Scobie these instructions:

> Do not hesitate to fire at any armed male in Athens who assails the British authority...it would be well of course if your commands were reinforced by the authority of some Greek Government...Do not however hesitate to act as if you were in a conquered city where a local rebellion is in progress.[13]

On December 13, Roosevelt wired Churchill that "I regard my role in this matter as that of a loyal friend and ally whose one desire is to be of any help possible in the circumstances."[14]

From the beginning of the war until 1944 Roosevelt officially backed the French Nazi collaborationist Vichy government led by Marshal Henri Petain, a government that worked hand-in-glove with the Nazis, enforcing the anti-Semitic laws, rounding up Jews for the Nazi death camps and executing members of the French Resistance as directed by the Nazis. Roosevelt's top advisors were far more afraid of the French people than they were of the Nazis or their puppet Vichy government. In May, 1943, Secretary of State Hull voiced the problem he had with supporting the Resistance leader, Charles DeGaulle: "The issue at stake is not only the success of our future military operations, but the very future of France itself. DeGaulle has permitted to come under his umbrella all the most radical elements in France."[15] Even "as late as February 1944, [FDR's Chief of Staff Admiral] Leahy advocated leaving [Vichy's Marshall] Petain as head of France after D-Day."[16]

And in Yugoslavia the U.S. backed the Chetniks. The Chetniks were led by King Peter's strongman and Minister of War, General Draza Mihailovic. They were discredited as "Resistance" fighters for "supplying information on the Partisans [Communist Resistance fighters led by Josip Broz Tito] to the Germans" and because they "were preoccupied with fighting and containing Tito's growing power."[17] Tito's resistance fighters were the only ones who fought the Nazis, but the U.S. went out of its way to prevent them from getting arms.

The Allies Bombed Civilians To Destroy International Working Class Solidarity

Many people have wondered why FDR, and later Truman, committed mass murder of German and Japanese civilians by using conventional bombs and later atomic bombs to deliberately create firestorms to kill tens of thousands of people when there was no particular military purpose. That there was no military rationale has become far less controversial among those who have seriously studied the question. All of the military leaders in a position to know have weighed in on the atom bomb question and said very clearly that there was no need to drop those weapons whatsoever. This includes Major General Curtis LeMay, commander of the Twenty-First Bomber Command responsible for destroying Japan's military targets; Admiral William Leahy; General Douglas MacArthur, Supreme Commander of the Allied Forces in the South West Pacific Area (including Japan) during the war; and Dwight Eisenhower. For example, General MacArthur stated in a press conference in 1963: "We did not need the atomic bomb against Japan."[18] MacArthur later wrote that by June 1945: "My staff was unanimous in believing Japan was on the point of collapse and surrender. I even directed that plans be drawn 'for a possible peaceful occupation' [of Japan] without further military operations."[19]

Not even the "Cold War" excuse for using the atom bombs holds up. According to this theory it was necessary to drop the atom bombs in order to get a fast Japanese surrender so that the Soviets wouldn't have time to get a foothold in Japan. But if a fast Japanese surrender had been the object, then the U.S. would have made it clear from the beginning that the Japanese Emperor would be allowed to remain on the throne, since this was the only issue delaying the Japanese decision to surrender. But, despite warnings about the significance of the point, Truman deliberately rejected advice to reassure the Japanese that their emperor would remain on the throne, even though that was the plan all along.

The "Good War" story of the war makes it impossible to understand why civilians were targeted so deliberately. But if we keep in mind the true upper class objectives of the war, it becomes much more clear. The mass murder of Germans and Japanese was an attempt to make Americans cheer the killing of ordinary people just like themselves but living in a foreign country. It was an attempt to completely destroy the very notion of international working class solidarity.

The "War On Terror" Really Is Like WWII

The warmongers of today need the "Good War" mythology to remain firmly in people's minds so they can embed their "War on Terror" into its powerful story line that confers so much legitimacy on American rulers and their motivations. That's why they keep producing movies and TV shows about the Second World War. We can turn this strategy around by using the truth of World War II to expose the reality of the "War on Terror."

The "War on Terror" really is like World War II, just as George W. Bush and John Kerry keep telling us. Like World War II the "War on Terror" is based on a Big Lie. Like WWII it is an attempt by elite rulers to frighten and control people and manipulate them into cheering for the mass murder of innocent people in foreign lands. And like WWII it is being used to prevent us from making a more equal and democratic world.

Notes

1. Jeremy Brecher, *Strike*, South End Press, Boston, Massachusetts, 1997, p. 174, pp. 169-74.
2. *Ibid.*, pp. 188-90.
3. *Ibid.*, pp. 188-90.
4. *Ibid.*, pp. 190-92.
5. NYT, March 19, 1937, cited in Brecher, p. 227.
6. Lebow, R.N., *Between Peace and War*, 1981, Baltimore: John's Hopkins University Press.
7. Charles A. Beard, *President Roosevelt and the Coming Of The War: 1941*, New Haven, Yale University Press 1948, p. 419.
8. Charles Higham, *Trading With The Enemy*, Dell Publishing Co., New York, 1983, p. 184.
9. Sergio Bologna, *Nazism and the Working Class—1933-93*, [paper presented at the Milan Camera del Lavoro, 3 June 1993], p. 49.
10. Thomas Fleming, *The New Dealers' War: Franklin D. Roosevelt and The War Within World War II*, Basic Books (Perseus Books Group), New York, 2001, pp. 373-4.
11. *Ibid.*, pp. 175.
12. Gabriel Kolko, *The Politics of War: The World and United States Foreign Policy, 1943-1945*, Pantheon Books, New York, 1968, 1990, p. 173.
13. *Ibid.*, p. 188.
14. *Ibid.*, p. 190.
15. *Ibid.*, p. 70.
16. *Ibid.*, p. 68-9.
17. *Ibid.*, p. 131.
18. *New York Times*, 21 August, 1963, p. 30.
19. Douglas MacArthur, *Reminiscences*, McGraw Hill Book Company, New York, 1964, p.260.

by David Stratman

I.   IS IT REALLY A 'WAR AGAINST TERRORISM?'

IN THE WAKE OF THE HORRIFIC EVENTS OF SEPTEMBER 11 our political leaders declared a "war on terrorism" which they claim will last "for fifty years" and may include as many as 60 countries as enemies. President Bush's $379 billion Pentagon budget includes $48 billion for fighting terrorism.

Why would the government launch such a vast undertaking? Nothing is as it seems in this war. The government is lying about just about everything. Beneath the rhetoric about terrorism and "the clash of civilizations," their real goals are very different and have more to do with controlling the American people and working people around the world than they have with a real strategy to fight terrorism.

What is the U.S. government really trying to accomplish? Three things:

1) ratchet up social control in the U.S. to dramatic new levels;

2) project military power more aggressively to places around the globe where elite power is threatened;

3) establish a permanent U.S. military presence in Central Asia, to secure that region's vast resources—read "oil"—for U.S. needs.

Of these goals, number one is the most important. But since the other two are more easily explained, let's look at them first.

Playing "The Great Game" For Oil

For more than a century Afghanistan was the object of the "Great Game" played by the British Empire and Russia for control of this crossroads of Asia. When it recruited and armed the mujahadeen in Afghanistan to attack Russian invaders in 1979, the U.S. became a key player in the game.

Afghanistan has even more importance now than it did in the nineteenth century. Central Asia and the Caspian region hold the greatest proven reserves of oil and gas in the world after Saudi Arabia—from 60 to as many as 200 billion barrels of oil and 236 trillion cubic feet of natural gas, according to John Maresca, Vice President of UNOCAL Corporation, in Congressional testimony of 2/12/98. The difficulty is getting these vast reserves to market. Afghanistan is the best route for an oil pipeline to deliver these products. The chief obstacle to construction of the pipeline has been political instability: "Construction of the pipeline...in

Afghanistan could not begin until a recognized government is in place that has the confidence of governments, lenders, and our company."

The U.S. media have of course kept mum about the oil pipeline, lest Americans suspect that the real goals of the government in this war are not as pure as it claims.

Projecting U.S. Power

The ferocious bombing of Afghanistan, complete with cluster bombs and 15,000 pound "daisy cutters," the largest non-nuclear device in the U.S. arsenal, provided an awesome display of the military might of the U.S. elite and an object lesson to any country on Earth that may have ideas about bucking the New World Order. The message is pretty clear: the U.S. has unchecked, unmatchable firepower. Get out of line and you will get a taste of what Afghanistan has got.

The U.S. is also using the war to project military power more aggressively to "hot spots" around the globe. Since there is no longer a credible Communist threat, the U.S. is using "Islamic terrorism" to legitimize global intervention on behalf of local elites and U.S. and European investors. The U.S. is filling the power vacuum in Central Asia left by the collapse of the Soviet Union, establishing military bases at key points in Uzbekistan and Tajikistan, as well as in Pakistan in South Asia, where there is growing instability. The U.S. has announced that these military emplacements are long-term. In mid-January the U.S. dispatched 660 troops to the Philippines, having supposedly discovered a link between Al Qaeda and Moslem rebels there. The government has also found supposed links between Al Qaeda and Colombian "terrorists," by which it means not the right-wing death squads which work hand-in-glove with the U.S.-supplied Columbian armed forces, but the peasant guerillas who have been fighting for over thirty years against the wealthy elite of Columbia.

War and Social Control

Near the end of the Cold War, as the Soviet Union was about to self-destruct, Boris Yeltsin made a very revealing comment to the U.S. government. He said, "We are going to do something very terrible to you. We are going to deprive you of an enemy."

What did he mean? The 50-year long Cold War had proved extremely useful for both the Soviet and U.S. elites. The "Soviet threat" justified gigantic military budgets and a world system of U.S. military bases. It legitimized U.S. attacks on popular revolutionary movements in Central America and Indochina and other places too numerous to mention and the installation of U.S. client regimes by the CIA in Iran and Guatemala and elsewhere. The "Soviet threat" gave much-needed cover to repression in the U.S. against militant trade unionists and against the early civil rights movement and the anti-Vietnam war movement. The Soviets, of course, used the "capitalist threat" in similar ways, to justify anti-democratic repression in Hungary and Poland and throughout Eastern Europe and in the Soviet Union itself. If the Cold War had not existed, Soviet and U.S. ruling elites would have had to invent it.

The use of war by ruling elites for social control is hardly new. In a recent article in *Le Monde*, Philip Golub says, "Indeed, every war has both a foreign and a domestic agenda; Aristotle [writing 2400 years ago] reminds us that a tyrant declares war 'to deny his subjects leisure and to impose on them the constant need for a leader.'"

The U.S. has needed a new Cold War to take the place of the Soviet threat for over ten years. Sure, the government tried to pump up Saddam Hussein as "worse than Hitler," but how seriously can you take an enemy which is defeated in a few weeks with fewer than 80 American battle deaths? The government tried to scare us with images of "rogue states" like North Korea, but North Korea is on life support. Not a very credible threat.

Why Now?

The "war on terrorism" represents a dramatic escalation of the strategy of social control undertaken by the corporate elite in 1972 as a counteroffensive to the revolutionary upsurge of the 1960s and early '70s. The essence of that strategy was to introduce insecurity and fear into people's lives at every possible point. Now the government has taken the extraordinary step of promising us "a generation of war." This war on terror is designed to terrorize us, with threats of a sinister enemy from whom we have to be protected, and to grant the government limitless powers to police us. If we raise our voice against the government, we ourselves are under threat of being identified as "with the terrorists."

It is important to see this new elite strategy in historical perspective. At the close of WWII, governments here and in Western Europe adopted a "welfare state" approach to pacify their citizens. While there were still great inequalities and injustices, the lot of most Americans improved. But what was expected to be a period of social peace erupted in the 1960s into a "revolution of rising expectations" here and abroad.

In 1972 the government and corporate leaders went on the counteroffensive, to lower expectations and tighten their hold on society. For 30 years now they have attacked people in every area of their lives in the name of "the free market" or "globalization."

In the last few years, however, this strategy has reached a dead end. Everywhere they look, the corporate and government elite see growing resistance to their rule:

- *The growing anti-capitalist, anti-"globalization" movement.* The mass demonstrations against the World Trade Organization that took place in Seattle, Quebec, Sweden, and Genoa represent the emergence of something which has not been seen for 100 years: an international anti- capitalist movement not controlled by Communists. The demonstrations are concrete expressions of the emerging agenda of people around the entire globe. It is true that this movement is an extremely mixed bag and has not formulated any clear answers or widely-accepted vision of what a new society to replace capitalism might be or how we might get there, but these are the questions with which it is concerned. As the depredations of capitalism on human society become ever more obvious, the tendency of the movement to pose revolutionary answers to these fundamental questions will only grow.

- *An end to belief in capitalism as a system.* Millions of people, perhaps billions worldwide, have lost their confidence in the future under capitalism. This ironically is an inevitable effect of thirty years of corporate attacks on people's security, but the rulers had no other choice. They had to lower people's expectations and they did. The absolute conditions of life for most of the world's people have worsened dramatically in the last decades, and their relative conditions, compared with the wealthier people in their own societies, have grown even worse. Loss of confidence in the system is very dangerous for elite rule; it leads people to search for alternatives.

- *A growing willingness to see the system as the problem.* Ten years ago, when the few of us who founded New Democracy began talking with each other, it struck us that the problems people were then experiencing—high unemployment, homelessness, health care priced out of reach—seemed to many people to be like the weather. No one was responsible for them, they were just there: "Shit Happens." Few people actually saw these things as functions of government or corporate policies. The political movements of the time mostly revolved around "identity politics"—gay rights, feminism, multiculturalism and such. Now this has changed. Millions are aware that the rich have stacked the deck. They see Enron executives cashing out and leaving their employees robbed of their life savings. They see the corporate hand behind attacks on health care and job security and public education.

This new restiveness isn't just in the U.S., of course. Capitalism has devastated wide swaths of the globe in these years. In Eastern Europe and the former Soviet Union, promises of a better life through capitalism have proved hollow. China has experienced decades of social dislocation and increasing inequalities which some experts believe presage uncontrollable social upheavals. The standard of living in Mexico and some other Central and South American countries is less than a third of what it was in 1982. In Argentina mass resistance to capitalist measures toppled four governments in December, 2001 and threatens to spread to other countries.

Where is all this leading? It's not clear. It is not that the elite expect revolutionary upheaval tomorrow, but they see the possibility of revolution growing larger on the horizon. The elite understand that they cannot continue to rule in the old way, with democratic liberties and a world at substantial peace. The "war on terrorism" is how they are preparing for the future in a society which is rapidly discovering that it has no future. This new elite strategy is an admission of profound, potentially terminal weakness.

The fact that capitalism has nothing to offer but endless war does not mean that the system will collapse of itself or that we necessarily will succeed in creating a new society. Revolutions are built on hope, not despair. We can only find our way to a new society if we make this our goal and if we have a path to take us there.

II. WHAT ELSE COULD HE HAVE DONE?

MANY AMERICANS SUPPORTED THE BOMBING OF Afghanistan because there simply didn't seem to be any other course our government could pursue after the terrorist attacks. But another course did lie open to the U.S., one that would have expressed our very best values, that would have been more effective in eliminating terrorism, strengthened support for the U.S. around the globe, and would not have caused the deaths of any innocent people.

Assuming that bin Laden is guilty as charged (and the government still hasn't presented proof beyond the questionable "confession video"), what our government should have done and still should do is to isolate bin Laden as a criminal guilty of crimes against humanity and then bring him to justice. How would it isolate him? By removing the real injustices caused or supported by the U.S. which bin Laden uses to rally support for himself.

When Bush made his address to the nation shortly after September 11, after accusing bin Laden of the crime (and offering hard evidence), he should have said something like this:

> The terrible attacks of Sept. 11 are crimes against humanity, and we are determined to bring the criminals to justice. We know, however, that these crimes had roots in other crimes that have been visited upon people in the Middle East and in Afghanistan. Therefore, I have ordered that this government will begin immediately to do the following things:
>
> 1) Rebuild Afghanistan, a country that has been devastated by years of war funded largely by the CIA. We will begin this effort by bringing sufficient food aid to the 5 to 7 million Afghans now reported to be near starvation.
>
> 2) Order Israel to abandon its illegal settlements on the West Bank and Gaza, with a timetable fixed for rapid and orderly withdrawal, and order Israel to dismantle the cruel apartheid regime that it has established over Palestinians. Since the U.S. finances the Israeli government to the tune of $3.5 billion per year, we are confident that it will accede to our demands.
>
> 3) Stop the sanctions against Iraq that have resulted in the deaths of over 500,000 children while doing nothing to dislodge Saddam Hussein. Offer food and medical aid to the people of Iraq.
>
> 4) Withdraw from the 'temporary' U.S. military bases in Saudi Arabia established during the Gulf War.

What would have been the effects of such a pronouncement by Bush? Billions of people the world over, including most Muslims, felt shock and revulsion at the September 11 terrorist attacks. If Bush had taken steps to alter U.S. policies in this way, bin Laden would have been thoroughly isolated and political support for terrorism—support without which terrorism cannot exist—would have dried up. Our chances of actually capturing bin Laden, which seem now to be slim, would have risen astronomically. Such steps undertaken by the U.S. government would have changed the character of our relationship to 1.2 billion Muslims and would have won the respect and admiration of people the world over—without the loss of a single human life or the dropping of a single bomb.

Unfortunately Bush chose a very different course. The massive bombing of Afghanistan has already resulted in about 5,000 civilian deaths—more than the number of innocents murdered on September 11—and the numbers continue to mount. Rather than isolating bin Laden, the U.S. has made him a hero to many Muslims, symbol of all the outrage felt at the injustices the U.S. continues to support. It remains to be seen whether bin Laden was killed in the massive bombing of Afghanistan or, as the U.S. military believes, he escaped. But it was clear from the start that whatever terrorist network exists, it is not a centralized, hierarchical structure which bin Laden somehow directed from deep in a cave. It is a widely dispersed group of small cells and networks acting largely independently of one another. It cannot be bombed out of existence.

As in so many other things, you have to wonder why the U.S. government chose a course that seems counterproductive to its declared goals. The answer is that the government's goals are not what the politicians claim:

1) Rather than destroy him, U.S. leaders wanted to build bin Laden as the leader of the Muslim resistance to the U.S., because he is the perfect enemy —a Saudi millionaire and religious fanatic with very reactionary political ideas who has long worked with the CIA (and, according to foreign news reports, met with the CIA as recently as this July, two months before Sept. 11). The U.S. wants as leader someone who can be depended upon not to build a democratic movement. From this point of view, bin Laden is our government's man.

2) The U.S. government wants Israel to continue its seizure of Palestinian lands and its vicious apartheid regime, because the ethnic hatred that Israeli and Arab elites foment is crucial to controlling Jews and Arabs.

3) The U.S. government wants Saddam Hussein to remain in power, to control Iraq and to be another reactionary "enemy." This is why U.S. forces did not go all the way to Baghdad in the Gulf War, and why Bush the Elder abandoned the Kurds and Iraqi opposition when they followed his encouragement and tried to overthrow Hussein. Saddam Hussein was a loyal U.S. lackey for many years, funded, armed, and supported by the U.S. He still serves U.S. interests well, being another unsavory "leader" of the opposition to U.S. policies in the region.

4) Establishing permanent "temporary" bases in Saudi Arabia was one of the goals of the Gulf War to begin with. The Gulf War was a phony war, like this one—phony in the sense that it was deliberately triggered by the U.S. The

U.S. gave an apparent green light to Saddam Hussein to invade Kuwait. When he fell for the bait, the U.S. used the invasion as a pretext to attack Iraq and achieve its policy goals in the region—cut Hussein down to size while building him as a leader of Arab popular opposition to the U.S. and Israel; establish a greater U.S. military presence in the oil-rich Middle East; overcome the "Vietnam syndrome" at home, trying to win a new generation of Americans to support war for America's self-interests.

A humane, pro-people, common-sense course did lay open to our government—if the politicians were actually trying to do what they claim. But they aren't. A truly democratic government in a democratic society could easily choose a humane and popular path and easily achieve all the goals that ordinary decent people agree upon. The solutions to these problems are not so hard. The difficulty is that the problems themselves serve elite power. That's why they exist and why the ruling elites will never solve them.

III.   INVENTING THE ENEMY

IT USED TO BE SAID DURING THE COLD WAR that, "If the Communist threat did not exist, the U.S. would have to invent it." The threat of nuclear war and the notion of a Communist (or capitalist) under every bed provided American and Soviet ruling elites excellent means to frighten and control their own citizens, justify enormous arms expenditures, and legitimize power projection abroad in the name of saving the world from Communism (or capitalism).

The same thing can be said now with a good deal more accuracy of political Islam, which the U.S. ruling class has been courting and nurturing since it first allied in 1947 with the House of Saud. The line of strategic relationships between the U.S. and political Islam runs through Saudi Arabia, Iran, Pakistan, Bosnia, Afghanistan, and now Iraq. If the U.S. did not actually invent modern political Islam, for over half a century it has encouraged it, promoted it, funded it, trained it, armed it, and furnished it with a political rationale for its existence.

U.S. ruling circles and reactionary forces acting in the name of Islam are in a co-dependent relationship: they need each other and work together covertly, even while they publicly attack each other in word and deed. This relationship is part of grand strategy, in which U.S. rulers are playing for the highest of stakes: their continued control over the American people, as well as elite domination of the world. Ruling elites in Muslim nations use political Islam and the threat from the U.S. to control their own people with an iron fist concealed in a glove of religious fervor.

The Perfect Enemy

Political Islam perfectly suits the needs of America's rulers for an enemy. The lands of the Middle East and Central Asia occupied by Muslims are the most strategically important regions of the world, sitting astride the world's largest reserves of oil and gas; the U.S. could never justify attacking these nations without first convincing Americans that Muslims need either to be attacked—because they are dangerous terrorists—or liberated. Seeing Islam as the enemy also supports Israel's role as an outpost of Western colonialism in the Middle East; according to this script, Christians and Jews supposedly share a common Judeo-Christian heritage which is meant to exclude Muslims, and we are encouraged to support a Jewish state based on savage ethnic cleansing against Islamic fanatics.

The greatest benefits to America's rulers of political Islam as the enemy, however, are ideological: religious demagogues like Osama bin Laden and Iranian mullahs channel the poor and oppressed of the Muslim world into politically reactionary rather than revolutionary formations and legitimize the power of elites acting in the name of Islam; at the same time, they make the ugly face of contemporary capitalism look by way of contrast almost desirable to non-Muslims and many Muslims, in much the same way that Soviet Communism did. U.S. rulers would like the world to perceive the choice before it in effect to be between an admittedly decadent capitalist civilization with unlimited freedom to do your own thing and a pre-modern theocratic state.

Political Islam derives much of its effectiveness from the failure of communism as a revolutionary ideology. That failure left widespread despair in the Middle East and around the globe and an ideological void which militant Islam, assisted by the U.S., has rushed to fill.

A History Of Collaboration

Iran

The U.S.'s favored antidote to revolutionary ideology among desperate workers and farmers in the turbulent Middle East, Central Asia, and Muslim Africa, especially since 1979, has been the idea that God's will as expressed in the Koran requires people to submit to 'holy' dictatorships. That pivotal year marked the overthrow of the Shah of Iran, the most powerful U.S. client except Israel, and also the Soviet invasion of Afghanistan. In both cases the U.S. turned to Islamic fundamentalism to achieve its strategic goals.

The Iranian revolution was capable of establishing a secular, anti-capitalist revolutionary democracy and sweeping the Middle East. Instead *Time*'s 1979 Man of the Year, Ayatollah Khomeini, and the mullahs successfully channeled the mass popular movement into a right-wing theocracy, using nationalism and religion to crush the revolution and consolidate the class nature of Iranian society.

There has been a strong collaborative relationship between the theocratic rulers of Iran and U.S. rulers ever since. In November, 1979 Iranians took over the U.S. Embassy in Tehran, taking 50 Americans hostage. Focusing on the Great Satan allowed the Ayatollah Khomeini to put up a show of radicalism to satisfy his followers while he liquidated tens of thousands of worker and student revolutionaries in the spring and summer of 1980. In October, 1980 emissaries of the Republican Party met secretly with the Ayatollah's regime and persuaded it not to release the hostages until the election was over, thus guaranteeing the defeat of Jimmy Carter. From 1983 through 1988 the Reagan Administration, in collaboration with Israel, sold arms to the Khomeini regime in Iran and sent the proceeds to CIA-supported Contras fighting the Sandinista revolution in Nicaragua, in defiance of Congress.

Afghanistan

In 1979 the U.S. began another remarkably ambitious collaboration with Islamic fundamentalists after the Soviet Union invaded Afghanistan. With Jimmy Carter's express approval, under CIA direction, and with massive funding from the U.S. and Saudi Arabia, the U.S. undertook to recruit, train, and arm over 100,000 mujahadeen—Islamic freedom fighters, as President Reagan styled them —from Saudi Arabia, Pakistan, Iran, and Afghanistan, to make war against the Soviet invaders. The U.S. funded madrassas—Islamic religious schools—in Pakistan and Afghanistan to promote political Islam and it set up camps to train the mujahadeen in guerrilla tactics and terrorism. A key CIA asset in the struggle was a man of the fundamentalist Wahhabi Islam sect from Saudi Arabia, Osama bin Laden. The U.S.-backed Islamic fundamentalist movement was successful. In 1989 it drove the USSR from Afghanistan in ignominious defeat, a loss from which the USSR never recovered. On September 27, 1996 the Taliban, an Islamic fundamentalist guerrilla organization backed by the U.S., Saudi Arabia, and Pakistan, took control of the Afghan capital, Kabul.

Bosnia and Kosovo

In the mid-90s, with explicit approval of the Clinton Administration and the assistance of the Pakistani ISI (Inter-Services Intelligence) and Osama bin Laden, the U.S. channeled Iranian arms, Iranian Revolutionary Guards, Iranian intelligence agents, and thousands of mujahadeen from around the Islamic world to the Muslim government in Sarajevo during the fighting in Bosnia, greatly enhancing Iranian and fundamentalist influence in the region. The U.S., working closely with Osama bin Laden, then supplied the Kosovo Liberation Army with funding, arms, and Muslim fighters. Prof. Michel Chussodovsky of the University of Ottawa sums up the alliance between the U.S. and Islamic militants: A major war supposedly against international terrorism has been launched, yet the evidence amply confirms that agencies of the U.S. government have since the Cold War harbored the Islamic Militant Network as part of Washington's foreign policy agenda.[1]

Pakistan

The U.S. has covertly championed Islamic power in the Islamic Republic of Pakistan under a succession of leaders, most recently ex-General Musharraf, who led a military coup against the elected government in 1999 and proclaimed himself president. U.S. military forces and the CIA have maintained particularly strong ties with the Pakistani military and with ISI, the Pakistani intelligence service, which played a major role in directing Islamic mujahadeen against Soviet forces in Afghanistan in the 1980s and continues to have strong ties with the Taliban. The military and the ISI threw crucial support to the six-party alliance of Islamic parties, the Mutahidda Majlis-e-Amal (MMA), enabling it to triumph in the October, 2003 Pakistani elections. Ahmed Rashid writes:

> [T]he Islamicists see their moment to turn Pakistan into a theocratic state. The MMA are banking on their support within the army and the intelligence services. They have gone out of their way to revile Musharraf as a stooge of the Americans, while praising the army's commitment to Islam. Emboldened by its successes, the MMA has also declared that it will demand that the government impose Sharia law throughout the country...[U.S. policies] will only hasten Pakistan's turn towards Islamic fundamentalism as the MMA gets stronger and more strident in its demands.[2]

Iraq

This desire to bolster militant Islam may explain why U.S. military forces have been producing with every atrocity new guerilla fighters with which to frighten the American people and to make the war on terror and threat of terrorism more convincing. "Anonymous," a CIA analyst for 22-years who has just published *Imperial Hubris: Why the West Is Losing the War on Terror*, writes that the United

States has "waged two failed half-wars and, in doing so, left Afghanistan and Iraq seething with anti-U.S. sentiment, fertile grounds for the expansion of al-Qaeda and kindred groups." He adds that "There is nothing that bin Laden could have hoped for more than the American invasion and occupation of Iraq."

Before the first Gulf war, Iraq had been a secular state, with the highest standard of living in the Middle East. Health care was free, as was education up through secondary school. Iraq had a high degree of equality between the sexes, with laws against gender discrimination; there were more female than male university students.[3] After two wars and 12 years of U.N. sanctions, with its infrastructure in rubble, millions of its people malnourished, and 70% unemployed, the living standards of Iraqis have gone dramatically backwards. Iraqis have been subject to savage U.S. attacks on civilians and widespread torture and humiliation of a sort calculated to make even those Iraqis most initially supportive of the removal of Saddam Hussein see America as an enemy.

The U.S. has succeeded in consolidating the Iraqi resistance—the only future leadership with any legitimacy in popular eyes—increasingly under militant Islamic leadership, virtually guaranteeing an Islamic future for once secular Iraq. The U.S. strategy of encouraging Islamic fundamentalism may explain what otherwise seem like incomprehensible blunders in the war on Iraq, not to mention the invasion itself.

For example, the U.S. apparently deliberately provoked the Shi'ite uprising in southern Iraq in April, 2004 and thrust radical Islamic leader, Moqtada Sadr, into the position of being a national hero to Iraqis. Sadr is a Shi'ite Muslim, the same sect as that of the late Ayatollah Khomeini. In April, 2004, when Israel assassinated Shaikh Ahmed Yassin, Sadr's newspaper gave the story prominent coverage and promised to act as a wing of Hamas in Iraq. The U.S. promptly shut down Sadr's paper, arrested thirteen of his top aides, and, through an Iraqi court, issued a warrant for Sadr's arrest for murder. Though Sadr had a militia of his own, the Mahdi Army, it had never acted violently towards any Americans. Juan Cole, Professor of Middle Eastern Studies at the University of Michigan, asked,

> How did the CPA [Coalition Provisional Authority] get to the point where it has turned even Iraqi Shi'ites, who were initially grateful for the removal of Saddam Hussein, against the United States? Where it risks fighting dual Sunni Arab and Shi'ite insurgencies simultaneously, at a time when U.S. troops are rotating on a massive scale and hoping to downsize their forces in country? Someone in the CPA sat down and

thought up ways to stir them up by closing their newspaper and issuing 28 arrest warrants...This is either gross incompetence or was done with dark ulterior motives that can scarcely be guessed at.[4]

Naomi Klein, reporting from Baghdad, reacted with wonderment at the U.S. deliberately provoking a Shi'ite uprising. In an article titled "The U.S. Is Sabotaging Stability in Iraq," she wrote:

> Mr. al-Sadr is the younger, more radical rival of the Grand Ayatollah Ali al-Sistani, portrayed by his adoring supporters as a kind of cross between Ayatollah Khomeini and Che Guevara. He blames the U.S. for attacks on civilians, compares U.S. occupation chief Paul Bremer to Saddam Hussein, aligns himself with Hamas and Hezbollah and has called for a jihad against the controversial interim constitution. His Iraq might look a lot like Iran.[5]

Klein calls the U.S. provoking of an uprising in Shi'ite southern Iraq mystifying, and reckons that the CPA is trying to create chaos in the south to make the handover of power impossible. More likely, however, is that the U.S. is trying to create what Professor Cole calls a Shi'ite International, as demonstrations erupted throughout the Shi'ite world, including Lebanon, Bahrain, Iran and Pakistan, against continued U.S. fighting in Karbala, a key holy city for Shi'ite Muslims. "Bush is in the process of turning the Shi'ite world decisively against the U.S."[6]

After claiming that it would defeat Sadr and wanted him dead or alive, the U.S. backed down and negotiated with him. One of the concessions was that Sadr would order his militia fighters to return to their homes; meanwhile Sadr announced his intentions to form a political party and run in the elections scheduled for January, 2005.[7] This arrangement, one analyst put it, would signal that the United States has just christened the newest Islamic theocracy in the World.[8]

The pattern we see developing in Iraq is familiar. The U.S. covertly encourages militant Islamic opposition movements throughout the Muslim world. This means that U.S.-backed Islamic movements often find themselves in opposition to U.S.-backed governments. When Islamic forces eventually become powerful enough to take over, then secular allies can be dispensed with. This was the pattern in Iran, and it is the developing pattern in Pakistan and Iraq, both of which will likely become theocracies on the Iran model. In Iraq, given the former power and prestige of the secular and socialist Ba'athist Party, it has taken an invasion and brutal occupation to remove the secular leader and develop Islamic forces; still the model is the same.

I should point out that the U.S. is not alone in funding Islamic militants. Israel funded and promoted the Islamic terrorist group Hamas in the 1970s and 1980s and may still. Israel funded Hamas to undercut the popularity of the secular PLO (Palestine Liberation Organization) and the Palestinian cause, which it has done very effectively with suicide attacks on Jewish civilians in Israel.[9]

Organizing Permanent War

U.S. rulers need to create a frightening, ubiquitous, and apparently powerful enemy against which to wage endless war. They seem to be succeeding. We will likely soon see a Muslim world populated by Islamic theocracies in Iran, Iraq, and nuclear- armed Pakistan. These theocracies will impose harsh controls on their own people, crushing dissent in the name of religion, at the same time as they will be invoked by the U.S. and Israel as terrorist threats to world peace. The U.S. government has been laying the groundwork for a turbulent future of war and terrorism.

I do not mean to imply here that all has gone according to plan for the U.S. or that the U.S. government is all-powerful in foreign affairs. On the contrary, U.S. actions, especially in the war on Iraq, have been at enormous political cost. Millions of people in the Middle East, perhaps billions worldwide now see the U.S. war-maker state for what it is. Millions of Americans now understand the ruthless nature of their government more clearly than ever, and many now see the need for the overthrow of the war-makers.

At the same time, arranging for a future of endless war is not a sign of the rulers' strength but of weakness. War has always been a method of controlling restive populations, but it is the most extreme method, high in its political costs and unpredictable in its outcome. The rulers of the U.S. and the Muslim nations—and indeed of world capitalism—are being forced towards a future of endless war out of their fear of revolution, as billions of the world's people lose faith in capitalism and seek an alternative. America's most powerful elites are rolling the dice and hoping that fear of militant Islam and possible terrorism will make Americans line up dutifully behind their leaders and get them to accept life in an ever more unequal, undemocratic society without complaint or struggle.

U.S. and Islamic rulers hope to set Americans and Muslims against each other, inflame irrational hatreds, and blind people to their real enemies, the ruling elites of their own societies. Ordinary Iraqi and Pakistani and American workers have more in common with each other than they have with the ruling rich of their societies. To be effective the antiwar, anti-Empire movements in every country must have strong internationalist values and seek to build ties between workers of the U.S. and Muslim and other countries. The answer to division is solidarity. The answer to communism and capitalism is truly democratic revolution. The answer to imperialist war is to turn the guns around and overthrow the war-makers.

Notes

1. See: http://www.globalresearch.ca/articles/CHO110A.html.
2. See: http://yaleglobal.yale.edu/display.article?id=1766&page=1.
3. See: http://www.michaelparenti.org/DefyingSanctions.html.
4. See: http://www.antiwar.com/cole/?articleid=2246.
5. See: *Globe and Mail*, Toronto, Canada, 4/5/04.
6. See: http://www.antiwar.com/cole/?articleid=2642.
7. See: http://www.philly.com/mld/philly/news/world/8939749.htm?1c.
8. See: http://www.financialsense.com/editorials/duarte/2004/0710.html.
9. See: http://www.upi.com/print.cfm?StoryID=18062002-051845-8272r.

IV. THE U.S. AS FOURTH REICH

THE U.S. IS MAKING ITSELF AN OBJECT OF FEAR and hatred throughout the world. Bush Administration spokesmen have promised the world "endless war" against as many as sixty countries, have claimed for the U.S. the right to launch pre-emptive war on any nation which the U.S. suspects may become a threat in the future, and have reserved the right to first use of nuclear weapons. The U.S. now seems about to launch a pre-emptive war against Iraq which is likely to result in tens of thousands of civilian deaths, not to mention substantial U.S. military casualties, a war for which the U.S. has support only from U.S. Pekinese Tony Blair and Israel.

Has the Bush regime become unhinged? Or do its extremely bellicose policies serve some hidden strategic purpose which U.S. ruling circles believe make them worth their enormous political and economic costs?

I submit that, as ill-considered as these war-like policies may seem, in fact there are powerful strategic reasons behind them. U.S. ruling circles have determined (whether with the connivance of their elite partners in other countries is not clear) to serve a role similar to that of the Nazi regime in the 1930s and '40s. The U.S. will play Fourth Reich to the other governments of the world, in particular to those most likely to be threatened by mass insurrections and revolutionary upheavals in the coming years: China, certain Western European powers, and South American nations. The U.S. will go on the attack against many of the world's people—especially those who have the misfortune to be sitting on top of a lot of oil—to insure elite control of world resources and, more importantly, to police against revolutionary movements, all in the name of "fighting terrorism." Ironically though it will be the excessive violence and lawlessness of the U.S. approach that will be most useful to governing elites.

To understand this rationale, we need to review a bit of history. As dangerous as World War II was for world capitalism, war for and against the Third Reich was meant to save the world system of elite rule. The world was deep in Depression in the 1930s. Anti-capitalist sentiment was on the rise and workers' movements were increasingly powerful. Germany was on the verge of civil war when Hitler was appointed Chancellor by the German elite on January 30, 1933 to crush the growing workers' movement, which he proceeded to do with concentration camps for 100,000 Communists and militant workers. Japan was riven by strikes and anti-capitalist sentiment when the military leadership invaded China in 1937 in a desperate drive for natural resources and national unity. French capitalists were besieged by factory occupations and welcomed the Nazi invaders. Industrial unionism and sit-down strikes were sweeping the U.S. In the USSR Stalin was holding onto power through ferocious repression, with executions or the gulag for millions of workers, peasants, and Old Bolsheviks.

War gave the Nazi regime a national purpose and an external enemy to justify Gestapo domination of German life; while Hitler and many of his closest henchman died or were imprisoned after the war, the industrial elite which had placed him in power prospered. War brought unity and national purpose to a British society riven by class conflict. The French Vichy government collaborated with the occupying Nazis to break French workers' unions. U.S. corporations imposed a No-Strike Pledge on workers for the duration of the war and consolidated corporate power in American life. The German invasion came close to shattering Soviet power, but national resistance to the Nazis in the end saved Stalin's rule and helped keep the USSR from internal collapse for another fifty years.

Mobilization for war led these economies out of Depression. In the U.S., FDR's New Deal programs had negligible effect. What saved the U.S. economy was producing tanks and ships and planes for WWII. Mobilization for war led Nazi Germany from massive unemployment to a labor shortage. More important, mobilization for war solidified support for the government of each of these countries and provided an acceptable pretext for reigning in working class movements.

How does the history of the Third Reich apply to the present situation? The media are full of stories about Israel and Iraq and other arenas where the overwhelming military might of the U.S. and its client state leads many people to feel utterly powerless and hopeless about the possibility of ordinary people changing the world. Missing from the mainstream media are stories about the rising levels of mass resistance to capitalism around the globe: general strikes in Italy and Spain; labor unrest of historic proportions in China; South America in flames, with unrest in Brazil, insurrections and factory seizures in Argentina, strikes and riots in Uruguay, insurrections against privatization in Peru, mass mobilizations in Venezuela; and a level of disillusionment with corporate thievery in the U.S. not seen since the 1930s. Couple all these with growing danger of financial collapse and global deflation, and the future of capitalism begins to look shaky indeed.

The war plans and rhetoric of the Bush administration are meant to distract attention from capitalism's profound strategic weakness and focus instead on its overwhelming military strength, with the result that, even as capitalist economic and ideological power unravels, it appears to be insuperably strong.

But the bellicose policies of the U.S. have in addition more profound goals than to serve as diversionary emblems of overwhelming military power. This is what gets us to consideration of the U.S. as Fourth Reich.

The growing anti-capitalist movement among the world's workers and other people presents the world business elite with a deeply threatening situation. The elites of each of the countries in which resistance is growing need an external enemy against which they can lead their own people, either in real battle or in moral indignation. They need to be able to say that the problem in Italy or Spain or China is not Italian or Chinese leaders or the capitalist system: the problem is the Americans.

The role of the U.S. will be to act as a stimulant and target of world anger so that the burgeoning world anti-capitalist movement can be turned into an anti-American movement, in which the working classes of China and Spain and Italy and France and South America can be recruited into movements of national unity—Popular Fronts—against the Americans. In this way—or so it is hoped—potentially revolutionary working class movements will be transformed into nationalist movements under elite leadership.

Does this strategy seem far-fetched? In fact it is nothing new for the U.S., but merely playing out on a world scale its strategy in the Middle East. The U.S. has long used Israel as a lightening rod to deflect the class anger of impoverished Arab workers away from their own rulers, thus keeping in power shaky U.S. client regimes throughout the region.

This is also the strategy the U.S. used in Iran to prevent the revolution against the Shah from sweeping away capitalist control there and sparking a prairie fire of democratic revolution in the Middle East. The U.S. secretly colluded with the Ayatollah Khomeini, even as he attacked the U.S. as the "Great Satan" and took over the U.S. Embassy in Teheran and held Americans captive. The U.S. was perfectly willing to permit, even encourage, this storm of anti-Americanism, since it deflected popular anger away from capitalism and class rule itself and permitted the reactionary regime of the mullahs to consolidate its grip on Iranian society.

Playing the role of the Fourth Reich will have an added benefit for the U.S. elite. As Fourth Reich-like policies bring the U.S. under attack from terrorists and lead to real war, they will be used to justify tighter and tighter government control of the U.S. population. Constitutional protections will prove as flimsy as the prisoners' huts at Guantanamo.

The U.S. strategy amounts to a very serious gamble with enormous stakes. While it is intended to intimidate people and make them feel powerless, it does so at the cost of calling into question the ability of capitalism to offer them a secure future. In other words, embarking on endless war will intensify the strategic erosion of capitalist ideological control while strengthening the capitalist state. While making war will immediately strengthen the hand of the rulers, over time it will undermine their position.

It is worth recalling here the complicated history of WWII and of nations which succumbed to German or Japanese invasion. While people were initially stunned into defeated silence by invasion and occupation, over time they organized Resistance movements which rose up not only against their foreign occupiers but also against their own business and aristocratic classes which had collaborated with the enemy. As the German occupiers were routed in France, Italy, and Greece, sweeping social revolutions were only narrowly prevented when Communist parties obedient to Stalin succeeded in disarming triumphant Resistance forces. Communist-led partisan forces under Tito in Yugoslavia refused Stalin's order, defeated Nazi occupiers and native Fascist forces alike, and took power. The Chinese Communist Party likewise refused Stalin's orders to desist; after waging civil war from 1946 to 1949, Mao's forces defeated Chinese Nationalist armies and seized state power.

Even peoples who had not suffered occupation emerged from the war with greatly raised expectations of what their societies should be like, expectations which threatened their rulers. British voters swept Churchill and the Tories from power at war's end and established a welfare state. Workers in the U.S., which had suffered none of the ravages of war that European countries had endured, in 1946 embarked on the greatest strike wave in our history. It took the Taft-Hartley Act, the declaration of the Cold War, and a ferocious anti-Communist campaign to bring labor under control. (Communists in the labor movement were particularly vulnerable to attack since they had vigorously supported the No Strike Pledge during the war and had led the attack on rank-and-file militants who resisted it.)

Will elite strategy lead to another world war? Given the embattled situation of world capital and the trajectory of history in the last fifty years, a war involving, say, China and perhaps India or some other Asian powers vs. the U.S. or some mix of European powers, may be more possible than we would like to think. Capitalism is running out of options. The future depends largely on how threatened governing elites feel and to what lengths they believe they must go to protect their rule. One can imagine, for example, a Chinese Communist government threatened by domestic upheaval attacking Taiwan in a desperate bid for national unity, realizing that this will bring war with the U.S. The consequences of such possible developments are unforeseeable.

As the air waves ring with threats by U.S. officials against Iraq, it is sobering to reflect that the Bush regime has staked its entire credibility on more terrorist acts occurring; indeed Administration policies in Israel and Afghanistan and Iraq seem calculated to stir up more attacks on Americans. Cheney, Rumsfeld, and Ashcroft have promised us some new terrorist outrage. Let us hope that this Administration does not decide to furnish us with the terrorist catastrophe that it has promised.

Will the elite strategy succeed? Only time will tell, but the facade of Bush's post-September 11 power-grab seems to be cracking, as more and more Americans connect the dots between the "war on terrorism," attacks on Constitutional rights, Wall Street thievery, and government promises of endless war. No one likes to admit that entities as powerful as the U.S. government and Corporate America are not our friends but our enemies, but many people are coming to this conclusion and are finding their voice. What seems undeniably true is that the world has entered a new and dangerous period of war and revolution in which the fate of humanity hangs in the balance.

V. BEWARE THE LIBERAL WAR ON TERROR

MANY PEOPLE WHO OPPOSE THE WAR IN Iraq are living under a dangerous illusion: that the war is the work of a cabal of fundamentalist Christians and Jewish neo-conservatives who have hijacked the government for their own purposes—that the war, in other words, represents not the policies of the core American Establishment but the zany doings of some interlopers.

There have been plenty of indications that this view is mere wishful thinking. The war in Iraq had resounding support at its inception from both Democratic and Republican politicians and the media. Only now that the situation in Iraq has dramatically deteriorated have some politicians and editorial writers begun to backpedal. Even so John Kerry, the presumptive Democratic nominee, has continued to give the war vigorous support, calling for 40,000 more troops.

But the war in Iraq has been so much the focus of the antiwar movement that we are in danger of accepting by default the larger "war on terror" of which the Iraq war is merely one part. While the war on Iraq has held horrors aplenty for the people of that tortured land and for U.S. servicemen and women there, it is the war on terror which holds the greatest long-term threat for Americans and for the people of the Middle East and the world. As far as I am aware, no politician of any note, no mainstream media personality or outlet has called into question the war on terror or challenged the rationale which it provides for a future of permanent war; rather, what criticism has been raised of Bush's war on Iraq often has been on the basis that it has detracted from the war on terror and the search for bin Laden, as Richard Clarke famously charged. In his National Security address of May 27, 2004, Senator Kerry outlined the defense policies he will pursue if he is elected, all of them premised on fighting the war on terror more effectively, so that we can "honor the legacy of the Greatest Generation and restore respect to the greatest country—the United States of America." The war on terror is the framework within which all his security policies are forged.

A recent and, I think, very disturbing article by commentator Bill Moyers puts the centrality of the war on terror in perspective. Along with John Kerry's speech, Moyers' article suggests that the war on terror is the fundamental strategy on which the U.S. ruling elite has placed its hopes for controlling the American people and the world in the 21st century.

Bill Moyers, former White House press secretary to Lyndon Johnson, is America's most respected journalist. His "NOW with Bill Moyers" on PBS reaches millions of viewers with in-depth pieces on such issues as income inequality, the environment, women's reproductive health, COINTELPRO, nuclear proliferation, and White House secrecy. Moyers is a strong advocate for racial equality, for civil liberties, for the duty of government to protect the weak from the strong and the average citizen from unrestrained corporate power. He is a model of progressive thinking.

Moyers' "Winning the War on Terror"[1] is a lament over President Bush's leadership. Moyers accepts Bush's narrative of the war on terror without question. He doesn't point out that Bush's war on terror has done nothing but multiply terrorists, or that Bush could easily have isolated terrorists after 9/11 by addressing the authentic grievances of Arabs, or that Bush in fact needs terrorists to justify Administration policies. On the contrary, Moyers has no doubts about who the real enemy is: "Islamic fanatics have declared war and seem willing to wage it to the death. If they prevail, our children will grow up in a world where fear governs the imagination and determines the rules of life." Apparently to Moyers' mind we are always at Orange Alert or worse; it's almost as if it is Americans—rather than, say, Iraqis or Palestinians—who live under constant threat of being bombed or strafed or tortured or starved; the brutal realities of life for many Muslims are transformed somehow into omnipresent dangers for Americans. And so, writes Moyers, "Like most Americans, I want to do my part in the war." He makes clear that this war is not just another issue *du jour*. In language evoking the grand old days of World War II, Moyers agrees with Bush that the war on terror "is an inescapable calling of our generation."

The problem, according to Moyers, is that "the president makes it hard for us to do our part. Bush confused us when he switched from chasing Osama bin Laden in Afghanistan to hunting Saddam Hussein in Iraq. He undermined his own credibility when he justified the invasion of Iraq with so many patent lies." While Moyers is well aware that Bush's justifications for the Iraq war were false, his response is not to call the whole enterprise into question but to chide Bush for weakening popular support for the war on terror with his lying. Bush stands to lose public confidence in Iraq in the same way that Lyndon Johnson lost public support for that great liberal war in Vietnam. (Moyers was Lyndon Johnson's press secretary until 1967 and was tasked with defending the war to reporters and the public.)

Moyers does not question the goals of the president in this war of aggression, much less raise awkward questions about war crimes and the murder of innocent civilians. It doesn't seem to occur to him to wonder what the president is really up to. Instead the crucial question for Moyers is, "How to assure we win this war?"

His answer: a bipartisan wartime Cabinet. "Why not a wartime cabinet to serve a wartime nation? Al Gore as head of Homeland Security. Gary Hart at Defense. The independent-minded John McCain or Warren Rudman at State. The world would get the point: This time we mean it, all of us—the war on terror no longer a partisan cause." Americans need to show a united front in the face of world criticism.

But, Moyers continues, a wartime Cabinet of national unity is not enough. The president has called on all of us to unite in a common purpose, "But so far sacrifice has been asked only of the men and women in uniform and their families." Ever the compassionate liberal, Moyers writes:

> Even now the privates patrolling the mean streets of Baghdad and the wilds of Afghanistan, their lives and limbs constantly at risk, are making less than $16,000 dollars a year in base pay. Here at home, meanwhile, the rich get their tax cuts—what Vice President Cheney calls 'their due.' Favored corporations get their contracts, subsidies and offshore loopholes. And as the president praises sacrifice he happily passes the huge bills that are piling up on to children not yet born.

Never mind that Iraqis and Afghanis have disappeared from this picture, much less that off-stage they are being bombed and slaughtered and tortured. What really upsets Moyers is that there is so much inequality in the war on terror; some corporations are getting rich, while soldiers have to get by on poverty wages. Apparently we should not seek to end the war but to distribute its rewards more equitably. Moyers would like to see "the moral equivalent of the draft" imposed on all of us, so that the sacrifices are truly shared.

Moyers' lament is not that President Bush has led us into a war of aggression based on lies or that he has undermined our Constitutional rights or that he has caused untold suffering and death for a great many innocent people or that he has made America an object of fear and hatred around the world. No, his lament is that Bush is failing "to lead all of us, and not just a partisan few, to answer...the inescapable calling of our generation." Bush has failed to rally all Americans to the glorious cause of the War on Terror.

Bill Moyers, as Andrew O'Hehir put it in *Salon*, "has arguably become the lone radical on television, openly challenging our national failure to confront fundamental issues of class, money, and power." This is why his fervent call for support for the war on terror comes as such a shock, and it is also why his call is so important to interpreting the significance of the war on terror. We are not here dealing just with one man's views, but with the views of a personage who has spoken for and had the ear of those at the center of power in American society, and who has often been one of their greatest critics.

Are Moyers' views on the war on terror inconsistent with his liberal political ideals? Not really. Liberalism is the dominant philosophy of social control of America's ruling elite. Liberalism does not challenge the structure of power in society or question elite goals. Instead it aims to disguise real power relationships while it mitigates or obscures their effects, with programs ranging from the Great Society agenda of the Johnson years to the affirmative action/gun control/multiculturalism/gay marriage agenda of the past decade. None of these programs poses the least threat to America's financial elite. They are rather weapons of mass distraction. They encourage those without power to see each other as the enemy. They make the people seem to be the problem and the government or corporations the solution.

I don't mean to suggest that Moyers' declared sympathy with the underdog and his campaigning against the excesses of corporate power and big money are in any way insincere. But these sympathies don't in any way challenge the most powerful in our society any more than they truly help those in need. The man whose heart bleeds for underpaid GIs in Iraq while cheering the strategy that put them there is not a threat to any elites.

More to the point, the warm glow of Moyers' folksy and egalitarian patter can be put to use by the monied interests to rally the American people to permanent war against "Islamic fanatics" or, indeed, against any purported enemies government leaders want to name. Anti-warriors should take heed: our enemies are not just some cowboy oilmen or Likudnik neocons, but the Eastern bloc of corporate and financial power which dominates U.S. foreign and domestic policy. Should John Kerry become our next president, expect to see the "war on terror" waged ever more aggressively, but with more sophisticated, pervasive, and liberal PR to rally Americans to the cause.

Only a Democrat with liberal credentials can lead the American people in sustained military conflict. This is true for two reasons. Only the Democratic Party has deep and extensive ties with labor unions and with black, white, and Hispanic workers—in other words, with the people who will do the fighting; without effective working class support, no military effort can long be sustained. In addition, of the ruling parties, only the Democrats have a seemingly generous and uplifting ideology capable of summoning a majority of Americans to a cause demanding blood and sacrifice. Republicans can call frequent Orange Alerts and remind SUV drivers of the need for Arab oil ("How did our oil get under their sand?") as motivating factors, but these can't inspire most people for long, and calls for "democracy in the Middle East" don't ring true coming from Republican moneybags like George Bush or Dick Cheney. However dishonest or manipulative they may be, Democrat leaders waging the war on terror can at least attempt to dress that war in their party's long-abandoned first principles and paint the war as progressive. Making a convincing case for permanent war on Islam will require huge efforts of propaganda and deceit, but this is clearly the strategy on which the ruling class is embarked, and it is not clear what other options they have. Given the strategy, U.S. success in the war depends on liberal leadership.

Aristotle some 2400 years ago said that the tyrant declares war "to deny his subjects leisure and to impose on them the constant need for a leader." The war on terror is meant to serve the purpose for which wars have been waged by rulers from time immemorial. It is not mainly about oil or about projecting American power into the Middle East and Central Asia or supporting Israel, however important these goals may be to the elite. It's key purpose is more central.

The war on terror is the new strategy for elite domination of U.S. society. It is their desperately-needed successor to the Cold War, which for fifty years legitimized government power and Pentagon budgets and held people in thrall to Mutually Assured Destruction. The war on terror is intended to strike fear in the hearts of Americans, so that they sacrifice liberty for security and mobilize behind their leaders to smite the foe wherever and whomever he may be. It is meant to justify the far-flung bases of Empire and to make Americans eager to sacrifice their sons and daughters and treasure in the noble cause. It is meant to turn an alienated and ever more unequal and undemocratic society towards unthinking, patriotic zeal. Most of all, it is meant to focus on carefully-selected foreign enemies the anger and revolutionary solidarity which should be focused on the enemies of democracy and peace here at home.

If it is the case that the war in Iraq is only one element in a broader elite strategy, the antiwar movement must have much more ambitious goals than just military disengagement from Iraq. It must challenge the rationale and motive force behind the Iraq war: the war on terror. Our goals must be to shut down the war on terror with mass popular action, dismantle the worldwide phalanx of U.S. military bases, and bring about a day of reckoning for the war criminals responsible for these policies.

Notes
1. See: http://www.truthout.org/docs_04/printer_040904A.shtml.

VI.   NO TO POLITICS, YES TO MASS REFUSAL

The war against Iraq brought out the biggest protests in world history.
More than 30 million people worldwide publicly demonstrated against
war, and hundreds of millions more silently opposed it. But protest is-
n't enough. Instead of letting the killing machine disempower and de-
vour us, we must strike back in peace against the killers.

—Ramzy Kysia[1]

WE'RE AT A PIVOTAL POINT IN THE STRUGGLE to resist the U.S. war machine.
The movement is poised to be deepened by a new sense of power and purpose or
derailed into the electoral swamp. We have to decide what we are trying to do
and how we are going to do it.

The wars in Iraq and Afghanistan served as crucial diversions from other
historic events. One is the development of the first worldwide anti-capitalist
movement not under Communist domination for nearly 100 years, in reaction to
the World Trade Organization and "globalization." Another is the unmasking of
corporate criminality and popular disillusion with business leaders that have
made Enron and WorldCom household names. Another is the eruption of popular
unrest around the globe, including two general strikes in Italy, one in Spain, and
mass strikes in France. China in spring, 2002 witnessed its largest strikes since the
Communist accession to power in 1949. Unrest is sweeping South America, with
uprisings in Argentina and Bolivia, general strikes in Chile, massive popular
struggles in Venezuela and Brazil. The world capitalist offensive against working
people of the last thirty years has lost much of its power to subdue. The bloom is
off the capitalist rose.

The wars may have been about oil, but they were also about social control.
The U.S. went to war in Afghanistan and Iraq not only for a route to lay a pipeline
to the Caspian Basin or to seize the world's second largest oil reserves. It went to
war to frighten into submission a world of people who have begun too actively to
question and resist the power of capital, too actively to seek an alternative. It
went to war to silence them with its awesome and brutal power.

The successes and failures of the antiwar movement and its next steps
should be judged in this context. True, the antiwar movement did not stop the attack on Iraq—a goal that, in my view, was never really achievable; nothing in history suggests that ordinary citizens, short of revolution, can stop an executive in
command of a powerful army from waging war when it is determined to do so.

But the world antiwar movement succeeded brilliantly in other, less clearly defined goals. It brought real information to millions about the course of U.S. foreign policy. It assured the many Americans who opposed the war that they were not alone, and it showed the people of other countries that there is a huge and vital movement of ordinary Americans who oppose their government's policies.

Most important, the huge numbers involved in the antiwar movement around the world dramatized the contrast between the values of ordinary people and the values of the war-makers. The war exposed the huge chasm which separates the rulers of the world from ordinary people. This deep divide suggests that the only way to end wars is with real democracy and ordinary people in charge.

The rulers are now trying to hide that chasm from view by suggesting that the war was a function of the policies and personality of George Bush or of the cabal of advisors around him—Cheney, Rumsfeld, Wolfowitz, Perle, Kristol, et al.,—rather than a strategic move which had the backing of the U.S. ruling elite. In fact there was little or no visible dissent from Democrats or Republicans and almost total media complicity in selling the war and deeply misinforming the population on the motives and realities behind it.

The rulers are using the 2004 presidential campaign to restore the facade of democracy, pretending that voting for Dean or Kerry or Kucinich will change the course of U.S. society and rescue it from a future of permanent war. But, *Boston Globe* columnist James Carroll writes,

> By timidly giving the vague appearance of opposition while assuming the broad necessity of America's ongoing military presence in Iraq, the candidates are Bush's effective collaborators.[2]

The 2004 elections are being used to co-opt the antiwar movement and prevent it from seriously questioning the system from which have sprung this and countless other wars and social wrongs. They are using the elections to get people off the streets and back into the fold, just as Gene McCarthy declared his purpose to be in his antiwar election bid in 1968.

The electoral system is a mechanism of social control designed to suck people into an illusion of democracy to prevent real democracy from ever emerging. It is the last great illusion of American society. We cannot create democratic change in America unless we expose the electoral fraud and liberate people from its control.

I suggest that we call on people to do two things: 1) Refuse to participate in the 2004 presidential elections, as the first step in a campaign to expose, undermine, and challenge the system. As James Carroll puts it, "Instead of politics, it is time for resistance." 2) Deepen the antiwar movement into a coherent, anti-capitalist, revolutionary movement.

Mass refusal to vote in a fraudulent electoral process is the first step to build a movement to collapse the system from within by withdrawing our support from it. We should call on people to hold house parties not for candidates but for discussion among neighbors and friends of what real democracy would look like and what it would take to get it. We should hold teach-ins about war and the attack on working people here at home in all its guises. We should raise money not for candidates but for literature and radio and TV ads calling for Mass Refusal to Vote. We should go to the polls armed with literature calling on people not to vote. We should bring a glaring light to bear on the chasm between the ruling elite and the people and withdraw from the system its political lifeblood. We should expose the electoral system and its role within the capitalist system.

Politicians are front-men for the system. The great theme of our Mass Refusal to Vote should be that we are going not to the politicians but to the people as the source of change. We will not talk to the politicians, we will not support the politicians, we will not plead with the politicians, we will not give them our money or our votes. We will instead talk to our fellow country-men and -women. We will approach our neighbors, our friends, our families, our townspeople to talk about the great issues of war and peace and democracy. We will find in ourselves and our friends and neighbors and co-workers the democratic virtues and strengths and force for change that have lain dormant too long. We will find in our communities the power to move mountains and in our people the vision to create a new world.

From this great refusal to cooperate in a fraud we will move on to build Mass Refusal to cooperate with the system in every area of life that we are able: Mass Refusal to military recruiting; Mass Refusal to military demands from schools for information on draft-age students; Mass Refusal to speed-ups at work, to longer hours and overtime, building eventually to strikes and Mass Refusal to cooperate in any way with the giant corporations that control the government; Mass Refusal to support high stakes testing and other "standards-based" reforms at school; Mass Refusal to permit attacks on pensions and health care.

At the same time we should deepen the antiwar movement and other reform efforts into one revolutionary movement. It's pointless to keep trying to put out one fire after another. Why not deal with the problems at their source? The issues of war and peace, capitalism and revolution, are inseparable, as are other key issues in our society. War is the most perfect expression of capitalist society, competition taken to the point of blowing away other human beings with all the technological might that human ingenuity and endeavor have produced. Peace without revolution is impossible. The same may be said of unemployment, lack of health care, pension insecurity, attacks on the education of our young, and countless other problems: they exist because they serve the needs of the rich and powerful. They exist, in other words, because of the lack of democracy in our society. The only solution is revolution to create a real democracy based on equality and mutual aid. We need to expose the system, de-legitimize it, refuse to co-operate with it, and overthrow it. It is time that we put the issue of real democracy on the table.

Notes
1. From "Building Tomorrow's House" by Ramzy Kysia. Antiwar.com, August 22, 2003.
2. *Boston Globe*, 9/16/03.

VII. THE MOVEMENT NEEDS A PLAN

THE ANTI-WAR, 'ANTI-DIRECTION IN WHICH our country is moving movement' desperately needs a coherent plan of action.

Voting—for Dean or Kucinich or "anybody but Bush"—is hardly a satisfactory strategy, even if Kerry were not the front runner. Not only do politicians invariably do in office what they swore not to do while on the stump. Electoral politics by its nature goes against two essential elements of democratic movement-building: expanding people's sense of social possibility and developing in people the confidence that they themselves are the key force for change. The "lesser-of-two-evils" nature of electoral politics is not about expanding possibility but contracting it, promoting not the most desirable candidate but the most "electable": bye-bye, Kucinich, hello Kerry. Aside from this problem, voting is still about choosing someone who will presumably solve our problems for us—the opposite of mass democratic action. It is a strategy which in the entire course of American history has never worked.

Marches on Washington and local demonstrations are useful to a point, but that point has been passed. Such demonstrations typically involve the highly-committed traveling far from home to express their commitment and pressure government officials. They involve a huge expenditure of energy and money for relatively little return. Except for fleeting media coverage, demonstrations mainly affect their participants, assuring them that they are not alone. This is no small achievement. But it is not enough.

We need a strategy, if not to replace demonstrations, at least to supplement them with something more politically far-reaching and less limited to activists.

To be effective, a strategy must meet certain requirements. It must have the potential to include many millions of people. It must make a powerful political statement. It must strengthen people's faith in themselves and each other as agents of change. It must not require individuals engaged in it to take excessive risks. And it must embrace a long-range democratic vision, beyond its immediate goal of stopping the next war or other disaster. It must be a small step making a big statement that many people can take together to strengthen them to move further along a path to fundamental change.

New Democracy is proposing a strategy that meets these requirements. We are calling on people to refuse *en masse* to vote in the 2004 presidential election—and to say why they are doing it. This is a strategy that can include the entire electorate, including the 50% who already do not vote. It makes a powerful statement: that the electoral process is a fraud. Its mass character and its message will strengthen people's understanding that real change must come from them, not from some front-man for the monied elite. The only risk it poses for individuals is the combined thrill and fear that come from admitting to ourselves that we're on our own: no man on a white horse is going to save us.

Our strategy, which we call Mass Refusal/2004, is obviously geared to the election-year context. It is meant to be developmental, a small step millions of people can take together which makes a powerful political statement and prepares them for further action. Mass Refusal/2004 is only one step in a continuing campaign to build a mass democratic movement in the U.S.

What are the next steps? In her recent address to the World Social Forum in New Delhi, noted Indian author Arundhati Roy called for a world movement to challenge the occupation of Iraq. She said,

> We have to become the global resistance to the occupation. Our resistance has to begin with a refusal to accept the legitimacy of the U.S. occupation of Iraq. It means acting to make it materially impossible for Empire to achieve its aims. It means soldiers should refuse to fight, reservists should refuse to serve, workers should refuse to load ships and aircraft with weapons.

We can begin our mass resistance with Mass Refusal to choose which candidate will continue the occupation, as they all promise to do in one form or another. After the election, strengthened and refreshed by our collective rejection of fake democracy, we can build the movement to undertake refusals which entail more risk, including direct refusals to do the work of Empire.

In the short time since we first proposed it, our strategy proposal has gotten decidedly mixed reviews. Some people have felt liberated at not having to vote "for the lesser of two weevils." Others have reacted with shock and outrage. "Have you completely lost your minds?" was one of the more temperate comments we received from a young Democratic Party activist in response to a recent fund-raising letter. We have had similar reactions even from people not wed to the Democrats, who simply don't have a great deal of confidence that millions of ordinary people feel exactly as we do about the society and can be mobilized to change it.

The shock and awe our strategy proposal has caused among activists is actually a sign of how badly it is needed. Belief in the electoral system is the last great illusion in American society, an illusion typically more deeply cherished by political activists than by the broader community, who have learned from experience that politicians lie. Activists also know this—how could they not?—but they refuse to give up hope that Howard or Dennis or John might somehow be different and might somehow save us all. The touching but misplaced faith of activists in political hacks and a fraudulent process is a measure of their lack of faith in ordinary people as the force for change. We must never forget what happened before the invasion of Iraq: millions of ordinary people here and abroad rose up to oppose the war, while the Democrats collaborated with the war-makers.

This MassRefusal strategy can reach far beyond the already-engaged to what one friend calls "the people on the sidelines"—the majority of people in our society, who have been demobilized by undemocratic institutions operating in an undemocratic, atomized culture; people whom the media, the political parties, the unions, the schools, the governing agencies at every level have discouraged from participating in society and have left deeply alienated. These millions of people know very well that they are unrepresented in the political process. Political scientist Walter Dean Burnham has shown that the characteristically low turn-out rates in U.S. elections are not a sign of apathy or laziness on the part of the electorate but of political understanding; the profile of non-voters in the U.S. matches that of those who vote communist or socialist in European elections. Burnham writes, the "huge 'hole' in American participation [in elections...] seems insepara-

bly linked…to the total absence of a socialist or laborite mass party as an organized competitor in the electoral market."

Our strategy proposal is the outgrowth of an earlier campaign. In 2001 New
Democracy proposed a strategy to a committee of large teacher union local presidents in Massachusetts to counter what is known here as MCAS, a high stakes
test administered at most grade levels in the public schools which tenth graders
must pass to earn a diploma. We called the strategy MassRefusal. We explained to
the local presidents that MCAS is part of a broader corporate plan of social control, aimed at getting people to accept their place in an increasingly unequal and
undemocratic society. Our proposal was that teachers vote in their local unions
not to administer the MCAS tests. Our hope was that at least a few locals would
refuse the test and start a groundswell of refusal. An anti-testing movement already existed in Massachusetts, but was hamstrung by its reliance on politicians
and the legislative process; MassRefusal was a strategy for teachers to take their
and their students fate in their own hands through collective action.

The union presidents on our committee were terrifically excited by the proposal. Janet Dufault, president of the Education Association of Worcester, ex-
claimed, "Teachers will be dancing in the streets if we do this." We issued our "Call
for MassRefusal," signed by six local union presidents, a former state teacher union president, and several other educators, calling on teachers to refuse to administer the MCAS. This writer addressed the building rep committees of five large
union locals about MassRefusal.

And then…nothing happened. Not only did no teacher local vote not to administer the MCAS; no local even met as a whole to consider the question. There
were a number of reasons for this outcome—the culture of their unions has demobilized teachers in important ways—but the overriding reason was fear. Many
teachers have expressed outrage at the MCAS, and none of them has been fired for
refusing to administer the test. But the accumulated fear and cultural conditioning of years of deferring to authority has left its mark.[1]

My point in this example is not to single out teachers but to point out the
fear that pervades American society. People in every walk of life have been under
attack in manifold ways by the corporate beast, and people have lost much of
their sense that they can fight back. Millions of relatively high-paying manufac-
turing jobs have been lost through automation or shipped overseas, while many
white collar jobs are being outsourced to India and elsewhere. Many other jobs
have been reduced to temp work. Teachers have been told for decades that they

have failed, and have been subjected to ferocious educational "reforms." People are under the gun and they know it.

We cannot build a successful movement unless we can overcome fear. In his 1991 book, *Breaking the Barrier: The Rise of Solidarity in Poland*, Larry Goodwyn points out how rare are mass democratic movements in human history. There are a great many barriers to the rise of such movements, the most fundamental of which is the internalized fear which people accumulate over years of cultural conditioning. The "necessary condition [of social movements]," writes Goodwyn, "is the conquest of fear and an overcoming of social habits generated by fear. When a handful of people find a way to achieve this conquest, a political sect appears; when a great number do, a large-scale social movement can form."

The fear that Polish workers had to overcome in creating Solidarity had very real roots: a Communist party-state that dominated every area of life, from the factory floor to the unions to the schools and media and security police to the government itself. The party ruled by insuring that there was no "democratic space," in Goodwyn's phrase, in which popular forces could assemble and reinforce each other, no institution which working people themselves controlled where they could gather their ideas and strength. Individuals challenged the party-state only at their peril and few did so openly. While police beatings and black-listings and worse were always available to keep workers in line, there often was little need to apply these measures, since people had learned to censor their own words and behavior.

While we don't live with the same level of threats that ordinary people faced in Communist Poland, still there is rising fear, and there is precious little "democratic space" where people control their own institutions organized around their own shared values and ideas where they can overcome their fear. MassRefusal/2004 is a movement-building step designed to help overcome fear and encourage people to see themselves as the great force for change. Our past attempt to shut down high stakes testing in Massachusetts was defeated by fear and passivity within unions dominated by conventional politics; through MassRefusal/2004 and other movement-building steps, we hope the movement will become strong enough to see successful mass refusal by teachers in the future.

A final word here about the long-range vision of the movement. Underlying the "anti-direction-in-which-our-leaders-are-taking-us" movement is a positive vision of human life and values fundamentally different from the vision which drives the war-makers and ruling elites. The positive elements of this vision are perhaps too seldom evoked, as people scramble to stop the next atrocity. But as the movement grows and matures, it will more consciously project its vision of a better world implicit in the values which drive it.

If we are to succeed, this vision must find its source and sustenance not in new elites, whether Left or Right, but in the lives and values of ordinary working people here and around the world. It must imagine a new world rooted in the already existing struggle of ordinary people in the face of a profoundly anti-human culture to create relationships which reflect human life as they believe it should be. In a society based on inequality and selfishness, most people try, in the little piece of the world that they think they can control, to create relations based on love and trust and mutual respect. The most intimate acts of kindness and the most public acts of mass resistance and revolution are on a continuum of struggle to humanize the world. Solidarity and equality are the best values which drive the movement today, and they are the values which should shape the whole world in the future. The more aware of its own implicit vision the movement becomes, the stronger it will be.

Notes
1. I should note that our campaign for MassRefusal reached its height in the spring of 2001, shortly before 9/11—an event which redoubled the climate of fear and made it much harder to focus on the tests

VIII.   THE ANTIWAR MOVEMENT IS NOT PROGRESSIVE—AND THAT'S A GOOD THING

THE MOVEMENT AGAINST WAR IN IRAQ BEFORE the war began offers us an unprecedented opportunity to change the direction of American society, but only if we understand who is in this movement and what it stands for.

The movement included the expected voices on the Left, such as Noam Chomsky and Howard Zinn, who produced searing indictments of the imminent war. But vocal opposition came also from the Right—Pat Buchanan, Lew Rockwell, and a host of others.

The mass antiwar movement in the streets reflected a similar breadth. Huge marches took place not only in Washington, D.C. and New York City, but also in towns and cities across the country, and included many people who had never before protested. More than 90 U.S. city councils passed resolutions against the war.

The marchers did not represent the full scope of antiwar feeling. Leslie Gelb, president of the Council on Foreign Relations (CFR), the premiere elite policy organization in the United States, after traveling the country in late 2002 to advocate war on Iraq, reported that "I have encountered enormous opposition to my terribly persuasive arguments...80 to 90 percent of audience members were against an invasion." Thomas Friedman, a pro-war *New York Times* columnist, wrote eighteen days before the invasion,

> [D]on't believe the polls. I've been to nearly 20 states recently, and I've found that 95 percent of the country wants to see Iraq dealt with without a war.

The range of antiwar opinion is reflected in the scope of the lies that the administration, with its Republican and Democrat and media allies, felt compelled to deploy to justify war. It is true that, once the invasion began and American troops were in harm's way, antiwar sentiment faltered. But the startling fact remains that, even after twelve years of propaganda calling Saddam Hussein "worse than Hitler," even after the national trauma of 9/11, even after the Bush Administration and the media had created the completely false impression of a link between Saddam Hussein and Osama bin Laden, the antiwar movement encompassed a huge majority of the American people.

The movement's amazing breadth developed in spite of the fact that many of the leading antiwar organizations share a "progressive" outlook. The scope of the progressive agenda varies, but it generally includes such programs as gun control, affirmative action, "diversity," abortion rights, feminism, and now gay marriage. While one may agree or disagree with this agenda, it is surely much narrower in its appeal than the antiwar position itself.

The progressive wing of the antiwar movement is now being courted by Dennis Kucinich and Ralph Nader, who will be joined in June by Green Party candidates—progressives all. We need a much bigger tent for the antiwar movement than these campaigns can possibly provide if we are to bring inside everyone who belongs there.

If the movement gets defined by its progressive agenda, the vast antiwar population which does not share that agenda may well become invisible to the organized movement, if it is not already. The tendency will be to ignore and possibly alienate the "non-progressive" part of the movement.

The ruling class constantly works to divide us on issues from the trivial to the profound. To attempt to fit the antiwar movement with a particular candidate or party with a progressive agenda is to limit its appeal, undermine its power, and fail to realize its democratic potential. We should not impose this strait jacket on so vital a movement. That is why I believe an election boycott is the best way to nurture this movement.

The antiwar movement should focus not on candidates but on the underlying decency of the vast majority of Americans and their moral superiority to the ruling, war-making class. Never again should we allow the war-makers to claim to speak for "the silent majority."

Mass opposition to the war revealed a vast chasm between the ruling elite and the people. This fault line between war and peace, between elite rule and democracy, runs very deep in our society—far deeper than the myriad issues which usually divide us.

What separates us from the rulers is what binds us together as people: a sense of human values, a sense of decency, a sense of what is right and fitting that led us to cry out against the war and to call on our government to stay its hand.

We should look to our common rejection of the war as the basis for a redemptive movement in America, a movement in which we overcome divisions among people of varying backgrounds and beliefs to focus on the most important division: between the war-makers and the people. Our mass rejection of the war demonstrated conclusively that most Americans at some fundamental level share common values. We should discover in these shared values a new democratic vision, more powerful and more real than the democratic vision on which the nation was founded. In it lies the redemptive vision for a second American revolution.

IX. THE TRIUMPH OF LIBERALISM

THE ELECTORAL CAMPAIGN HAS FINALLY CRAWLED to its dreary and foreseeable end: the victory of George W. Bush, anti-"red state" hysteria and despair among Kerry supporters, and the effective end of the antiwar movement.

Those millions of Americans appalled at the continuing carnage in Iraq must step back from the electoral debacle and draw the right lessons from it, beginning by examining the role of the Democratic Party and the liberal agenda in the anti-war movement.

The struggle against the War on Terror, or whatever name we wish to give the policy of pre-emptive wars endorsed by both candidates, is the most important struggle of our lifetimes. To succeed in it, we need now to establish a new antiwar movement on a broader popular basis than the one which chose to self-destruct in the Kerry campaign. To do this we must first step outside the mind-set which dismisses as mere bigotry the moral concerns of Americans who oppose gay marriage and abortion and other items on the liberal agenda such as gun control and affirmative action, but who are also deeply opposed to this criminal war.

The new movement must welcome into the fold people from the right and the left. It must use no liberal litmus test for membership. Opposition to the war must be the only criterion.

The bleak outcome of the electoral campaign shows the enduring effectiveness of liberalism as the key strategy of social control by the U.S. ruling elite. In a nation where people from all walks of life and political philosophies opposed a war based on lies, the organized antiwar movement embraced a narrow liberal agenda which excluded millions of people opposed to the war. Because of the perceived weakness of this self-isolating self-definition, all but a few elements of the antiwar movement then allowed themselves to be corralled into the Democratic Party and to accept as their leader a pro-war candidate.

By its astonishing docility the liberal antiwar movement proclaimed loud and clear to the U.S. corporate elite that it had nothing to fear, that liberals would be loyal and true even to a candidate calling for mass murder and victory in Iraq, as long as he kept reasonably ambivalent about gay marriage and abortion.

The post-election U.S. onslaught on Fallujah should come as no surprise to anyone. It wasn't Bush's 51-49% win that made more devastation in Iraq a certainty, but the fact that the antiwar movement allowed the Democratic Party to define the movement's goals and methods and its relationship to the people. With both candidates promising victory in Iraq, what else could happen once the polls closed, whoever the victor may have been? It was not Bush but the War Party, comprising both Democrats and Republicans, that was unleashed by the electoral campaign.

The Democratic Party and John Kerry performed exactly the task they set out to do and for which they received hundreds of millions in corporate largesse: they wed the antiwar movement to the pro-war Democratic Party, and thereby deprived it of life and purpose—until the movement is organized on a new basis.

Since the days of FDR, the role of the Democratic Party has been to undermine the self-confidence and unity of the working class and lead it away from direct action, like the sit-down strikes that swept the nation and had governors and industrialists in the1930s in fear of impending revolution. In the 2004 campaign it performed its role to perfection. Bush as candidate was vulnerable as few incumbent presidents have been. He had lied his way into a war rejected by most of the American people. He had led an assault on civil liberties alarming to citizens of all stripes. He was the first president since Herbert Hoover to bring American workers a net loss of jobs over his term. He had demolished the greatest federal surplus in history to create the greatest deficit. He had created in No Child Left Behind a federal assault on public schools that engendered unprecedented opposition from parents, teachers, local school boards and state legislators.

But the Kerry campaign refused to mobilize the huge majority of Americans who have been severely harmed by these policies. On the contrary, the campaign demobilized people, sucking the life out of issues that people cared deeply about and leaving them with nothing but "Anybody But Bush" hysteria. Kerry went out of his way to support the war in Iraq and to protect Bush from serious attack. Kerry refused to expose the Patriot Act and its assault on the Constitution. He endorsed the "War on Terror" and said that he would pursue it more vigorously than Bush. Kerry declined to propose measures to reverse the ravages of NAFTA on American working people and the outsourcing of jobs. He failed to criticize the No Child Left Behind atrocity, instead calling for it to be fully funded.

Why did Kerry not lead the way in opposing the war and loss of civil liberties and loss of jobs and the attack on public education? Why did he not further energize a base that was already in motion, already crying out for action on these issues?

The answer is obvious: Kerry did not lead on these issues because he and his party in fact support all these attacks on ordinary Americans. Kerry voted for the war in Iraq (as did the Democratic leadership in Congress) and for the Patriot Act (as did most Democrats) and for NAFTA (engineered by Bill Clinton) and for No Child Left Behind (co-sponsored by Ted Kennedy) because he believes in them and because they represent the interests of the wealthy class he serves. The primary goal of the Democratic Party and Senator Kerry in the campaign, more important even than gaining the presidency, was precisely what they achieved: to demobilize and demoralize working people and split them into hostile camps.

The real problem, of course, is not with people who found themselves voting or working for Kerry but with a political system which has made people feel powerless to take any action themselves beyond voting. Change has never been achieved in the U.S. through voting. It has always taken mass popular action by millions of people in their workplaces, their schools, their communities, their streets to create change. This has always been true in the past—in the labor movement, the civil rights movement, the anti-Vietnam War movement—and it is true now.

What next for the millions of Americans who remain deeply opposed to this war and to the whole set of anti-democratic policies in which it is enmeshed?

We need to step outside the Democratic Party to form enduring, popularly-controlled, democratic organizations with which we can challenge the direction of our society. The new antiwar movement must find its energy and its power in the ability of millions of people across the country to take concrete action themselves in the communities and workplaces against the War Machine. We need to build a mass movement of refusal to cooperate with Empire, and we need to figure out practical ways to do it. Never again should the antiwar movement line up behind a pro-war candidate because we prefer his Eastern liberal style. Never again should we let our goals be set by capitalist politicians. Never again should we abandon direct action to let politicians act for us.

We have a huge task before us. That task is not to elect another politician to office—even one who, unlike Kerry, might actually oppose Empire. Our task is much larger but doable. That task is to dismantle the Military-Industrial Complex and disarm the War Machine. If we are serious about this task and stay focused on the issue, we will find ourselves surrounded by many millions of new allies —new not because they weren't there before, but new because we just couldn't see them.

Part Two

PALESTINE / ISRAEL

by John Spritzler

I.   SHOULD THERE BE A JEWISH STATE?

> I would much rather see reasonable agreement with the Arabs on the
> basis of living together in peace than the creation of a Jewish state.
> —Albert Einstein[1]

> A state cannot be Jewish, just as a chair or a bus cannot be Jewish…The
> state is no more than a tool, a tool that is efficient or a tool that is defec-
> tive, a tool that is suitable or a tool that is undesirable. And this tool
> must belong to all its citizens —Jews, Moslems, Christians…The con-
> cept of a 'Jewish State' is nothing other than a snare.   —Amos Oz[2]

TED KOPPEL'S NIGHTLINE ABC-TV SHOW April 18, 2002 featured the question,
"Is it anti-Semitic to criticize the Israeli government's policy towards Palestinians?" Koppel was interviewing the head of the Jewish Anti-Defamation League,
who replied that Israel was a sovereign state and of course it was permissible to
criticize its policies. But, he warned, to oppose the idea of a Jewish state went over
the line and was pure anti-Semitism. Koppel smiled agreeably and gave no hint
that a reasonable person might disagree.

The idea of a Jewish state (whose Jewish proponents call themselves "Zionists") is sacrosanct in the mainstream U.S. media, which does not give voice to the
troublesome questions raised by the issue, in particular that many Jews have historically opposed the idea of a Jewish state. The establishment of Israel has been
far more controversial among Jews than most Americans are aware. Jewish opponents of a Jewish state believed in democracy with equal rights for Jews and
non-Jews, and thought a purely Jewish sovereignty would be disastrous for ordinary Jews.

The Apartheid State

What is Jewish about the Jewish state of Israel? It's not that Israel is a state where
only Jews live. One fifth of the Israeli population is non-Jewish. The Jewishness
of Israel is embodied in a set of laws which confer rights and benefits on Jews but
not on others. Were this not true, Israel would not deserve to be called a Jewish
state. But because it is true, Jews and non-Jews are not equal before the law in Israel.

The *Declaration of the Establishment of the State of Israel*, Israel's declaration of independence, signed May 14, 1948 is a two page document which clearly defines Israel as a Jewish state. The document stresses that the sovereign authority in Israel is the Jewish people: "This right is the natural right of the Jewish people to be masters of their own fate, like all other nations, in their own sovereign state." It repeatedly uses phrases to emphasize this point: "Jewish people...in its own country," "Jewish people to rebuild its national home," "Jewish state," "right of the Jewish people to establish their state," "Jewish people in the upbuilding of its state," "sovereign Jewish people."

Where does this leave Arabs, who are currently 20% of the population inside Israel (not counting the Gaza Strip and the West Bank)? The Declaration makes a clear distinction between Jews, who are the sovereign authority in Israel, and the Arab inhabitants who are not. The second-class status of Arabs inside Israel is enforced by laws that privilege being Jewish, rather than by a formal denial to Arabs of citizenship or the right to vote and hold office. Thus the document says that Arabs shall have "complete equality of social and political rights" and "full and equal citizenship and due representation in all its [Israel's] provisional and permanent institutions." But the Law of Return, passed in 1950, begins: "Every Jew has the right to immigrate to the country." Yet one of the central grievances of Palestinians is that they cannot do the same thing; they cannot return to their homes of many generations in Israel. Even Arabs who never left Israel, but who only stayed for a few days in a nearby village with relatives to wait for the fighting in 1948 to end, are now categorized in Israel as "present absentees," a category in which they remain forever, and in consequence of which their homes and property remain in the possession of the Custodian of Absentee Property, who puts the property at the disposal of Jews.[3]

Private organizations serving only Jewish interests hold quasi-governmental authority in Israel for policies that affect non-Jews. The main example of this is the Jewish Agency, which calls itself "the agency for Jewish interests in Eretz ["the land of"] Israel...[it's] role is defined...as a voluntary, philanthropic organization with responsibility for immigration, settlement and development, and coordination of the unity of the Jewish people."[4] The (Jewish) Jerusalem Center for Public Affairs describes the Jewish Agency as "a quasi-public, voluntary institution sharing many, often overlapping, functional jurisdictions with government."[5] Yes, Arabs could set up a private "Arab Agency," but it would not have the quasi-governmental power, for example, to dispose of Jewish property the way the law allows the Jewish Agency to dispose of Arab property: the state's Custodian of Absentee Property hands Arab property to the Jewish Agency, but it does not hand Jewish property to any Arab agency. Jews don't have their property confiscated as "present absentees" because Jews, unlike Arabs, enjoy the "Right of Return."

From "Letter to a Deportee"

For twenty years, I knew nothing of the Palestinian problem. I was one year old when my parents arrived among the 50,000 Bulgarian Jews who decided to immigrate to the new Jewish state. That was in 1948 when Israel was just born. We settled in Ramle, in a big stone house that had belonged to an Arab family...In the back of the house was a lemon tree, which almost collapsed each year under its fruit... One morning, right after the Six-Day War, a young Arab man turned up at the front door. He said: 'My name is Bashir el-Kheiri. This house belonged to my family.'

He was 26; I was 20. It was the first time I had ever met a Palestinian.

One day—I shall never forget it—Bashir's brother came to Ramle with his father. The old man was blind. After entering the gate, he caressed the rugged stones of the house. Then he asked if the lemon tree was still there. He was led to the backyard. When he put his hands on the trunk of the tree he had planted, he did not utter a word. Tears rolled down his cheeks. My father then gave him a lemon. He was clutching it in his hands when he left. Bashir's mother told me, years later, that when her husband couldn't sleep, he used to pace up and down their apartment holding in his hand an old, shriveled lemon. My father had given the same lemon to him...

I had always believed that the Arabs of Ramle and Lod had fled from the Israeli soldiers in 1948, that they had abandoned their houses like cowards...After the 1967 war, an Israeli who had participated in the expulsion from Lod and Ramle told me what really happened in July of 1948. He told me about the cars with loudspeakers driving through Ramle, instructing the inhabitants to leave. I didn't stop loving my country because of that, but my love lost its innocence.[6]

The U.N. Conciliation Commission estimated that about 80 percent of the land in what is today Israel is property formerly owned by Palestinians that was confiscated by Jewish organizations like the Jewish Agency.[7] Palestinians are forbidden by Israeli law from owning it. Of all the land that may be legally sold in Israel, 67% of it may not legally be sold to Arabs, while none of it is barred from being sold to Jews.[8] Thus, while Palestinians may be citizens in Israel, they are second class citizens, which is precisely what it means to live in a "Jewish state" when one is not Jewish. Yet another feature of Israel that makes it an apartheid state is that it aims to separate Jews and Arabs on a personal level. For example, a Jew and an Arab cannot legally marry each other in Israel; such marriages, if performed outside the country, are not recognized under Israeli law.

Section 7A(1) of the Basic Law of Israel explicitly prevents Israeli citizens —Arab or Jewish—from using the "democratic" system of Israeli elections to challenge the inferior status of Arabs under the law; it restricts who can run for political office with this language: "A candidates' list shall not participate in elections to the Knesset if among its goals or deeds, either expressly or impliedly, are one of the following: (1) The negation of the existence of the State of Israel as the State of the Jewish People..." In a 1989 Israeli Supreme Court ruling (reported in the 1991 Israel Law Review, Vol. 25, p. 219, published by the Faculty of Law at the Hebrew University of Jerusalem) Justice S. Levine, speaking for the majority, ruled that this law meant that a political party could not run candidates if it intended to achieve the cancellation of one of the fundamental tenets of the State—namely "the existence of a Jewish majority, the granting of preference to Jews in matters of immigration, and the existence of close and reciprocal relations between the State and the Jews of the Diaspora."

One can either be for a Jewish state or be for full equality of Jews and non-Jews inside Israel, but one cannot logically be for both. Israel's Zionist leaders use this logic as a weapon against people (Jew and non-Jew alike) who want equality and democracy in Israel. If you say you want Israel to be a truly democratic state in which Jews and non-Jews have equal rights, then the Zionists accuse you of wanting to abolish the state of Israel, because Israel is a Jewish state, not an "everybody who lives here" state. The Zionists have made "supporting the existence of Israel" (as a Jewish state) a litmus test; anybody who fails it is labeled either an anti-Semite or a Jewish "self-hater." This puts everyone who believes in universal concepts of equality on the defensive, and stifles free expression of views calling for solidarity between Jews and Arabs.

Israel is very different from virtually all other states today. If you are French or American or Chinese or Nigerian and you say you want your nation to be one where everybody is equal under the law and collectively constitute the highest authority in the land, nobody would accuse you of wanting to abolish France, the United States, or whatever. That is because, no matter how undemocratic or discriminatory these governments may be, they justify their existence by claiming to be a state resting on the assent of all their inhabitants. Nobody, for example, who opposed Jim Crow in the United States was ever accused of thereby denying the right of the United States to exist. But those who make analogous demands in Israel are—with good reason—accused of denying Israel's right to exist.

The right of the "Jewish state" to exist is indeed incompatible with universalist values of equality and democracy. Israel in this respect is similar to apartheid-era South Africa. Just as Israel accuses advocates of Arab-Jewish equality of wanting to abolish the state of Israel, South Africa accused advocates of black-white equality of wanting to abolish the South African state. The reasoning is the same: Arab-Jewish equality challenges the idea that only Jews are the sovereign authority in Israel, just as black-white equality challenged South Africa's basis in an exclusively white sovereignty.

Undemocratic From The Start

The first person in modern times seriously to call for the creation of a Jewish state was Theodor Herzl, the founder of the World Zionist Organization, who wrote The Jewish State in 1896. From its modern origin in Herzl's book, the concept of a Jewish state rests on a rejection of the democratic principle that states derive their right to rule from the assent of the people who live in them.[9] Herzl had to reject this democratic principle because Jews were not a majority in Palestine. Instead, he asserted that the Jewish state derived its legitimacy from the need of the Jewish people for a guardian. That is, he intended a government in Palestine, where Jews were a minority among Arabs, to be the sovereign power over all the inhabitants (both Jews and Arabs) and yet act in the name only of Jews scattered around the world.

The Zionists' break from the idea of democracy has had disastrous consequences. Today, Israel's leaders are in a real bind. They need the legitimacy that derives from being perceived as a democracy. But the presence of large numbers of Arabs inside Israel makes it impossible for Israel to be both a "Jewish state" (meaning only Jews are the sovereign authority) and a democracy (meaning all inhabitants equally are the sovereign authority.) This is one reason Israeli leaders cannot conceive of allowing Palestinians to return to the homes from which they were driven by Jewish military forces in 1948.

Jews With Opposite Goals

The idea of a Jewish state has historically been backed by Jewish and other elites, but not by most Jews. In 1903 Theodor Herzl traveled to Russia for two lengthy meetings with the Czar's interior minister, Wjatscheslaw Plehwe, the man believed responsible for the notorious massacre of Jews at Kishinev. According to Herzl's diary (August 10 and 14) Plehwe told him, "You don't have to justify your movement to me. You are preaching to a convert…The creation of an independent Jewish state capable of absorbing several million Jews would suit us best of all." Israeli historian Yoram Hazony explains, "As Herzl had long suspected, the czarist government, ruling 7 million Jews, many of whom were increasingly drawn to socialism, was predisposed to support any scheme that might encourage Jewish emigration."[10]

In the 1920s and '30s a great many Jews were involved in Socialist and Communist working class organizations fighting to create socialist revolutions in Europe, not to emigrate to Palestine. For instance, in 1938, Henryk Erlich, the leader of the Bund—the Polish Jewish working class organization which swept the large Jewish vote in the last free municipal elections before the Nazi invasion —declared, "Zionism has always been a Siamese twin of anti-Semitism and of every kind of national chauvinism." Working class Polish Jews rejected the Zionists when they saw Zionist leaders making deals with the most anti-Semitic politicians in Poland for the evacuation of Poland's Jews to Palestine.

Unlike the Zionists, the Bund made no demand for territory. They fought for equality for ordinary people as opposed to the establishment of a Jewish state. They believed in strengthening the trade union movement and working for unity between Jewish and non-Jewish workers in Poland, and from 1939 to 1945 they organized underground resistance to Nazis in the ghettoes, in concentration camps and as partisans in the forests.[11]

In contrast to the Bund's role during the Holocaust, the World Zionist Organization (WZO, headed by Chaim Weizmann) continued to cooperate with the most reactionary and anti-Semitic elements of European society to gain favor for its project in Palestine. For example:

- The head of the WZO's Zionist Rescue Committee in Budapest during the war, Rudolf Kastner, later a prominent member of Israel's government under Prime Minister Ben Gurion, collaborated with the Nazis. Kastner was made a V.I.P. by the Nazis and not required to wear a yellow Star of David because, in exchange for being allowed to hand pick a small number of educated Jews to emigrate to Palestine, he helped lure thousands of Hungarian Jews to their death without a fight by arranging for phony postcards "from other Jews" to convince them that the trains to the death camps were merely taking them to be "resettled."[12]

- The Zionist leader Yitzhak Shamir, a future Israeli Prime Minister, in 1941 proposed an alliance with the Nazis against Great Britain, writing to Nazi leaders: "In the matter of concept, we identify with you. So why not collaborate?"[13]

"A Loyal Jewish Ulster"

The British and U.S. elites who supported the Palestine Mandate in 1922 and the creation of Israel in 1948 had no particular regard for Jews; in fact, they were quite content to stand by while millions of Jews were murdered in death camps during WWII. When they did support the Mandate, their purposes were not altruistic but political and strategic. Sir Ronald Storrs, the first governor of Jerusalem under British rule in the 1920s, explained that the value of a Jewish sovereignty lay in its "forming for England a 'little loyal Jewish Ulster' in a sea of potentially hostile Arabism."

Thus Israel's role in the Middle East from its inception has been to act as a lightning rod for class struggle in the region, provoking Arab hatred and fomenting ethnic war so that the oil-rich Middle Eastern regimes—all of which are anti-democratic and sitting on a powder-keg of rebellious workers—can stay in power by directing the anger of their populations against Israel. Great Britain originally, and now the United States, wants anti-democratic governments to remain in power in the Middle East because only such regimes will keep oil money out of the hands of ordinary people in countries like Saudi Arabia, Iraq and Iran and safely in the hands of big corporations and local elites. For Israel to play its role in this social control strategy for the long-term, it has to be made militarily strong enough to repulse any Arab attack, which is why the U.S. arms Israel so heavily. U.S. corporate and government leaders would never be able to muster public support for turning Israel into a highly-militarized garrison state if they revealed to the American people their true purpose: to use the Jewish state to control the Middle East's vast and rebellious working class and its oil.[14]

To function as a lightning rod, Israel must provoke Arab hatred; it cannot be simply a state where Jews live and prosper in peace along with Arabs the way, for example, non-Mormons and Mormons live together in Utah, or Jews and non-Jews in the U.S. It must be an ethnically divisive state, a state only "of and for the Jews," a state whose "very existence" drives Arabs off the land and incites ethnic war. Some Jews saw this from the beginning of the state of Israel. Judah Magnes, the first Chancellor of Israel's Hebrew University, opposed the "Jewish state" idea because, as he expressed it in his diary in 1942, "The slogan 'Jewish state' (or commonwealth) is equivalent, in effect, to a declaration of war by the Jews on the Arabs."[15] From the elite's perspective, provoking ethnic war is precisely the function of a Jewish state.

Corporate and government leaders do not care how many Jews die in the ethnic fighting. As a result, ordinary Jews in public bus stops, restaurants and dance clubs are now at greater risk in Israel than in any other nation. This is why, according to a January 2002 poll conducted by Market Watch for the Israeli *Ma'ariv* newspaper, 20 percent of adult Israelis say they have recently considered living in a different country, and 12 percent of Israeli parents would like their children to grow up outside Israel.[16]

Dealing With Anti-Semitism

Zionists claim that the Holocaust demonstrates what they have asserted since 1896—that non-Jews are innately anti-Semitic and that, to survive in a hostile world, Jews need a state of their own. But the real history of the Holocaust demonstrates no such thing. In fact most Germans opposed anti-Semitism, and working class Germans actively fought the Nazis on the streets and at the polls before Hitler was handed power by German industrialists and aristocrats, precisely to crush the growing working class movement. In the last free election (Nov. 6, 1932) before Hitler's appointment as Chancellor, the German working class parties (the Social Democrats and the Communists)—both of which were known for being outspokenly opposed to anti-Semitism—out-polled the Nazis by 221 to 196 seats in the Reichstag. Most German workers recognized anti-Semitism for what it was: a strategy by the German elite to divide and attack all working people.

The Holocaust does not demonstrate that non-Jews are innately anti-Semitic any more than slavery demonstrates that whites are innately racist against blacks. If such innate prejudice were a fact, it would be hard to explain why any incident of racist or anti-Semitic graffiti in American towns today is met with public revulsion. The appropriate response to racism and anti-Semitism is to strengthen equality and solidarity among working people of all races and nationalities, not to erect ethnically pure states based on tribal and inherently divisive principles. The Holocaust is no more a reason for Jews to have a state of their own than slavery is a reason for African-Americans to have a pure "Black state" of their own.

Most Jews who survived the Holocaust, when given a choice between going to Palestine to create a Jewish state or going to the United States, chose the United States because it seemed to offer what they really wanted—a society where people are equal before the law and Jews are treated the same as everybody else.

What Now?

The very concept of ethnically pure states is divisive and destined to stoke conflict. The so-called "two state solution" in the Middle East—establishing a Palestinian state to counter the Jewish state—is a conceptual and political trap that prevents Arab and Jewish working people from uniting around their common interests and values. The situation in the Middle East cannot be solved within this framework; it leads nowhere except to more destruction and hate and more elite control.

The solution is not to establish another ethnic state but to disestablish the ones that exist now. Israel, as well as states that are just for Muslims or any other ethnic group, must cease to exist as states based on apartheid and ethnic domination. They must be replaced by secular democracies with equal rights for all, regardless of their ethnic background, and with equal tolerance for all religions.

Will this be easy to accomplish? Certainly not. Some of the most powerful elites in the world depend on continued conflict in the Middle East to maintain their power. To establish a real democracy in Palestine will require ordinary people joining together to defeat Israeli, Arab, and U.S. elites. Real democracy will take a revolution. Is this possible? Yes, with great difficulty. Is it necessary? Absolutely, because there is no other way. The first step is to think about the problem and its solution in a new way. It is time we began.

Notes

1. In *Ideas and Opinions*, Crown Publishers, New York, 1954, p. 190.
2. Amos Oz (Israel's pre-eminent writer of fiction), in "A Laden Wagon and an Empty Wagon? Reflections on the Culture of Israel," *Free Judaism*, October 1997, p. 5 [Hebrew], cited by Yoram Hazony in *The Jewish State*, pg. 338.
3. Tom Segev, 1949: *The First Israelis*, Free Press; ISBN: 0029291801; (February 1986)
4. See: http://www.jafi.org.il/mission/eval.htm.
5. See: http://www.jcpa.org/dje/books/projren-ch1.htm.
6. From "Letter to a Deportee," originally printed in *The Jerusalem Post*, January 14, 1988, quoted in Rene Backmann, "The Letter to Bashir," *New Outlook*, May 1988 http://www.vopj.org/personalnarr.htm.
7. Donna E. Arzt, professor of law, Syracuse University, presentation at the December 7, 1999, meeting of the Sadat Forum at Brookings, cohosted by Richard Haass, vice-president and director of Foreign Policy Studies at the Brookings Institution, and Shibley Telhami, the Anwar Sadat Chair for Peace and Development at the University of Maryland. http://www.bsos.umd.edu/sadat/publications/Forum/12-7-99.htm.

8. Alexander Safian, associate director and research director of the pro-Israel Committee for Accuracy in Middle East Reporting in America (CAMERA), a Boston-based media-watch organization, "Can Arabs Buy Land in Israel?", http://www.meforum.org/meq/dec97/safian.shtml

9. Theodor Herzl, *The Jewish State*, Harry Zohn, trans. (New York: Herzl Press, 1970), pp. 69, 92-3. Cited by Hazony.

10. Yoram Hazony, *The Jewish State: The Struggle for Israel's Soul*, Basic Books, a New Republic Book, USA, 2001, pp.136-7

11. David Rosenberg, *In Defiance of History*, http://www.redpepper.org.uk/intarch/xbund.html

12. Ben Hecht, *Perfidy*, Milah Press (Jerusalem, New London); ISBN: 0964688638; (April 1997)

13. David Yisraeli: "Le probleme palestinien dans la politique allemande, de 1889—1945," appendix 11. Also see Lenni Brenner, *Zionism in the Age of Dictators*, http://www.marxists.de/middleast/brenner/ch26.htm, noting that Shamir's organization (NMO) stressed that, "The NMO is closely related to the totalitarian movements of Europe in its ideology and structure."

14. Lenni Brenner, *Zionism in the Age of Dictators*, http://www.marxists.de/middleast/brenner/ch08.htm, citing Ronald Storrs, Orientations, p.405.

15. Cited in *The Jewish State*, by Yoram Hazony, p. 248.

16. "Escaping the Hell of the Holy Land," by Sylvana Foa in *The Village Voice*, February 13-19, 2002, http://villagevoice.com/issues/0207/foa.php .

II.   WHAT WILL THE NEW PALESTINE BE?

AMONG THOSE SINCERELY SEEKING A PEACEFUL resolution to the Palestine/Israel conflict, there has lately been a marked shift from advocacy of a two-state solution to advocacy of a one-state solution. This changed outlook has been driven primarily by a recognition of "facts on the ground." The material basis for a genuine independent state of Palestine is now a thing of the past, due to Israel's successful policy of using settlers and Jews-only highways and military force to drive the Palestinian population into isolated "bantustans" within the West Bank and Gaza Strip. There is no contiguous area of Palestinian-occupied land that could constitute a real Palestinian state.

The problem with the two-state solution, however, is not simply that it is no longer possible by reason of "facts on the ground." More importantly, the two-state solution is a conceptual and political trap that prevents Arab and Jewish working people from uniting around their common interests and values. The situation in the Middle East cannot be solved within a two-state framework; it leads nowhere except to more destruction and hate in a situation manipulated by Arab, Israeli, and U.S. elites. In contrast, there is every reason to be optimistic about a framework calling for replacing Israel and the West Bank and Gaza Strip with a single democratic Palestine in which all persons—no matter what their religion or ethnicity—are equals and live together in peace. That is why the growing consensus on a one-state solution is a development of historic proportions with new and inspiring possibilities.

Decades of conflict between Jews and Arabs in the Middle East have caused many to despair that there could ever be a just resolution that would end the violence. But a solution is not inherently impossible, as claimed by those who characterize the problem as "two peoples for one land." A solution is possible, and the apparently hopeless situation can be seen to be full of hope. For this transformation to occur, however, it will be first necessary for popular movements in Israel/Palestine to perceive the situation in a new way. Namely they must rethink who are their friends and who are their enemies.

The Key Obstacle To A One-State Solution

The key obstacle to achieving a one-state solution is the fact that the rulers of the United States and the Arab and Jewish rulers in the Middle East do not want ordinary Jews and Arabs to live together peacefully. The control of oil in the Middle East by foreign corporations depends upon preventing popular democratic movements from taking control of the region's resources and using them to meet the needs and aspirations of the working class. The key elite strategy to prevent such popular democratic movements from succeeding has been to foment conflict between Jews and Arabs. The more Jews and Arabs are pre-occupied with fighting and fearing each other, the easier it is for their respective rulers to control them, to strengthen their undemocratic regimes and preserve a status quo in which the few enrich themselves at the expense of the many. Class solidarity between working class Jews and Arabs threatens elite control. From the elite's perspective, peaceful and friendly relations between ordinary Jews and Arabs must be prevented at all costs.

This is why American presidents, Israeli prime ministers and Yasser Arafat over the decades have never negotiated a peaceful settlement of the Israeli-Palestine conflict. It is not that they tried and failed. It is that they have only pretended to try. The tacit agreement among all of these leaders is to keep the conflict going. This is why the United States gives Israel money and weapons and diplomatic backing no matter how flagrantly Israel violates UN resolutions and Geneva Agreements in carrying out its ethnic cleansing of Palestinians. The elite's social control strategy requires Israel to behave this way. The strategy requires Israel to provoke Arab hatred. For the plan to work long term, Israel needs to be armed to the teeth so that, on the one hand, the Arab governments can pretend to champion their people's anger at the Jews while, on the other hand, they can point to Israel's military might as a credible excuse for not actually "driving the Jews into the sea."

Those who envision a one-state solution as the result of a negotiated settlement between the PLO and Israel brokered by the United States are totally unrealistic. They are ignoring the most important "fact on the ground"—the elite's strategy of social control in the Middle East. In this unrealistic vision the PLO and the Israeli government will agree to set up a new state of Palestine (or some other name) with some kind of representative democracy with elections and so forth and with some kind of guarantee of equal rights under the law for Jews and Arabs. The new Palestine would be a capitalist society with class inequality, just like the United States and most other countries, but this would be, supposedly, a tremendous improvement over the present horrible state of affairs.

The problem with this scenario is that it will never happen. It will never happen for exactly the same reason that the elites could never afford to permit any solution—two state, one state or anything else—which entailed peaceful relations between ordinary Jews and Arabs. We need an entirely new way of thinking about how to achieve our goals.

How Can A One-State Solution Be Achieved?

How then can a viable one-state solution be achieved? It can only happen in spite of, not because of, the actions of American, Israeli, PLO and other regional leaders. A viable one-state solution can only happen if ordinary Arabs and Jews build a movement that sweeps the elites aside and makes society conform to their desire for a just peace. Such a movement can only succeed by mobilizing masses of people to challenge elite rule. In other words, only a revolutionary movement can succeed. It must make its goal a new Palestine where all forms of elite rule are abolished. This means replacing capitalist relations which benefit a small class of "owners" at the expense of a large class of "employees" with relations of equality and mutual aid where people work and live. In such a society ordinary people —not mullahs, priests or rabbis and not corporate CEOs or politicians beholden to them—would decide what kinds of behavior are proper and what kinds are not. Most importantly, in such a society matters of social importance would be decided by regular people who want to live together in peace, not by elites whose real aim is to control people with fear and lies.

The role of the United States in arming and funding Israel to make it a regional super-power, and more recently invading Iraq and establishing a long term U.S. military garrison of at least 100,000 troops there, shows that the American ruling class is committed to having its way in the Middle East. Any popular movement seriously aiming to win a viable one-state solution in Israel/Palestine will need to defeat the American rulers over an issue of strategic importance to them. This can only happen if the American public sides with ordinary Jews and Arabs in the Middle East against the entire American corporate elite (switching a Democrat for a Republican will not suffice.) To make this happen we need a radical break from old ways of trying to make change. We need to think about how to build a revolutionary movement, and about why this requires rejecting nationalism in all its forms—American nationalism, Jewish nationalism and even Palestinian nationalism.

A revolutionary movement based on class solidarity can only succeed by defining "we" and "they"—friend versus foe—in terms of the kind of society people want. "We" are the millions who want a society based on equality and solidarity and democracy. "They" are the few who want a society based on top-down control, inequality, exploitation and pitting people against each other. For every fanatical Zionist settler there are hundreds of Israeli Jews who, if they had any hope it were possible, would gladly trade their Zionist leaders' ethnic cleansing and the endless cycle of violence for a society where Jews and Arabs lived peacefully as equals. For every suicide bomber attempting to kill innocent civilian Jews there are hundreds of Palestinians who want to live peaceably as equals with Jews.

Nationalism is the enemy of any movement based on class solidarity. By nationalism I mean any ideology which defines "we" and "they" in terms of nationality or race or ethnicity or religion. Nationalism is the chief weapon elites use to control people by keeping them in fear of others like themselves who want the same thing. Jewish nationalism is Zionism waving the Star of David and telling Jews they need a "homeland of their own" because non-Jews and especially Arabs are all anti-Semites. Hamas and the PLO are two sides of the same coin of Arab nationalism, each leading Palestinians into an elite trap by different means which reinforce each other. Hamas does the bidding of Zionist rulers by waving the Palestinian flag and telling Palestinians to kill ordinary Jews standing at bus stops. This keeps Jews frightened enough to look to the Zionist elite as their protectors. The PLO fronts for the U.S. and Zionist elite by waving the Palestinian flag and lying to Palestinians that Zionist and American leaders will give them a better life in a "state of their own" as soon as Yasser Arafat charms them with his great negotiating skills. A revolutionary movement can only succeed by explicitly denouncing nationalism in all of its forms.

President George W. Bush advocates a "two state solution" not because he wants a peaceful resolution of the conflict but because framing the solution as "two states" reinforces the ideology of nationalism. It cements the notion that "we" and "they" are Jews versus Arabs, with each group needing "its own" state ruled by "its own" rulers. The two-state solution is dangled in front of the various opposition peace groups by Bush and Arafat and Israeli leaders as a means of preventing the notion of working class solidarity among Jews and Arabs from even being articulated within these groups. It's a way of nipping in the bud any chance that a revolutionary movement with any realistic chance of solving the conflict might develop.

A Revolutionary Movement Based on Class Solidarity

By breaking free from the shackles of nationalism in all of its forms, a revolutionary movement in the Middle East based on class solidarity can reach out to ordinary people across all national borders—including the borders of the United States!

The Middle East is a powder keg of class conflict. The oil-producing nations import cheap labor from all over the world and exploit these laborers ferociously. Unemployment for Saudi-citizen workers in Saudi Arabia is 27%. *Aljazeera* interviewed Dr Saad al-Faqih, a London-based dissident, and reported on November 3, 2003:

> "Homelessness is part of poverty and when we say poverty we mean real poverty," he said. "People estimate at least 30% are living below the poverty line," added the head of the Movement for Islamic Reform. Saudis are lining up at the royal palaces pleading for help, he said, adding the royal family is consuming 60-80% of the country's revenues. "Their dignity prevents them from begging," he said. More and more Saudis are unable to meet their basic essentials. "They are unable to pay water bills. They are unable to pay electricity bills. Meals are hard to come by," said al-Faqih. "We're talking about major areas in the big cities," he said. While there are no official figures, more than 12,000 beggars were arrested in Saudi Arabia in 1998 of which 9000 were foreign and expelled.[1]

Huge strikes in Israel are frequent. The latest one occurred November 3, 2003 when "a nationwide strike against plans to overhaul Israel's welfare state shut down government services, banks and train service."[2] One of the largest occurred from December 3rd through 7th, 1997, when 700,000 Israeli workers mounted a general strike against the government. The country was paralyzed, with airports, seaports, banks, government offices, state-owned industries and the national stock exchange effectively shut down. After the first day of the strike, the nation's teachers joined in the walk-out and the national journalists' association declared their support for the strike. The strike was a response to indications that the Treasury was attempting to violate wage and pension agreements signed in 1995 and 1996. Israeli workers were also protesting government privatization plans which would entail large-scale lay-offs.

Workers in Egypt confront the very same kinds of attacks from the Egyptian elite. Despite a no-strike law, public sector workers in Cairo and Alexandria staged over ten strikes in the single month of April 1999. Egyptian laws punish strikers with two-year jail sentences and more for "inciting a strike." Nonetheless, in just the months from June to December 1999, there were four sit-down strikes and nine hunger strikes by government workers in Egypt. During the entire year there were a total of 52 work strikes and 32 sit-down strikes.

The PLO talks about freeing Palestine. Its actions, however, are not only about making a few Palestinians rich at the expense of the rest but, even worse, providing a fig leaf to cover up the fact that the Israeli government, not Palestinians, rules the West Bank and Gaza Strip. Frank Kortmann, MD, PhD, a mental health consultant on trauma and trauma counseling in Palestine, wrote in a report dated October 14-26, 2002, that the corruption of the Palestinian National Authority was so bad that "people in the street notice it everyday." Kortmann noted that some of his informants in Gaza "even said that they were better off during the occupation by the Israelis." And he reported on data presented at the Palestinian conference on poverty held that year:

> The number of millionaires grew in the last nine years from zero to 500, whereas 50% of the Palestinian population has to live on less than $2 U.S. per day, with prices comparable to those in the Netherlands. According to an informant, at that conference the poor did not ask for more money, but for land to cultivate and to live on, and for equal opportunities for jobs for their children, as the children of high governmental officials have.[3]

The PLO's role reinforcing Israeli occupation was expressed very well by Gordon Levy who wrote of the leaders of the Palestinian Authority in *Haaretz* November 9, 2003:

> If they were more concerned about the subjects they are supposed to be in charge of—the well-being of their nation—they would have resigned and thereby torn the mask from the false impression of the supposed government and the "state in the making." They would have ceased to be the fig leaf that serves and perpetuates the Israeli occupation. Instead, they cling

to the few honors and benefits that Israel continues to confer on a few of them, and they go on lending a hand to the great deception that a sovereign Palestinian Authority and a government with powers exist.

Nationalism has been the key factor sustaining elite rule in the Middle East. The idea that, no matter how bad they may be, rulers of one's own nationality give protection from "the real enemy"—Israel or Arabs or Christians or Muslims, as the case may be—is pure poison. It subverts the efforts of ordinary people to make a better world without elite domination. And all top nationalist leaders without exception spread this poison and understand very clearly the role it plays. Thus far nationalism has enabled the ruling elites to prevail. The PLO and Hamas and the Zionists as well as the peace groups embracing a "two state solution" have all worked to promote nationalism and thus strengthen the grip of all the elite rulers. This nationalism has gone virtually unchallenged. But a class-based revolutionary movement that attacked the nationalist leaders—all of them without distinction—could turn the tables and solve the Middle East conflict for real by releasing the pent-up energy of millions of ordinary working people all across the region and even the world.

Such a movement would give Americans an entirely different way of thinking about their own government's role in the Middle East. Defining the conflict in terms of the conflicting values of ordinary Jews and Arabs versus the Jewish, Arab and American elites would resonate with Americans who, like working people all over the world, are coming under sharper and sharper attacks from their leaders in the form of joblessness, cuts in schools and other social services (to pay for military aggression abroad), vanishing health care availability, and increasing inequality in all walks of life. What formerly seemed to be a regional conflict between "terrorist Arabs" and "democracy-loving Jews" would be seen by ordinary Americans as a struggle of people like themselves who want the same things they do, against the same corporate elite who are attacking Americans as well. In this new context it is quite realistic to hope for defeating the American ruling class on its own territory.

The hopelessness produced by unmitigated failure to achieve peace in the Middle East has benefited the rulers of the world by demoralizing and demobilizing millions of ordinary people who want a different way. Certainly the persistence of the violence has contributed to making people all over the world more cynical about the possibility of a world without ethnic conflict or the possibility of changing the world with class solidarity. No doubt the rulers intend for the Middle East to have exactly this depressing effect on people everywhere. In the United

States the media play up all the Arab-Jewish violence in the Middle East and hardly mention the huge general strikes and other forms of class solidarity that take place around the world from Italy to Bolivia.

In this sense, the elite's success in controlling people in the Middle East by whipping up hatred between Jews and Arabs has been one of their great global victories. But it is also their Achilles heel if only we recognize it as such and turn it to our advantage. We should expose the real enemy in the Middle East—all of the nationalist leaders who wave their flags to lead "their people" into attacks on other working class people.

We need to do whatever it takes to make sure that ordinary Jews and Arabs come to fully understand the role of nationalism as an elite weapon against them. We need to do whatever it takes to develop a revolutionary movement that breaks out of the trap of nationalism and champions the values and aspirations shared by ordinary people of all nationalities. And what does it take? Nothing that we can't start doing immediately: Speaking out clearly about who are our friends and who are our enemies. Describing the conflict in terms that reveal rather than mask the truth. Articulating working class values and aspirations shared by ordinary Jews and Arabs. Exposing and attacking the elite values, lies and aims of all the nationalist leaders.

The few could never impose all of the terrible "facts on the ground" on the many if they only had guns and tanks. They dominate the people of the Middle East because they have relied on unchallenged nationalism to confuse and muddle the thinking of everybody who is trying to make a better world. We must break out of the nationalism trap that has enslaved the people of the world for so long. This is the only way to achieve the one-state solution. It is the only way to give renewed hope to millions of people in the Middle East. It will constitute one of the greatest global victories of working people in history. It will resonate across the planet and mark the beginning of the end of elite rule altogether. Let us work to make it so.

Notes
1. See: http://english.aljazeera.net/NR/exeres/004D25AC-86AF-4C51-9575-E98564967AF4. htm.
2. Peter Enav, *Canadian Press*, November 03, 2003.
3. Report: Identification Mission to Palestine, Prevention of trauma and trauma counselling interventions, 14-26 October 2002 by Frank Kortmann, MD, PhD Mental Health Consultant.

III.   DO JEWS REALLY RULE THE WORLD?

AT THE OCTOBER MEETING OF THE ORGANIZATION of the Islamic Conference, Malaysian Prime Minister Mahathir Mohamad declared that "today the Jews rule this world by proxy." Not unexpectedly, the Prime Minister was charged with "blatant anti-Semitism" by the governments of the United States, Israel, the European Union and Australia.[1] More unexpectedly, some Jews came to the defense of the Prime Minister's remarks. The Israeli, Israel Shamir, an outspoken foe of Zionism and a prolific writer about the Israel/Palestine conflict, reported shortly after the Malaysian Prime Minister's speech that his good friend, Elias Davidsson, of Jerusalem, wrote:

> As a Jew myself (but opposed to Zionism) I need no encouragement from
> Malaysian PM Mahathir Mohamad to observe what should be obvious
> to the blatant eye: Namely that Jews effectively rule U.S. foreign policy
> and thus determine to a great extent the conduct of most countries.[2]

Those of us who oppose Zionism, who want to stop the United States from backing Israel's ethnic cleansing against the Palestinians, and who want to build a movement that can defeat the anti-democratic elites who rule over people virtually everywhere on the planet, need to ask two questions: 1) Is there any truth to the Malaysian Prime Minister's claim that Jews rule the world by proxy? and 2) Even if all Jews stood against us, would it help our efforts to categorize "the Jews" as our enemy?

I believe the answer to both of these questions is "No." Since Israel Shamir articulates the contrary position so clearly, I want to examine what he says closely and respond.

Do Jews Determine U.S. Foreign Policy?

Let us start with the first question: Do Jews rule the world by proxy? The actual question, to be precise, is "Do Jews determine U.S. foreign policy?" Shamir weighs in on this question by criticizing Nat Weinstein's assertion that, "[Former U.S. Senator Patrick J.] Buchanan's insinuations of a Jewish conspiracy in the service of Israel echo a similar claim that lay at the heart of Adolph Hitler's brand of fascism."[3]

Shamir responds:

> However, an open Jewish 'conspiracy' of supporting Israel is a hard fact,
> and it is expressed by almost every Jewish newspaper by slogan 'Jews
> stand steadfast behind Israel'. This slogan is not an empty word: recent

survey shows 86% of the U.S. Jews support Israel. In a recent discussion on the Web, Jeff Blankfort, a consistent antizionist, made a sober conclusion: "the distinction that we are always careful to make between being Jewish and being Zionist is essentially deceptive and that while all Jews are not Zionists, the organized Jewish communities throughout the world, despite whatever differences they may have, are totally behind the Zionist project. To pretend that these organizations do not speak for the overall Jewish community, one, that without any doubt, supports Israel as a Jewish state, is illusory."[4]

Shamir acknowledges that "all Jews are not Zionists" but he chooses to emphasize that the Zionists not only have the backing of most Jews, but that they also "rule the world" or at least the part of the world necessary to control the U.S. government's foreign policy. Shamir writes:

[T]he Jewish Lobby is not a 'small group of pro-Zionist Jews' but an extremely powerful group of billionaires, media lords, and their supporters in the left and the right, from the *New York Times* to the *Nation*, from Wolfowitz of Pentagon to Rabbi Lerner of *Tikkun*.

To refute Weinstein's claim that it is absurd to believe that a small group of pro-Zionist Jews could dictate foreign or domestic policy to the hard-nosed, quintessentially-pragmatic American capitalist class, Shamir argues that:

'Hard-nosed American capitalists' are indeed 'quintessentially-pragmatic', and they understand what is good for them personally. That is why even the dedicated antisemite Henry Ford preferred to scrap his book when he had met with the irresistible force of Jewish boycott. That is why the American parliamentarians are united in their support of Israel, as it was recently confirmed by the Senate vote 89 to 4 against Syria. The Iraqi war was a disaster from the point of view of American capitalism: as it was predicted, it brought them no oil, no weaponry orders, no new friends; but the capitalists are not idealists Weinstein presupposes: they know that their stand against Israel would ruin them personally, and they disregard 'the general interest of capitalist class.'

Like many people trying to understand why the U.S. government so consistently backs Israel, Shamir has concluded that the explanation lies in the power of the "Jewish Lobby" in the United States and specifically in its ability to put pressure on powerful individuals in government and business to force them to carry out pro-Israel policies which they would otherwise reject. But the premise of this reasoning is false. The pro-Israeli policies of the U.S. government are in fact highly beneficial to U.S. corporate interests in the Middle East, and American politicians beholden to these corporate interests would carry out these policies even absent any pressure from the "Jewish Lobby."

U.S. rulers, acting on behalf of big corporations, back Israel because it is the key to their strategy for controlling the oil of the Middle East. To control the oil these corporations need to ensure that the rulers of the oil-producing nations in the Middle East are corporate-friendly regimes able to prevent ordinary Arabs from taking control of the oil and other resources and using it to benefit ordinary people instead of enriching foreign and domestic elites. The Middle East is a powder-keg of class struggle. The U.S. and the anti-democratic regimes in nations like Saudi-Arabia fear any popular revolutionary movement directed against Arab elite rule getting started anywhere in the region. To prevent such a movement developing, U.S. and Middle East rulers have all relied on the key strategy of directing the anger of the Arab masses against Israel. The strategy is for Israel to serve as a "lightning rod" of class struggle for the whole region. In order for the strategy to work, Israel must provoke Arab hatred by doing exactly what it presently does—carry out brutal and naked ethnic cleansing against Palestinians. The strategy also requires that the U.S. arm Israel to the teeth so that Arab rulers can pretend to champion "their people's" hostility to Israel while at the same time pointing to Israel's overwhelming military superiority as an excuse for not actually "driving the Jews into the sea."

The "Jewish Lobby" in the U.S. and the Zionists in Israel, of course, have their own reasons for supporting the U.S. rulers' pro-Israel strategy of social control in the Middle East. The Zionists in Israel benefit by receiving enormous military and economic aid from the United States and by setting themselves up as the ruling elite in Israel. The Arab hatred of Israel only helps the Zionist elite stay in power, as every suicide bombing of Israeli Jews at a bus stop only makes Jews more fearful of Arabs and more convinced that, no matter how anti-working class the Zionist rulers are (massive strikes of working class Jews against the Zionist government are frequent), the Zionist rulers are the only ones who can protect Jews from Arabs. Were it not for their strategic value to U.S. corporate interests, the Zionists would no doubt have remained today what they were from their modern beginnings at the turn of the century until World War II—a rather small cult, with followers from only a very small minority of Jews, whose leaders sought an audience with one imperialist power after another begging for a plot of land to call a Jewish state.

Like their Zionist counterparts in Israel, powerful Jewish business and religious leaders in the United States also have their reasons for backing the U.S. rulers' Middle East policy. Chief among them is the fact that Zionism helps these Jewish leaders to maintain their position in society as powerful and privileged elites. Zionism is Jewish nationalism, and nationalism—be it American, Chinese, Jewish or whatever—is an ideology that tells ordinary people to defend those of the same nationality or ethnic group (and obey them when they are heads of government) because national identity is more important than "secondary" issues like class inequality and exploitation. Jews who hold positions high up in American society want very much to be seen by working class Jews as "defenders of the Jewish state of Israel" and not as upper class individuals who happen to be Jewish but who benefit from class inequality and hardships that hurt all working class people whether they are Jewish or not. Additionally, American Jewish leaders cannot fail to appreciate that their admission into the top tiers of American society is made far more secure if they advocate rather than oppose the Middle East foreign policy pursued by the most powerful American families who, like the Rockefellers and Mellons and Gettys and Fords, are not Jewish.

There is no evidence that the U.S. government has been "taken over" by Jews. That many of the government officials advocating a "pro-Israel" foreign policy are Jewish merely reflects the fact that the policy has the support of many Jews, not that it exists because of Jews. These facts give the lie to the notion that "the Jews" rule the world by proxy.

How Committed To Zionism Are Ordinary Jews?

But even if Jews do not "rule the world," it is undeniable that many Jews are indeed pro-Zionist to one degree or another and most of the large organizations that speak for Jews are today pro-Zionist. By "pro-Zionist" I mean they support the existence of a Jewish state, of Israel. And they go along, to varying degrees, with the logic of a Jewish state—in other words they accept the notion that only Jews should be the sovereign authority in the land of Israel even though non-Jews make up a substantial proportion of the population. Thus the great debate in Israel and among diaspora Jews is (after being stripped of euphemisms) whether Israel should continue to occupy the West Bank and Gaza Strip, which requires ruling over Arabs without any pretense of being democratic; or whether Israel should end the occupation and withdraw to the pre-1967 "green line" inside of which Arabs form a minority of only 20%, thus enabling exclusive Jewish sovereignty to more easily masquerade as a "democracy." The dominant institutions in Israel exclude from the public arena any debate or expressions of doubt among Jews regarding the more fundamental question: Should there be a Jewish state? Should Israel exist, as it is now defined?

I grant that there is much support for Zionism among Jews. I recall my (Jewish) great-aunt, a secretary barely making ends meet who, on the occasion of the 1967 war, sent her entire week's paycheck to the government of Israel. Only the blinders of Zionism can explain why so many Jews perceive themselves as staunch foes of racism and champions of the universal values of equality and democracy and at the same time see nothing racist or anti-democratic about the fact that the Israeli government bulldozes down the homes of Palestinians just because they are Palestinians, that it builds super-highways for Jews only, that it destroyed, depopulated and occupied at least 418 Palestinian villages in 1948,[5] or that it provides each Jewish settler four times as much water as a Palestinian so that Palestinians sicken and die of thirst while the settlers enjoy lush lawns and swimming pools, to cite just a few of the crimes that Zionism routinely justifies in the name of defending the Jewish state against its Arab enemies. I do not deny the seriousness of the problem of Zionism's hold over Jews. Nonetheless, ordinary Jews are not unalterably pro-Zionist and their present loyalty to Zionism does not run as deep as one might suppose. From the perspective of Yoram Hazony, a passionately pro-Zionist Israeli historian and author of *The Jewish State*, it is nothing short of alarming how rapidly Israeli Jews are abandoning their Zionism. Here is how Hazony describes his generation of Israelis in contrast to the founding fathers' generation:

> This generation of the sons certainly paid its dues in military service, but its members' failure to ignite like their fathers had for the cause of the Jewish state was gradually to become an open scandal, perhaps the open scandal of the years after Ben-Gurion had been expunged from public life.[6]

Hazony was most alarmed by his experience when serving in the Israeli Defense Force in the late 1980s:

> Perched atop a rooftop in Hebron with a Netanya businessman for a twelve-hour watch; or guarding a communications relay on a mountain peak for days on end with a newly immigrated Russian poet; or on patrol in an Arab village with a kibbutznik officer in command of the jeep—during one stint or the next, you gradually get to see and hear ev-

erything. And the "everything" was something rather shocking, but also unambiguous: The Jews of Israel are an exhausted people, confused and without direction. This is not to say that they are unwilling to fight. Israelis still agree that they will carry on their struggle if they must. But in no end of discussions, it was made clear to me that there was a vast gulf between their willingness to fight and sacrifice and their ability to understand why they should do so. Certainly, they all knew that we were at war—including those who believed we could and should get out of it— but as soon as the discussion skidded close to the reasons that it might be worth being in this fight, the screen went blank. Of what value is the Jewish people? What can it contribute to mankind? What is to be gained by joining in its struggle? Why should one sacrifice on its behalf? Why should the Jewish state exist at all?...And then there was the pudgy young officer, days before finishing out his four-year tour of duty, who objected when I inadvertently referred to him as a Jew. "Don't say that to me," he said huskily, putting his hand up like a traffic cop. "If you want, you can talk to me as a human being. But don't talk to me as Jew. That doesn't speak to me." From him I understood that one had to be careful whom one implicated in being a Jew in the Jewish state.[7]

Ordinary Jews, an "exhausted people, confused and without direction," far from being "rulers of the world" are like working class people of any other nationality. They are manipulated and controlled by their elite rulers with an avalanche of nationalist propaganda which is made particularly effective by the suicide bombings orchestrated by Hamas (with the tacit if not covert encouragement of Israel's rulers.) They are confused because all of the alternatives they hear in what passes for public discourse are confined within the parameters of nationalism which frames everything as a conflict between national (or racial/ethnic/religious) groups, such as "the Arabs/Palestinians" versus "the Jews." They are demoralized about breaking out of the trap of nationalism because the last great attempt to do this—the Communist movement with its call for international working class solidarity —created anti-democratic regimes that offered absolutely no hope for a better world. Every natural inclination they have to look for a solution based on the working class values that ordinary people share and which elites attack—equality and solidarity and democracy—is branded as disloyalty to their nation. Working class Jews seeking to make common cause with Arabs like themselves are accused of advocating the destruction of the Jewish state.

Jews drafted into the Israeli Defense Forces are not that different from American soldiers drafted to fight in Vietnam. American G.I.s too became "exhausted, confused and without direction." In boot camp the young soldiers learned that the enemy was "gooks" and Communists. This made it easier for American G.I.s to follow their orders to attack the Viet Cong. Similarly, Israeli soldiers find it easier to shoot at Palestinians and bulldoze down their homes after all the efforts by Zionist leaders—and their Hamas helpers in this regard—to convince them that Arabs are bloodthirsty Jew-killers. But American soldiers also saw that they were being ordered to attack the entire Vietnamese peasantry, and they had no idea why. Troops were told it was treason against the United States if they sided with ordinary Vietnamese against U.S. rulers. So there was little overt rebellion by G.I.s against the U.S. government. But G.I.s "fragged" (i.e., killed, typically with a fragmentation bomb) their "gung ho" (i.e., very enthusiastic and dedicated) officers in the field to avoid obeying orders to attack the peasants. This and other forms of resistance to the U.S. high command eventually made it clear to President Nixon that he could no longer rely on American soldiers to fight Vietnamese peasants, and it forced the U.S. to pull out of Vietnam in disgrace.

In Israel today IDF soldiers are engaging in more than just passive resistance. They are organizing overt resistance to Israel's occupation of the West Bank and Gaza Strip, with many speaking out publicly against the occupation and flatly refusing to serve in the occupied territories. The refuseniks have not, to my knowledge, challenged the idea of a Jewish state (which is a serious weakness in their efforts to achieve a real peace.) But a movement—were it to be organized—based on class solidarity between ordinary Jews and Arabs and calling for a one-state solution in which Jews and Arabs were truly equal would certainly appeal to many Jews looking for a way out of the trap into which they have been thrust by history.

Most of the Israeli population, when not diverted by fear of Arabs, already find themselves in conflict with their Zionist rulers. Huge strikes in Israel are frequent. The latest one occurred November 3, 2003 when "a nationwide strike against plans to overhaul Israel's welfare state shut down government services, banks and train service."[8] One of the largest occurred from December 3 through 7, 1997, when 700,000 Israeli workers mounted a general strike against the government. The country was paralyzed, with airports, seaports, banks, government offices, state-owned industries and the national stock exchange effectively shut down. After the first day of the strike, the nation's teachers joined in the walk-out and the national journalists' association declared their support for the strike. The strike was a response to indications that the Treasury was attempting to violate wage and pension agreements signed in 1995 and 1996. Israeli workers were also protesting government privatization plans which would entail large-scale lay-offs.

Many Israeli Jews experience Zionism in their daily life the way Yaffa Yosefian does. Yaffa Yosefian, according to the New Israel Fund's Fall, *2003 NIF News*, was

> ...one of Israel's 113,000 single mothers [who] doesn't know if she and her family will survive from month to month. On July 1, the Finance Ministry cut deeply into social support payments to Israel's needy, including single mothers, as part of its new economic austerity program...Yosefian is one of dozens of women who camped outside the Ministry of Finance in Jerusalem. She was motivated to protest not only by her own plight but also a sense of social responsibility for all the single-parent families hit hard by the cuts.

Some people say the Jewish religion itself is the problem. They claim that it turns Jews against the rest of humanity. They point to passages in the Old Testament and to the classical (i.e., Middle Ages until the end of the18th century) writings of acclaimed rabbis telling Jews that they are the "chosen people," that non-Jews are inferior and unworthy of rights that belong only to Jews, that Jews should not marry non-Jews and should not even encourage non-Jews to convert to Judaism. The holocaust survivor, Israel Shahak (not to be confused with Israel Shamir, cited earlier), provides strong evidence for these claims about traditional orthodox rabbinical teachings in his book, *Jewish History, Jewish Religion: The Weight of Three Thousand Years*. Such rabbinical teachings—a kind of Jewish nationalism pre-dating modern Zionism—were no doubt used by Jewish elites in the past to turn ordinary Jews against non-Jews, bind them to their "betters" and make them more controllable. The old rabbinical teachings also dovetail with modern Zionism, and (with the exception of the small Neturei Karta orthodox Jewish group, who, wearing their traditional black garb, go to demonstrations holding signs that read, "Zionist Spokesmen Do Not Represent World Jewry"[9]) Jewish orthodox religious leaders are pro-Zionist. The relevant point, however, is that however influential the chauvinistic aspect of the Jewish religion may have been in the past, it is rapidly losing its influence over contemporary Jews around the world. Of the approximately 13.5 million Jews in the world, 4.9 million live in Israel and 5.6 million live in the United States. Of all the Jews in Israel, 71% light the Hanukkah candles (which signifies no more religious persuasion than does decorating a Christmas tree for a Christian) but only 23% say they always attend syn-agogue on Saturday morning, and 56% say they never do.[10] Among the majority of Jews, who live outside of Israel (the "diaspora"), surveys done in 1998 indicate that fifty percent marry outside their faith, and in some American cities the inter-marriage rate reaches 80 percent. In the U.S. only about 20 to 25 percent of inter-married couples where one partner is Jewish raise their children as Jews.[11]

These demographic facts are cause for great anxiety on the part of Zionist leaders who, though largely secular themselves, rely very much on the orthodox religious Jews to provide the "moral" backbone of Zionism. But for those who want Jews to join a movement against Jewish nationalism and chauvinism it is only encouraging news.

Who Benefits If We Categorize "The Jews" As Our Enemy?

Even if all Jews stood against us, would it help our efforts to categorize "the Jews" as our enemy? Like many others, I find it discouraging to hear Jews (especially close friends) make apologies for Israel and defend Jewish nationalism with re-marks like, "No matter how bad its leaders may be, still, we Jews need a homeland of our own and must defend Israel from its enemies." I understand the temptation to lump all Jews together with their Zionist leaders and categorize "the Jews" as the enemy. I have sketched above my reasons for believing that ordinary Jews can be won to a class-based movement against Zionism.[12] But let us accept, for the sake of argument, that virtually all Jews will forever stand in support of Israel. Who would mainly benefit if we categorized our enemy as "the Jews?"

The answer is not ordinary Palestinians or working people anywhere. The an-swer is that the American ruling class and the Zionist leaders of Israel would be the real beneficiaries. The power of these elites is based largely on nationalism, and de-fining friend and foe with categories like "the Jews" only reinforces nationalistic thinking. It would in fact endorse the claim of elites to speak for all "their people," thereby greatly enhancing their control. In the Middle East the ruling elites need to prevent the Arab masses from coming to power, and they do that by turning Arab anger against "the Jews." President Bush and the entire corporate elite in the U.S. rely primarily on nationalism to stay in power despite the fact that they attack the values and living standards of most Americans. They rely on the idea that Ameri-cans must all stick together and obey their rulers because the "real" enemy is exter-nal—Islamic terrorists or North Korean Communists. Defining the enemy with a category like "the Jews" plays right into the nationalism that elites depend upon.

There is only one way to defeat the elites who truly rule the world. We must identify as the enemy all those who consciously aim to benefit at the expense of the many, who enforce inequality, who control people by pitting them against each other and lying to and manipulating them, who attack people's efforts to help each other and to stand in solidarity with each other, and who impose top-down control and use fake democracy to defeat real democracy. And we must reach out to all of the billions of other people, no matter what their race or nationality or religious beliefs, as friends or at least potential friends. In other words we need to build a movement that isolates our real enemy explicitly on the basis of the elite values they stand for, and unites everybody else on the basis of the positive values they share.

There is a strong association between these values and social class, which is why I use the phrase "class-based" sometimes as a shorthand. Most working class people try to shape the part of the world over which they have any control with the values of equality, commitment to each other and democracy. And most people in the wealthiest ruling families hold the opposite elite values of inequality, competition, and top-down control. But there are exceptions in both cases, which is why I disagree with the Marxist practice of formulating friend and foe based on social class membership. This Marxist approach stems from the fundamental flaw in Marxist theory—the idea that social change is not caused by people consciously fighting for conflicting values, but by impersonal economic "laws" driven by the supposed fact that everybody is motivated by self-interest and class conflict is merely a conflict of self-interests—the self-interest of workers who trade labor for wages versus the conflicting self-interest of owners who buy labor to make a profit.

It is impossible to accurately identify who are our friends and who are our foes if we resort to using nationalistic categories like "the Jews." Doing so obscures what our struggle is all about. It shifts attention away from the categories that precisely define who we are fighting and who we are asking to join us and what we are fighting for. A movement organized around such misleading and nationalistic kinds of thinking is easily misled by any skilled leader fronting for the elite. This is why mis-leaders have been able to sabotage real resistance to Zionism in the Middle East. Yasser Arafat, for example, denounces Israel and waves the Palestinian flag but his real role is to pacify Palestinians by lying to them that they will get all they want by waiting patiently for negotiations to work, and telling them that in the meantime they already have Palestinian rule (the "Palestine Authority"). The sham "peace process" of Oslo and the "Road Map" could not have succeeded in dampening Palestinian resistance without a nationalist mis-leader like Arafat, whose legitimacy depends on Palestinian confusion about who are their friends and who are their foes. Nationalism makes it hard for Palestinians to organize anything Arafat disapproves of, even though most Palestinians can plainly see that he presides over a corrupt Palestinian Authority that has enabled the number of millionaires under the Palestine Authority to grow from zero to 500 in the last nine years while 50% of the Palestinian population lives on less than $2 U.S. per day.[13]

There are moments in history when crucial decisions must be made that will affect the outcome of great struggles, and this is one of them. A very encouraging consensus is developing for a one-state solution in Palestine/Israel. This is a profound and inspiring rejection of George Bush's nationalistic propaganda calling for a "two state" solution based on the idea that Jews and Palestinians have inherently competing values and interests and therefore each needs a "state of their own" (ruled, it goes without saying, by "their own" elites). Our enemies will do everything possible to prevent ordinary Palestinians and Jews from uniting around their shared aspirations. In particular they will encourage our movement to label "the Jews" as our enemy. Let us avoid this terrible trap, and build a movement that unites all of our potential friends against all of our real enemies and wins.

Notes

1. See: http://www.abc.net.au/news/newsitems/s969056.htm.
2. See: http://www.adelaideinstitute.org/Dissenters/mahathir_mohamad2.htm.
3. See: http://www.socialistviewpoint.org/sum_03/sum_03_08.html.
4. See: http://www.israelshamir.net/ and http://www.israelshamir.net/english/the%20marxists.shtml.
5. See: http://www.columbia.edu/cu/museo/6/jacir/.
6. Yoram Hazony, *The Jewish State*, pg. xvi.
7. *Ibid.*, pp xvii–xviii.
8. Peter Enav, *Canadian Press*, November 03, 2003.
9. See: http://www.nkusa.org/.
10. See: http://www.jcpa.org/dje/articles2/howrelisr.htm.
11. See: http://www.washington-report.org/backissues/1298/9812056.html.
12. For more discussion of how this requires a clean break with Marxism see "The Communist Manifesto Is Wrong" http://www.newdemocracyworld.org/manifesto.htm.
13. For more on this see "What Will The New Palestine Be?" http://www.newdemocracyworld.org/new_Palestine.htm.

Part Three

The Meaning
of Class Struggle

by David Stratman

I. ORDINARY PEOPLE

NEW DEMOCRACY IS BASED ON THE IDEA THAT ordinary people's everyday lives have revolutionary meaning. Are we nuts?

Look at the striking Brockton nurses as an example. Nursing is known as one of the "caring professions" with good reason. When young women and men choose the profession, it is at least in part because they want to care for other human beings. There are a lot of professional skills that go into nursing; but beneath their technical competence there must be a caring quality in nurses, a quality of love and kindness, to tie their skills together and bring them to life.

These qualities of love and support for other human beings inevitably bring nurses into conflict with hospital authorities. The nurses are motivated by concern for their patients and for their own families, but the first concern of hospital management is the bottom line. This conflict over goals—human caring vs. the bottom line—simmers beneath the surface of hospital life and touches every decision over staffing, overtime, length of patients' stays, and other vital questions affecting the quality of care. The nurses' strike didn't create this conflict. It brought it into the open.

What does all this have to do with revolution and the meaning of people's lives? Nurses are not so very different from the rest of us. The qualities that the nurses bring home to their families and friends are the same qualities of caring and love that they bring to their patients. These are the same qualities that the rest of us bring to our own families and friends. The success of all of our relationships depends on love and loyalty and commitment to each other. These qualities may be "special," because we value them above all else; but they are qualities that we all share to one extent or another and that we all admire.

Are these qualities revolutionary? Yes, they are, in two important ways.

One, these values—our commitment to other people, our determination to do what's right—will always bring us into conflict with the authorities, just as the nurses' values bring them inevitably into conflict with hospital management. Whether we are auto workers or teachers or students or retirees, the authorities are trying to squeeze us and our families and friends. They are trying to attack our self-confidence, break our connections with other people, undermine our belief that we and the people we care about have the right or the power to change anything. To the extent that we remain true to our commitments, sooner or later we have to fight. Two, these values of support and solidarity are revolutionary because their extension to the rest of society would be a revolution, the transformation of society.

When we in New Democracy talk about revolution, we aren't talking about pie in the sky or something that's never existed. We're talking about reshaping the world with the very best values that we practice now, today, in our families, with our friends and co-workers, with our students and patients.

We believe that the smallest acts of kindness and the most public, collective acts of revolution are on a continuum of struggle to make the world the way we believe it should be. The nurses' strike is a perfect example of this; it is a more public and collective expression of values the nurses practice everyday at their patients' bedsides. It is an act of love and an act of class war.

What would the world look like if society were based on these best values of ordinary people? Imagine.

II.   LET'S BE PRACTICAL

KEITH THOMAS, A MACHINIST AT THE BOEING plant in Wichita, recently told me a very interesting story. Keith and a handful of co-workers in several Boeing plants organized a rank-and-file caucus, Unionists for Democratic Change (UDC). They exposed the union (International Association of Machinists-IAM) leadership and led the fight against the company. Their numbers grew to about 500 in locals in Wichita and Seattle. There are about 4,000 union members in Keith's plant, out of 8,000 hourly workers.

In the months leading up to their contract expiration in October, 1995 UDC frequently hand-billed their plants to inform members of contract issues. A few days before the contract expired, workers began actions to build solidarity and give management and each other a real taste of workers' power. In Seattle thousands of workers marched on the flight lines and around the plant. In Seattle and Wichita, workers spontaneously downed tools and began to beat on something, anything, that would make noise. At first they did this every hour on the hour. Then they began to do it every half-hour. Then every fifteen minutes. Pretty soon, Keith said, it got so loud in the plant that you couldn't hear somebody shouting in your ear. Management began to run around giving people other things to beat on than their machines or airplane wings. Finally, when the noise became too intense, management left the plant floor, in effect ceding control of the plant to the workers. The workers kept this up for several days. They rejected the new contract and went on strike. Members rejected concessions negotiated by the union. Finally Boeing caved in to sustained worker solidarity.

The story doesn't end here. The company and the union leadership were very threatened by the rank-and-file group. As Keith put it, "the caucus was under attack before the strike, during the strike, and after the strike." Several people had their cars vandalized. One activist had his brake lines cut. During the strike one member of the caucus had his life threatened. Shots were fired in the direction of Keith's house while children were playing outside in the street. An hour earlier a member was told down at the union hall that "UDC needs a good killing."

The level of threats and reprisals became more than many members of the rank-and-file group had bargained for. After awhile the leadership core decided to disband the larger group. They destroyed all their membership lists and computer files, and freed members of any obligations. They informed union officials of their move.

The original core group of four or five is thinking about what to do next. Keith has concluded that it's impossible to reform the labor movement. So what should they do? Keith's story is unusual for its drama, but its key elements have been experienced by many activists inside and outside the unions. Thinking about his situation brought me back to some of the thoughts that led me to write *We CAN Change the World*.

I have long felt that we need a revolution in the U.S.—and world—and that anything that stopped short of revolution, such as attempts at reforming the unions, or attempts to impose significant reforms on capitalism, were bound to fail. I have also long felt that building a popular revolutionary movement in the U.S. is very doable, far more than most people realize, and that, the more revolutionary the movement becomes—revolutionary in the sense of truly challenging capitalist goals, values, plans, and power with the values and goals and aspirations of ordinary people—the more popular it can be. My thinking, in other words, was the opposite of the left assumption that to be "revolutionary" means to be isolated. I was starting with some very different ideas about people from the left's and I had some very different notions of revolution.

I also felt that building a revolutionary movement would consist more of reaching out to other working people with the revolutionary message than it would consist of mounting direct challenges to capitalist institutions, such as corporations or union structures. Building the revolutionary movement would in fact pose far more of a long-range threat to the capitalist system than any challenge of union leaders or management of a particular corporation, but it would not bring about immediate reprisals or have the same high personal costs, since it would not pose an immediate threat to specific people or institutions.[1]

What about Keith's situation? Their success brought down a storm all out of proportion to what many people were prepared for, because it posed an immediate threat to some union hacks who like their jobs and are determined to hold onto them, and who play an important role for management.

Many people in the rank-and-file group were not prepared for the level of reprisal probably for several reasons, but I'd guess that two reasons were these: 1) they thought they were demanding what was only fair and right—that their union should represent them rather than the company—and were surprised when their entirely reasonable demands brought such a response; and 2) the level of risk they were taking was out of proportion to the change they thought they would make if they succeeded.

There is plenty of evidence that people will make terrific sacrifices and fight against incredible odds if they find themselves inspired by the goals of the struggle. The Vietnamese prevailed against B-52s and napalm because of their belief in the Revolution. People in this country engaged in bloody struggles to build industrial unionism because they thought they were taking an important step to changing the world. People in the Civil Rights struggle saw it as a struggle over what it means to be human, and were willing to sacrifice much to achieve an inspiring ideal.

If, however, the fight is not to change the world, but just to make the unions work the way they are supposed to (but never have), it's far more difficult to sustain the struggle. People can easily get cynical and feel, "Why risk my neck for something that isn't going to change things anyway?"

Probably a great many of the people who were joining Unionists for Democratic Change believed, as Keith came to think, that the unions can't really be changed. They were willing to be part of the struggle, however, because they believed they were in the right.

But even if the struggle could have reformed the IAM from within, it still wouldn't have affected the more profound problems of living and working in a capitalist society. The solution didn't match the problem, and it still brought ferocious attacks down on the people involved. The people recruited to UDC may not have spelled all these things out exactly in their minds, but they must have felt them to be true. At this point people very reasonably began to question whether the struggle was worth the cost.

Building a movement to destroy capitalism and create a society which truly reflects the aspirations of most people, though it may sound scary, is actually more practical than trying to reform a union:

- Building a revolutionary movement means reaching out broadly to other workers, in our own plant or school or office and beyond, to everyplace that people live or work or shop. The focus would not be on going toe-to-toe with union leaders or plant management, but on building the movement. The people involved would not be coming under immediate attack (see note above).

- While the organizing activities would be low-risk, at least at first, we would be proposing as a goal for the movement the creation of a world that reflects the deepest values and aspirations of the people involved—goals worth fighting for and worth risking all for, should it come to that.

- With more ambitious goals, our ability to talk about people's concerns would expand. People have goals as workers, as parents and grandparents, as members of a community, and in other regards. All these areas of life are under attack by capitalism. In all of them, we need to understand the attack more clearly and reach out to more people. As we move beyond dealing only with workplace or representation issues, our ability to reach deeply into people's feelings and to tap their energy and creativity would greatly increase.

- We would have a real chance of winning. Instead of not trying to win the class war but only trying to make a little adjustment in it, we'd be saying we're going to beat this system, and the movement in Wichita, Decatur and Detroit is part of a worldwide effort to create a fully human society.

Would a revolutionary movement engage in the kind of militant solidarity action practiced by the Boeing workers? Absolutely. But we would do so as part of building a long-range movement both inside and well beyond the plant, a movement the goals of which the participants were fully aware. People would then be able to turn reprisals to their advantage, to further expose union-company collusion and build the revolutionary movement.

Notes
1. Keith and his brother, who also works in the plant, think this particular point is incorrect, since "anything we do is a threat to their power and authority." They've got the experience, so they may well be right.

III.   CAN WE MAKE UNIONS STRONG AGAIN?

U.S. UNIONS, ONCE FIGHTING ORGANIZATIONS OF workers, have declined sharply. What's wrong with the unions? Can we turn them around?

Why Are The Unions So Weak?

Thousands of working people gave their sweat and blood to build the first industrial unions in the U.S. Once the CIO unions were established, however, the leaders changed from militant organizers to contract administrators working with management to ensure production. To gain greater control of the members, union officials discouraged membership participation and undermined shop-floor solidarity. Union officials turned from organizing workers against the company to managing workers for the company.

The problem with the unions was not just bad leaders. The problem was that there seemed to be no promising alternative to capitalism. Communism turned out to be a police-state. With no democratic alternative to the profit system, the welfare of workers seemed tied to the profitability of U.S. corporations. Union leaders saw no option but to work with the system. "What's good for General Motors is good for the country" was believed by union heads and government and business leaders alike. AFL-CIO leaders became eager supporters of capitalist power.

In the 1960s and early '70s, wildcat strikes swept the country, threatening the power of union bosses. The goal of union and corporate officials became the same: to destroy the growing power of the members.

Corporate and government officials soon went on the attack against workers. The attack succeeded because union officials cooperated with it. When Reagan fired 13,000 striking air traffic controllers, AFL-CIO leaders did nothing. The AFL-CIO has undermined numerous strikes, from Local P-9 to UAW 2036 to the recent grocery workers strike. The problem with the unions is not that they are weak but that they are on the wrong side.

Solidarity Values

The struggle in the workplace is part of a class war throughout society over what values will shape it, what goals it will pursue, and who will control it.

On one side stand corporate leaders, government officials, and masters of great wealth. They value inequality, competition, and dictatorial control. They slash wages, ship jobs overseas, pit worker against worker in bloody wars to control us. On the other side stand ordinary working people, who believe in equality, solidarity, and control from below. Every time workers slow down, or refuse overtime, or support each other on or off the job, or create supportive relationships with family and friends, they are resisting capitalist power and expressing their belief in equality and solidarity.

An Alternative to Capitalism

Capitalism offers only more war, insecurity, and fear. We need a revolutionary and democratic alternative.

Solidarity values rooted in the lives of working people offer an alternative to capitalism. Democratic revolution means changing all of society to reflect the best values already present in working peoples' lives.

Can We Change the Unions?

Decades of effort have shown that the unions cannot be reformed. Good people elected to union office get sucked into the pro-company culture of union officialdom. Unions linked to capitalism will always turn worker against worker and will always betray us.

We need a new organization which rebuilds the solidarity culture of friendship and support that is natural to working people and gives us our real strength. The new organization should:

- be independent of the unions;
- build solidarity across plants, across industries, across races and genders, across employed and unemployed, across generations, across borders;
- not try to change the unions, not run candidates for office, not negotiate contracts, not urge the unions to act but take action itself;
- unite working people in a struggle to revolutionize society and create a true democracy based on equality and solidarity.

IV.   HOW CAN WE STEP OUTSIDE THE BOX?

TIME AFTER TIME WE HAVE BEEN BETRAYED BY institutions that are supposed to represent us. Our unions work with management to keep us in line. The political parties are dominated by corporate money. Congress has been on sale to the highest bidder for years. The media are corporations themselves and surround us with the corporate message. The public schools undermine teachers and parents with corporate-led reforms like high stakes testing.

How can we break outside the box of corporate capitalist domination? How can we take some control of our own destiny?

The Need For An Organization

All of us in our daily lives are under great pressure to conform to capitalist ideas, ideas about success, about other people, about whether we have any power to change things. We want the world to be different from what it is, and we work in our own ways to change it, but our sense of the world and ourselves, our values, our way of life are under unremitting attack. We can be nagged by self-doubt: Does anyone object to the way things are but me? Am I crazy for trying to change the world? Can we really make a difference?

To sustain our efforts and help them to grow, we need a solid core of relationships and ideas that confirm the best of what we know and do against the pressure of capitalist ideas and values.

We have been talking for some months now in New Democracy about how to build the revolutionary movement. We know that our ideas have a wide appeal. But more is necessary to build the movement than just to promote the ideas. It has become clear to us that we cannot build the revolutionary movement unless we build the revolutionary organization.

Building an organization of our own, an organization not dominated by capitalist ideas or by anti-worker ideology or by creeps, is how we step outside the box of corporate and elite domination. Building New Democracy chapters is how we can give our efforts staying power; it is the only way to institutionalize our ideas and give them permanence.

New Democracy chapters will be the anchor and base for the new movement. They will be a place for people to come who are interested in our ideas. They will be a place where people can get confirmation of their best values and plan how to make them prevail. They will be a place for people to discover that they are not alone in their desire for a better world.

Stepping Outside The Unions

Labor unions provide one of the clearest examples of organizations which have betrayed ordinary people. If we can figure out how to deal with them, we can figure out anything.

Union leaders have played a leading role in the corporate attack on working people of the last twenty-five years. Part of this role has been very public, for example, when Machinist president William Winpisinger directed his members to cross the PATCO picket lines in 1980, keeping the airports open and breaking the air traffic controllers strike. But much of the union role has been more subtle. For example, AFL-CIO officials from "reform" president John Sweeney down to most local presidents promote the "Company Team" concept, the idea that workers and the company have the same interests and that workers should join "their" bosses to compete against other working people. Unions encourage workers to stand against their own brothers and sisters and against the values they believe in most deeply.

What have we learned from years of trying to change unions? That it can't be done. Unions and labor laws are designed to manage and control workers on behalf of the owners, not to lead workers against them. How many thousands of rank-and-file activists have burned themselves out over the years "trying to get the leaders to lead?" How many good, honest members have run for union office, only to get chewed up by the International once they're in office, or to change their stripes and become part of the problem themselves?

So what can union members do? How can they "step outside the box" of union control? This issue of New Democracy includes two letters from Tom Laney to fellow union members that point a way out. Tom has been an auto worker and member of UAW Local 879 for 25 years and was president for four years.

In one letter Tom says, "We need a network of auto workers, other workers, farmers, employed and unemployed talking not about the lean workplace and lean society but what kind of world we want for our kids and grandkids. We should talk about all the things that make auto workers feel good about each other and forget about the UAW except as the UAW applies to capitalism. And we should make clear that any system run by people who think they are better than other people, capitalism, communism, ANY system antithetical to democracy, solidarity and equality, is unacceptable."

What can union members do to "step outside the box" of union/management control? They can start to build a worker-to-worker network which:

1) Is not based on union structures.

2) Builds solidarity and exchange of ideas among workers across plants, across industries, across employed and unemployed, across races and genders, across generations, across borders.

3) Does not try to change the unions, does not run candidates for office, does not urge the unions to act but takes action itself.

4) Unites working people in a struggle to revolutionize society and create a true democracy based on equality and solidarity.

Why is it so important for workers to have their own organization? Many thousands of people have been involved in heroic actions against the corporations in the past decades, the Caterpillar and Staley struggles come to mind, but these efforts vanish like the wind if they do not result in building an organization of our own. We need an organization where we can draw the correct lessons from our struggles and use the lessons to build the movement.

Tom has mentioned that in his auto plant twenty years ago there was such a strong culture of solidarity among the workers that the occasional selfish, pro-company suck-ups "kept their heads down." Now, he says, all that has changed. After twenty years of union/management cooperation, pushing "The Company Team" and competition among workers, the shop-floor culture of worker solidarity has been forced underground. The suck-ups are now in charge. A revolutionary organization of workers, New Democracy chapters, is where people could come to plan how to reassert worker solidarity in the workplace and wage the class war against the company and union.

Starting From Scratch

After much discussion in the Boston chapter, we came to these conclusions: 1) There is no way to build a better society except with a movement for revolutionary democracy. 2) There is no way to build a movement for revolutionary democracy except by building an independent revolutionary organization which seeks to transform all of society. 3) There is no way to build an independent organization except by creating an infrastructure and recruiting people to it.

What does it take to start a chapter? Just two or three people who agree with the Statement of Principles of New Democracy (see newdemocracyworld.org) who meet regularly and plan how to grow.

V. AFFIRMATIVE ACTION—OR CLASS SOLIDARITY?

THERE ARE GOOD PEOPLE TRAPPED ON BOTH SIDES of the affirmative action debate. We think there is a way out of the trap which can unite working men and women of all races.

Two Sides Of The Same Coin

The liberal and conservative positions on affirmative action claim to be opposites. In fact they amount to the same bad idea. Liberals support affirmative action, saying that it is important to make competition between the races and genders fair; by favoring one group over another now, liberals say, affirmative action makes up for past discrimination.

Conservatives oppose affirmative action, saying that, by favoring one group over another, affirmative action unfairly affects competition between individuals.

The liberal and conservative positions on affirmative action both favor the idea of competition. They share the view that society consists of groups and individuals all competing in a war against everyone else for jobs and other goods. Liberal and conservative both accept class inequality as permanent and competition among working people as good.

What "Group" Do You Belong To?

The corporate and government elite always tell us to identify with one group against all others. "What group are you part of?" they ask. "Asian male?" "Black female?" "Angry white male?"

People care most about what they have in common, but the government stresses the differences. People know there has always been discrimination in job and other opportunities. Yet people also know that more discrimination, even in the name of "fairness," attacks people's natural inclinations to overcome differences and work together.

Affirmative action continues the game of pitting people against each other. It distorts what people mean by racial justice, which would require decent jobs for all. Instead the government promotes unemployment while it encourages competition among racial groups. There is only one "group" that the powerful do not want us to identify with—the working class. The ruling elite know that they can keep groups based on race or gender fighting each other forever. The elite cannot control a united working class.

Scarcity Is Artificial

The elite force us to compete for scarce jobs and necessities like medical care.

But the scarcity of jobs and other goods is artificial. The U.S. economy is more productive than ever. The corporate and government elite intentionally cut jobs and programs, while taking an even greater share of the wealth for themselves. While corporations lay off millions, the government gives them tax rebates to ship jobs overseas. The government cuts taxes on the rich, then slashes Medicare for workers, saying that there's no money to pay for it. The goal of job and program cuts is to control people by making them feel insecure.

Part Of A Larger Battle

The debate over affirmative action is part of a larger battle over the direction of society. Politicians may play roles as "liberals" or "conservatives," but they all have the same goal: to tighten elite control over working people. They promote competition in every way they can.

Most working people believe in equality and solidarity of all workers. We have been at a terrible disadvantage in this battle, however, because no working class leadership has firmly rejected both affirmative action and discrimination of all kinds in favor of solidarity of working people against elite rule.

Solidarity: The Answer To Discrimination

Solidarity is the answer to discrimination. The real struggle for equality has always come from the solidarity of working people in their everyday lives. Let's continue and extend the fight. Build bridges among people in your plant or neighborhood. Stand up if any of your brothers or sisters is treated unfairly. Fight against all layoffs. Slow down against speed-up. Refuse overtime, so businesses are forced to hire more workers. Support strikes and spread them. Fight for real equality: not the false equality of fighting each other for a handful of jobs, but a world where the wealth we create is ours.

VI.   A LETTER TO AN ACTIVIST

RECENTLY I RECEIVED AN EMAIL LETTER FROM A FRIEND of a friend. This person is a teacher and very active in the fight to change her union. She seemed to me to be experiencing some of the burn-out that sometimes affects us all. Below is my reply.

Hello,

You wrote me that: "As long as most of the teaching staff on our campuses is white, middle class, and the vast majority of our students in the public schools are people of color from various ethnic backgrounds and from working families and families in crisis, the schools will fail."

I don't really agree with this as an analysis. I mean, the problem in the schools is not the color of the teachers or even the class background of the teachers, in my opinion. Teachers don't become teachers because they want to fail at teaching; they want to succeed. The problem is that the education system is rigged against teachers and students. It is designed to reproduce and reinforce the system of inequality and class domination of the society. It would have the same outcome no matter what the color or background of the teachers. The problem with an analysis that gives such prominence to the color or background of the teachers, I think, is that it makes teachers the problem and makes them an enemy.

I appreciate you sending me notes on how things are going for you. You and I have never met, and I hope I'm not being presumptuous by offering my viewpoint.

I've been sorry to read how stressed out and isolated you seem to feel. It sounds like you're in a very tough position, and dealing with the union I'm sure is maddening. I don't know if I can say anything that will be helpful to you, except that it's very important to try not to see your colleagues too critically.

I speak from experience. As a young radical professor during the Vietnam war, I was so distraught by the war and so outraged that my colleagues weren't doing much about it that I managed to alienate just about everyone I dealt with. I'm not saying that this is what you're doing, I'm just saying that this is the biggest "occupational hazard" of activists/revolutionaries. We can get so involved in seeing what's wrong —and there's so goddamn much that is wrong—that we can lose sight of the basic goodness of the people around us.

The fact that our friends and colleagues aren't involved in the same ways as we are does not mean that they don't care about the same things or have the same values as we. It may simply mean that they don't see much possibility of change, or maybe they have other things going on in their lives that they have to focus on, or maybe we don't yet have a movement that is really inviting to people, because we are too frantic ourselves about the wrongs that we see and the changes we want to make.

We are living in a very difficult time. The revolutionary movements of the past have failed, and while the necessity for revolution seems ever more obvious to so many of us, the possibility of revolution seems very remote to most people. People like you and me and Gregg Shotwell and Tom Laney and others have a special task, which is historically very important. That task is to help find the basis for hope for a new world which can help inspire a new movement. I think it's pretty clear that we're not going to find that inspiration in a text of Marx or some other revolutionary thinker from the past. We have to find that inspiration in our own lives and in the lives of the people around us—our students, our colleagues, our families, the very people whom we may find maddeningly frustrating at times (and who no doubt find us maddening too). Finding our inspiration in other people is absolutely essential to the creation of a new revolutionary movement, and it's essential also, in my experience, to our personal salvation. Without it we are lost.

A few years ago, when three or four of us in Boston were talking together and were first starting New Democracy, we concluded that "revolutions are built on hope, and the basis of hope is confidence in other people." We also decided that we couldn't just be experts on what's wrong. Our most important task as revolutionaries is to see the good in people and in their lives. That's the only place we're really going to find hope.

We're all of us in this fight for the long haul. We all need friendships and relationships we feel safe with and can rely on. It's very clear that you feel a lot of stress right now. If I can offer some advice, I would say just focus for awhile on making and building friendships. You must teach with some good people. Forget about "politics." Or rather, if you truly believe as I do that "the personal is political," just concentrate on repairing relationships with your fellow teachers, gaining their confidence, learning from them, hearing more about what their concerns are, what their hopes are. Be a friend.

As I say, I hope I'm not being presumptuous. I don't know if this makes any sense, but I hope it does and that it is of some use to you. You have my very best wishes. Hang in there.

Dave Stratman

Part Four

HEALTH CARE

by John Spritzler

1. MARKET-DRIVEN HEALTH CARE AND SOCIAL CONTROL

> The organization of medicine is not a thing apart which can be sub-
> jected to study in isolation. It is an aspect of a culture whose arrange-
> ments are inseparable from the general organization of society.
> —Walton H. Hamilton, 1932[1]

AS PATIENTS, DOCTORS AND NURSES KNOW all too well, health care is being turned into just another commodity for sale in the marketplace. So-called "Health Maintenance Organizations" and hospitals, whether they are "for-profit" or not, are driven by market competition to keep their costs low and sell their "product" for as much as the market will bear. Because the central values of the marketplace are self-interest and the "bottom line," market-driven health care is in fundamental contradiction to the best values of the health professions expressed in the Hippocratic Oath, the Samaritan tradition, and the legacies of Florence Nightingale and Lillian Wald. All these affirm that medicine and health care should be driven not by self-interest but by that most humane of values—a commitment to each other's well-being.

There has been a dramatic shift in our health care system recently which has called these humane values into question. Corporate values have become ascendant in the health care system and are destroying what is best and strengthening what is worst in it. Physicians are being pressured to choose the corporate bottom line over their patients' health; if they resist, they are labeled as "problems" by HMO CEOs.[2,3] Nurses have been forced to go on strike to protect patients from hospital administrators who refuse to hire adequate numbers of nurses and who force nurses to work mandatory double shifts instead.[4]

To turn this fundamental, destructive shift in health care around we need to understand why it is happening and what forces exist that can defeat it.

Not Just the Insurance Companies

Why is market-driven health care being promoted so vigorously today? One theory is that insurance and health industry companies are the culprits. But the evidence, on the contrary, is that the people who made the decision to implement market-driven health care in the United States were corporate leaders from virtually all industries.

One of the principal policy-formulating organizations of corporate America is the Committee For Economic Development, or CED, which consists of about two hundred trustees, mainly CEOs of the largest corporations. The CED advocated HMO health care delivery as early as 1973.[5] In 1987 it issued a health care policy statement, "Reforming Health Care: A Market Prescription," which "offer[ed] a comprehensive strategy for reform of U.S. health care focusing on greater reliance on market incentives."[6]

Of the two hundred twenty corporations whose CEOs or board chairmen were members of the CED in 1987, only six were insurance companies. Of the fifty-five corporations represented on the CED's Research and Policy Committee, all of whose members participated in writing the health policy "Market Prescription" statement and all of whom approved it, only four were from insurance, health care, or pharmaceutical companies. The other members included Exxon, Procter & Gamble, General Electric, Philips Petroleum, Goodyear Tire & Rubber, Ford Motor Co., General Motors, AT&T, Chase Manhattan Bank and other non-health-related corporations.[7]

Public Opinion Has Been Ignored

Corporate leadership has been the only significant force backing market-driven health care. A majority of Americans replied "Yes" to a 1990 Gallup poll asking, "Would you be willing to pay more taxes to provide health care to all?"[8] and 73 percent answered "Yes" to the question, "Would you favor free government-provided health care?" When President Clinton made health care reform his first administration's priority, the great majority of Americans (69 percent according to a 1992 Harris poll[9]) favored a universal, comprehensive, publicly administered national health program.[10,11,12,13]

What Is at Stake?

Why are corporate leaders imposing market-driven health care despite the fact that public opinion opposes it, and despite the fact that most of the corporate leaders involved do not make their profits in health care or insurance? The answer can't be simply that corporations want the lower health insurance premiums that HMOs offer: with a single-payer system collecting the premiums as corporate taxes, corporations could lower their premiums as much, and even arguably more, than with a market-driven system. The administrative inefficiency of market-driven health care has been long known and well documented.[14] A 1990 U.S. Government Accounting Office report on health care costs reported that the Canadian single-payer system had proportionately much lower costs than the U.S. because Canadian spending on insurance administration was lower.[15] From the point of view of getting the most health care for their buck, corporations had no incentive to go with market-driven care.

If the corporate leadership's embrace of market-driven health care cannot be explained as a cost-cutting measure, then what does explain it?

In fact something more fundamental is at stake in market-driven health care than just the cost of the corporate benefits package. The real effects of market-driven health care on people's lives suggest that the primary corporate motive for imposing this type of health care system is to make people more controllable.

The Effects of Market-driven Care

What are the results of market-driven health care? First, market-driven health care makes people feel insecure about their prospects for receiving health care when they need it. Second, it destroys the trust that patients once had in their doctors by making doctors "gatekeepers" whose role is often to block access to care. Third, by making health care a commodity to be bought and sold like any other, it expands the growing economic inequality in the United States to include health inequality. Fourth, it pits health professionals against each other in competing physician groups and hospitals. These are four classic methods of social control: make people feel too insecure to challenge those in power, destroy people's trust in one another, make them more unequal, pit them against each other.

Even before the rise of market-driven health care, corporations relied on the insecurity of health care to control workers. For decades, large employers have preferred to link health benefits to employment, knowing it gave them more control over their employees. According to a *New York Times*/CBS poll in 1991, 32 percent of workers did not quit jobs they disliked because they were afraid of losing their health benefits.[16] In June, 1998 General Motors threatened to deny medical benefits to striking workers in Flint, Michigan in order to pressure them back to work.[17] Raytheon actually did cancel health insurance for striking workers in Massachusetts in August 2000, to force them back to work.[18]

Payback For The 1960s

More evidence that social control is behind market-driven health care comes from looking at its specific timing. Why did elite organizations like the CED begin advocating HMOs as the first step of their "market prescription," in the early 1970s?[19] That was when America's corporate and government leaders re-evaluated the way they would have to govern in light of the social upheavals of the 1960s. From the time of FDR to LBJ, elite social control had been based on policies like the New Deal and the Great Society that were meant to convince working class Americans that corporate leadership would give them a better and more secure future. These policies, however, led to rising expectations and a sense of security that emboldened people to challenge authority over issues like the Vietnam War, Civil Rights, conditions of work, and welfare. In other words, the elite strategy of improving social conditions as a means of controlling people back-fired.

How profoundly the 1960s affected the thinking of elite leadership can be seen in the writing of Samuel P. Huntington, Professor of Government and Director of the Center For International Affairs at Harvard University, and co-author of *The Crisis of Democracy: Report on the Governability of Democracies to the Trilateral Commission* written in 1975.[20] Huntington's Report noted that, "The essence of the democratic surge of the 1960s was a general challenge to existing systems of authority, public and private,"[21] marked by a "sharp increase in political consciousness, political participation, and commitment to egalitarian and democratic values."[22] What especially frightened the elite was the fact that, as Huntington wrote, "In recent years, the operations of the democratic process do indeed appear to have generated a breakdown of traditional means of social control, a de-legitimation of political and other forms of authority…The late sixties have been a major turning point."[23] The Report concluded: "Al Smith once remarked that 'the only cure for the evils of democracy is more democracy.' Our analysis suggests that applying that cure at the present time could well be adding fuel to the flames. Instead, some of the problems of governance in the United States stem from an excess of democracy…Needed, instead, is a greater degree of moderation of democracy."[24]

Corporate leaders abandoned the old method of social control embodied in the New Deal and the Great Society and began relying instead on a fundamentally different, "get tough," strategy designed to strengthen corporate power over people by making them less secure. This new strategy motivates corporate leaders' new enthusiasm for the "discipline" of the free market, which they use to justify not only market-driven health care but downsizing and attacks on the social safety net.

Market-driven health care is part of a pattern of government and corporate policy initiatives over the last several decades which have one thing in common: they strengthen corporate power over people by lowering people's expectations in life, and by reducing their economic, social, and emotional security. These policies include corporate downsizing and the "temping" of jobs; the elimination of the "family wage," so that now both parents have to work full-time and have less time with their children; drastic cuts in the social safety net of welfare and related assistance; the introduction of pension plans based on individualized investments that leave each older person to his or her own fate; and the use of high stakes tests in public elementary and secondary schools to subject children to the same stress and insecurity that their parents face on the job. In the workplace, employers have adopted anti-worker tactics that had not been used since the early 1930s, most notably firing striking workers and hiring permanent replacements, as President Reagan did during the air traffic controllers' strike. All these policies put people on the defensive and pressure them to worry more about personal survival than working together for social change.

Health Care and Social Values

The values of health professionals, who believe that a concern for other people and not self-interest should be the basis of health care, are shared by most people. Millions of Americans oppose elite values in health care and every other aspect of society. The majority of Americans who favor universal health care and who would willingly pay more taxes to make it possible demonstrate that most people value solidarity as opposed to the dog-eat-dog competition so highly praised by the elite in health care as in other areas. When people care for each other in their families and sacrifice for their children, when residents of flooded areas pile sand-bags to save their neighbors' homes and people far away send food and money, when full-time UPS drivers strike in solidarity with young and part-time workers fighting for equal hourly wages, when teachers try to raise their students' expectations above what corporations have in store for them: in these and countless other acts that never make the news, most Americans are struggling to make our society one where relations between people are based on a commitment to each other, on equality, trust, and solidarity.

The fight over the direction of health care is really part of a larger conflict, between most Americans and a small elite, over the core values that should shape our society. Ordinary Americans are an implicitly revolutionary force because the values by which they try to shape the world contradict the elite's capitalist values. This revolutionary force can defeat market-driven health care and re-shape our whole society. This will happen when people in and out of the health care professions connect with each other on the basis of a true understanding of the problem of corporate domination of our society and a true understanding of the solution. The corporate elite's fear of losing control is well founded.

The elite strategy for reasserting its domination over society has met with considerable success in these past two decades. That success has come about for a number of reasons, but perhaps the chief reason has simply been this: that the real meaning of the struggle has not been clear to people. Elites have been able, in the area of health care and elsewhere in society, to misrepresent as "efforts to control excessive costs" or "to remain competitive" or "to gain efficiency" what have in fact been measures aimed at destroying popular power and undermining democracy. They have largely been able to keep debate over vital issues such as health care out of the public arena and restrict discussion to policy elites and to health professionals who by themselves are not strong enough to challenge elite power.

In health care as in arenas such as education and labor, there is really only one way forward: to expose the real meaning of the conflict. We must show that the struggle over market-driven health care versus health care based on commitment to each other is part of a struggle over the values and direction of society. The fight is over the future of our society and can only be won by making this fundamental meaning of the struggle explicit. We must bring actively into the struggle the millions of people who share anti-capitalist values, and we must fight to win. Winning means defeating the power of the corporations and reshaping health care and all of society with democratic, humane, egalitarian values.

Notes

1. "Medical Care for the American People: The Final Report of the Committee on the Cost of Medical Care," Adopted October 31, 1932, Chicago: University of Chicago Press, cited in *The Future of Health Policy*, Victor R. Fuchs, Harvard University Press, Cambridge, MA, 1993.
2. Ad Hoc Committee To Defend Health Care, "For Our Patients, Not For Profits: A Call To Action," JAMA Dec 3 1997, Vol 278 No 21.
3. Peeno, Linda, "What is the value of a voice?" *U.S. News & World Report*, March 9, 1998.
4. For example, the nurses struck St. Vincent's Hospital in Worcester, MA in the spring of 2000 over this issue.
5. Committee For Economic Development, "Building a National Health-Care System: A Statement on National Policy by the Research and Policy Committee of the Committee for Economic Development," CED, April 1973, New York, NY, p 22-23.
6. Committee For Economic Development, "Reforming Health Care: A Market Prescription," CED, New York, 1987, p 6.
7. Committee For Economic Development, "Reforming Health Care: A Market Prescription," CED, New York, 1987.
8. "Opinions '90 Cumulation," Chris John Miko & Edward Weilant, editors, Gale Research Inc., Detroit, 1991.
9. Navarro V., *Dangerous To Your Health*, Monthly Review Press, New York, 1993, p 75.

10. Navarro V. "Where is the popular mandate?" NEJM 1982; 307:1516-8.

11. Pokorny G., "Report card on health care," Health Management 1988: 10(1):3-7.

12. Danielson D.A., Mazer A., "Results of the Massachusetts Referendum on a national health program," *Journal of Public Health Policy* 1987; 8:28-35.

13. Himmelstein, David U. and Woolhandler, Steffie A., "National Health Program for the United States," NEJM 320:102-108 (Jan 12), 1989.

14. Woolhandler, Steffie and Himmelstein, David U., "The Deteriorating Administrative Efficiency of the U.S. Health Care System," *NEJM*, 324:1253-1258 (May 2), 1991.

15. Executive Summary, U.S. GAO Report, June 1991, "Canadian Health Insurance: Lessons for the United States."

16. Navarro V., *Dangerous To Your Health*, p 50.

17. National Public Radio, June 29, 1998.

18. *Boston Globe*, August 30, 2000.

19. Committee For Economic Development, "Building a National Health-Care System: A Statement on National Policy by the Research and Policy Committee of the Committee for Economic Development," CED, April 1973, New York, NY, p 22-23.

20. Crozier, Michael J., Huntington, Samuel P., Watanuki, Joji, *The Crisis of Democracy: Report on the Governability of Democracies to the Trilateral Commission*, New York University Press, New York, 1975, p 36.

21. Crozier, p 74.

22. Crozier, p 106.

23. Crozier, p 8.

24. Crozier, p 113.

II. AN OPEN LETTER TO ADVOCATES FOR UNIVERSAL HEALTH CARE: WE NEED A WHOLE NEW APPROACH

FOR DECADES WE HAVE BEEN TRYING TO GET A health care system in the United States that provides good and equitable health care for all. Our efforts have been to no avail. Market-driven health care is moving in the opposite direction, making access to health care even more unequal by making it a market commodity.

We have spent decades trying to persuade big business to see the obvious advantages of universal health care, even from the standpoint of their stated corporate concerns for financial and administrative efficiency. But all we have experienced is bitter failure in these efforts. Our arguments are unpersuasive to corporate leaders because many of the most powerful corporate figures view the lack of an equitable national health care system as a means of increasing the dependence of working people on their employers (see "Market-Driven Health Care and Social Control").

Many of us have accepted the fact that we will never persuade big business to embrace universal health care. Now we're debating what to do. Some argue that, since big business will block the sweeping changes we all want, realism requires that we settle for incremental reforms of the current system acceptable to big business. Others argue that such incremental reforms do nothing to solve the fundamental problems: 1) Many people lack access to the health care they need and deserve; and 2) Health care dollars are needlessly wasted by the profit-making agendas and administrative inefficiency in our system of multiple competing health insurance companies. These people conclude that we should keep making rational arguments for the superiority of universal and equitable health care (most would agree this means a single-payer system with everybody included in one large risk pool) and hope for eventual success, despite our dismal record of failure so far.

We seem trapped: What big business permits is not good enough; and what is good enough, it won't permit. To escape this trap we need a whole new approach to winning universal and equitable health care. We must stop trying to persuade big business and start organizing to defeat it. To achieve this ambitious goal, we must see ordinary Americans in a new way, and make them our allies in a fight of crucial importance to us all.

Why Have We Failed to Recruit Ordinary Americans?

We need to understand why we have failed to recruit many Americans to becoming activists for universal health care. The commonly accepted explanation—that Americans fundamentally support the status quo ("free enterprise," "capitalism," etc.)—is wrong. Americans share our goals for health care. The reason they haven't actively joined our cause is because they have very little hope that it can win. Working people have been under attack in every area of their lives for over two decades. Their jobs have been "downsized" out of existence or sped up or reduced to temp work or shipped overseas. They work increasing hours at low pay to make ends meet. Their pension plans have been decimated, their children over-tested and over-stressed at school, the social programs on which they might have relied cut back. On top of all these things, the health care available to their families is increasingly at risk.

These enormous pressures on working people are not accidental. In the 1960s there was a worldwide revolutionary upsurge. People fought Soviet tanks in the streets of Prague. Over ten million French workers occupied their factories and schools and hospitals for ten days. In the U.S. militant movements for social equality and against the Vietnam War undermined elite control, while a rank-and-file labor movement challenged union officialdom and threatened corporate control of the workforce. The problems which ordinary people have experienced since the early 1970s, like the attack on health care, are part of a government and corporate strategy to strengthen elite control precisely by making people feel vulnerable and hopeless.

Let us not confuse lack of hope with disagreement over goals. If most Americans truly disagreed with us over goals, then universal health care in the U.S. would indeed be an impossibility. Lack of hope, on the other hand, is something which, as I will discuss, we can turn around.

Anti-Capitalist Values

As many articles by universal health care advocates have pointed out, the public agrees with us about health care. Most Americans want good health care to be equitably available to everybody. They say this in opinion poll after opinion poll.

We have a majority on our side, not just on the issue of health care but on the more fundamental question of which values should shape our society. When challenged that, in advocating removing health care from the market system, we are opposing capitalist values, universal health care advocates typically respond apologetically that, "in just this one area, health care, life should be exempt from market capitalism." The assumption behind this response is that most Americans support capitalism and that we will isolate ourselves and undermine our movement if we do not express our agreement with it.

Contrary to this assumption, most Americans in fact hold values that are the opposite of the corporate values of self-interest, dog-eat-dog competition, inequality and top-down control. Despite all of the pressure from corporate power to make people compete against each other and put self-interest above commitment to each other, Americans in their everyday lives and in occasional organized efforts do the very opposite. People try, sometimes with more and sometimes with less success, to create supportive relations of trust, friendship, love, and equality with family members, neighbors and co-workers all the time without giving it a second thought. They view this as simply normal human behavior, and generally don't see the significance of these efforts as implicitly resisting capitalist values.

Anti-capitalist values are the reason why people do the things they do. This is why workers stand together against company threats to lay off workers deemed "uncompetitive," why many students care more about friendships than about competing to prove that they are "better" than their peers, why teachers resist the standardized testing that corporate leaders are using to sort our children into winners and losers to make them fit into an increasingly unequal society, why nurses risk their jobs in strikes to prevent hospital managers from harming patients with nurse under-staffing, and why NYC firefighters sacrificed their lives in an effort to save the victims of the 9/11 attack on the WTC. Efforts like these, which spring from our shared humanitarian values, are the only reason why our society is not the dog-eat-dog jungle it would otherwise be.

We need to grasp the full import of this fact. Ordinary Americans are an implicitly revolutionary force. Properly nurtured, this force can be made self-aware, and thereby become confident of its power, and capable of defeating even the powerful corporate minority that presently blocks all of our efforts to make health care what it should and could be. Far more than health care is at stake, because when this revolutionary force is fully mobilized, it can change the world for the better in every walk of life, from what it means to "go to work," to education, the environment and every aspect of our lives that is affected by those values that shape our human relations.

The Real Problem

Working people know that the corporate and government elite are not on their side, and are not likely to provide universal health care just because people say they want it. They know that to win, it would take a mass movement powerful enough to defeat the elite. But this seems impossible because people opposed to capitalist values have been made to feel all alone: politicians, union leaders, schools and the media all insist that everybody is, and ought to be, motivated by self-interest and competition. People know that it takes large and powerful organizations controlled by working people to defeat the elite on any issue, and, given the dismal record of the labor unions, they also know that they do not possess such organizations.

The problem we face is not convincing people to agree with our goals, it is giving people hope that it is possible to win. We have a majority on our side. What we don't have is a majority who are convinced that they are the majority, sure that they are right, certain that they ought to be the ones to decide what values will shape health care, and confident in their power to defeat the elite who stand in the way. These are the real obstacles that we need to overcome. Unfortunately we have been focusing all our attention elsewhere.

To win universal and equitable health care we need to give Americans hope that it is possible to win a fundamental change in society that is directly opposed by the corporate and government elites who clearly hold the real power today. Explaining why universal health care is a great idea does not address this central problem.

How Can We Build Hope?

To have hope, people need to see that they are not alone and they need to be confident that they are right. Our task (and the task of everybody who wants a better world) is to help people see and feel this, so that they will have the confidence it takes to build large and powerful organizations which, unlike today's unions and political parties, explicitly fight for the revolutionary values of working people and against elite power.

Our most important allies resist market values like dog-eat-dog competition. They do it in their daily working lives in a Ford plant or a public school as much as in an HMO or hospital, but unfortunately many of us have been isolating ourselves from such allies by denouncing only HMO/insurance companies and by using pro-corporate arguments like, "Market values are fine in general, just not appropriate for health care."

Let's go to the blue collar workers and teachers and firemen in our communities, to the professionals in non-health as well as health fields, and to working people wherever we can reach them, and say to them, "When you and we try to create positive relations with others, no matter how small the scale or personal the context, we are resisting the competitive, unequal and selfishly exploitative relations that corporate leaders try to impose. What you are already doing, without necessarily thinking of it as political, and what we are already doing in our efforts to get a health care system based on a commitment to each other instead of corporate greed, are one and the same fundamentally."

Let's talk to people about their organized struggles, whether they are focused on work, education, the environment, or any other issue, and say to them not simply, "Join our movement for universal health care," but something like this: "The values underlying your struggle for _____ and our struggle for universal health care are the same: commitment to each other, equality and democracy. The elite corporate forces we are each fighting are the same. Our struggles are pieces of the same struggle. You and we are part of a large majority. You and we are the ones who are morally right and ought to be in charge. The elite are morally wrong and have no right to the power they now wield. Neither of us is alone! Help us spread this awareness to others so that one day enough people will have so much confidence that they are not alone and that they are right that they will begin making concrete plans to actually defeat elite power in real and lasting ways."

We haven't even begun to do this yet, but it is necessary to do this on a large scale to accomplish what leading activists Philip Pollner, Nancy Wooten, and Don

McCanne, have called for: "Reignite the spirit, reawaken hope, and foster a new campaign, permeated with trust, that will engage the cooperation and support of ordinary people and groups to commit to this cause, and no longer accept the inequities and injustice of the present health care system."

Wider Is Better

We need to stop defining our goal narrowly, and take to heart an insight that economist Walton H. Hamilton expressed so well in 1932: "The organization of medicine is not a thing apart which can be subjected to study in isolation. It is an aspect of a culture whose arrangements are inseparable from the general organization of society."

The general organization of our society is dominated by a corporate elite who use every institution to shape the world by their corporate values and to attack people's efforts to shape the world by anti-corporate values. The strength of our movement will come from embracing everybody who is struggling against elite values and domination, no matter in what walk of life or specific context, and appealing to their deepest feelings and motivations. If we focus narrowly—say, only on health care legislation—we will deprive ourselves of our greatest reservoir of strength. It will mean we are fighting with one hand tied behind our back.

As long as the corporate elite are in power, they will undermine any narrow reform we may win. They are now turning Medicare into a servant of HMOs, and in Canada and Europe they are pushing health care in the direction of the U.S. model.

A truly healthy society with a truly good health care system requires real democracy; and in a society such as ours where corporate wealth rules, real democracy is a revolutionary goal.

The great majority of Americans share our implicitly revolutionary goals and can be a mighty force. It is our task to help nurture this force into a self-aware, confident movement with explicitly revolutionary goals.

Part Five

EDUCATION
for DEMOCRACY

by David Stratman

I. SCHOOL REFORM AND THE ATTACK ON PUBLIC EDUCATION[1]

I HAVE TWO PROPOSITIONS I WOULD LIKE to put to you. The first is that the official education reform movement in Massachusetts and the nation is part of a decades-long corporate and government attack on public education and on our children. Its goal is:

- not to increase educational attainment but to reduce it;
- not to raise the hopes and expectations of our young people but to narrow them, stifle them, and crush them;
- not to improve public education but to destroy it.

My second proposition is that the education reform movement is part of a wider corporate and government plan to undermine democracy and strengthen corporate domination of our society.

What evidence do I have for these assertions? Let's look first at the long-standing campaign to persuade the American people that public education has failed. This has been a disinformation campaign based on fraudulent claims, distortions, and outright lies.

Since the publication of *A Nation at Risk* in 1983, there have been numerous reports issued, each declaring U.S. public education a disaster, and each proposing "solutions" to our problems. The sponsors of the many reports are a little like the con-man in "The Music Man," who declares, "We've got trouble, right here in River City…" and the chorus repeats, "trouble, trouble, trouble, trouble…" He just happens to be selling the solution to all their troubles. How do you sell radical changes that would have been completely unacceptable to the public a decade or two ago? You tell people over and over that their institutions have failed, and that only the solutions you are peddling offer any way out of their "troubles."

In the past couple of years, several excellent books have been published showing in detail that these claims are false. My purpose in this talk is not to cover the ground that these authors have already explored, but to answer the critical question: Why are the public schools under attack?

But let's look just briefly at a couple of the key pieces of disinformation to which the American public has been subjected.

The supposed dramatic decline of Scholastic Aptitude Test scores was a fraud. These scores did decline somewhat over the period 1963 to 1977. But the SAT is a voluntary test. It is not representative of anything, and it is useless as a measure of student performance or of the quality of the schools. The scores began to fall modestly when the range of young people going into college dramatically expanded in the mid-sixties.

Did this mean that there was a lowering of student achievement during this period? Absolutely not. The Preliminary Scholastic Aptitude Test, or PSAT, is a representative exam, given each year to sample student populations across the country. During the period in question, PSAT scores held absolutely steady.

Even more notable is the fact that scores on the College Board Achievement Tests—which test students not on some vaguely-defined "aptitude," but on what they know of specific subjects—did not fall but rose slightly but consistently over the same period in which for the first time in the history of the United States or any other country, the sons and daughters of black and white working families were entering college in massive numbers.

Berliner and Biddle comment in their book, *The Manufactured Crisis*, "the real evidence indicates that the myth of achievement decline is not only false—it is a hysterical fraud."

How different would have been the public's understanding of what was happening in the schools if the media and the politicians had told the truth! How different if they had announced that, during the period of the greatest turmoil in American society since the Civil War, in which a higher proportion of young people were graduating high school and going on to college than ever before, at a rate unparalleled in any other country in the world, representative tests showed that overall aptitude and achievement were holding steady or increasing? How different would have been the history of these last decades for educators and parents and students—and for public education?

What about the claim that U.S. business has lost its competitive edge because of the alleged failure of public education? Anyone who has been watching the triumphal progress of American corporations in the world market in the last two decades or has watched the unprecedented returns on the stock market knows that these claims are preposterous. Let me cite a few specific facts here:

- U.S. workers are the most productive in the world. Workers in Japan and Germany are only 80% as productive; in France, 76% as productive; in the United Kingdom, 61% as productive.

- America leads the world in the percentage of its college graduates who obtain degrees in science or engineering, and this percentage has been steadily rising since 1971.

- Far from having a shortage of trained personnel, there is now in fact a glut of scientists and engineers in the U.S. The *Boston Globe* reported on 3/17/97 that, "At a time when overall unemployment has fallen to around 5%, high-level scientists have been experiencing double-digit unemployment." The government estimates that America will have a surplus of over 1 million scientists and engineers by 2010, even if the present rate of production does not increase.

What explains the aggressive effort by corporate and government leaders to discredit public education?

To understand this, I believe we have to look beyond education to developments in the economy and the wider society. In the past decades, millions of jobs have been shipped overseas. Millions more have been lost to "restructuring" and "downsizing." This trend is not likely to abate. The U.S. is presently enjoying its lowest official unemployment rate in decades—4.9%, or about 6.2 million unemployed at the peak of a long period of sustained growth. But even this large figure is deceptive, because it does not include the millions of people who have been reduced to temporary or part-time work, without benefits, without job security, and without hope of advancement. The number of "contingent" workers in 1993 was over 34 million.

The future for employment is even more grim. Computerization will eliminate millions of jobs and deskill millions more. This is, after all, the attraction of automation for corporations: it downgrades the skills required of most jobs, and thereby makes employees cheaper and more easily expendable. I was talking recently with a chemist who works at a major hospital in Boston. She expressed dissatisfaction with her job. She said that, when she began the job ten years ago, she actually did chemistry. Now, she says, her job has been reduced to tending a machine which performs chemical analyses. A friend of mine wrote a book on the effect of computerization on work. She interviewed a vice-president of Chase Manhattan Bank who was a Loan Officer at the bank. He sat there smartly in his three-piece suit and complained that "He doesn't really feel like a loan officer or a vice-president." Why? Because, after he gets the information from the person requesting a loan, he punches it into a computer—which then tells him if he can make the loan or not.

The transformation of work through computers has really just begun. In his book, *The End of Work*, Jeremy Rifkin estimates that "In the United States alone, in the years ahead more than 90 million jobs in a labor force of 124 million are potentially vulnerable to replacement by machines." As Rifkin puts it, "Life as we know it is being altered in fundamental ways."

Now, what does all this have to do with education?

There were two little incidents which happened to me in 1976-77, when I was an Education Policy Fellow working in the U.S. Office of Education in Washington, D.C., which gave me a clue as to how to understand the attack on education. The first was a conversation with a man who was at the time a very highly-placed federal official in education. He put to a few of us this question. He said, "In the coming decade of high unemployment"—referring here to the 1980s—"in the coming decade of high unemployment, which is better? Is it better to have people with a lot of education and more personal flexibility, but with high expectations? Or is it better to have people with less education and less personal flexibility, and with lower expectations?" The answer was that it was better to have people with less education and lower expectations. The reasoning was very simple. If people's expectations are very high when the social reality of the jobs available is low, then there can be a great deal of anger and political turmoil. Better to lower their education and lower their expectations.

A second clue involved a man whom many of you may know. Ron Gister, who was Executive Director of the Connecticut School Boards Association at the time, began a speech in 1977 with this simple question. He said, "Ask yourself, What would happen if the public schools really succeeded?" What if our high schools and universities were graduating millions of young people, all of whom had done well?

In an economy with over 6 million unemployed by official count, in which millions more are underemployed or working part-time or in temporary jobs, in which many millions of jobs are being deskilled by computerization and many millions eliminated, and in which wages have fallen to 1958 levels, where would these successful graduates go? What would they do? If they had all graduated with As and Bs, they would have high expectations—expectations for satisfying jobs which would use their talents. Expectations for further education. Expectations about their right to participate in society and to have a real voice in its direction.

I think you can see that, for the people at the very top of this society, who have been instrumental in shipping jobs overseas and restructuring the workforce and downsizing the corporations and shifting the tax burden from the rich onto middle-class and working Americans—the class of people, in short, who have been planning and reaping the benefits of the restructuring of American society—for this class of people at the top, for the schools to succeed would be very dangerous indeed. How much better that the schools not succeed, so that, when young people end up with a boring or low-paying or insecure job or no job at all, they say, "I have only myself to blame." How much better that they blame themselves instead of the economic system.

The reason that public education is under attack is this: our young people have more talent and intelligence and ability than the corporate system can ever use, and higher dreams and aspirations than it can ever fulfill. To force young people to accept less fulfilling lives in a more unequal, less democratic society, the expectations and self-confidence of millions of them must be crushed. Their expectations must be downsized and their sense of themselves restructured to fit into the new corporate order, in which a relative few reap the rewards of corporate success—defined in terms of huge salaries and incredible stock options—and the many lead diminished lives of poverty and insecurity.

If my analysis is correct, it means that you—public educators, every person in this room, and all the staff and colleagues you have worked with these many years—you are under attack not because you have failed—which is what the media and the politicians like to tell you. You are under attack because you have succeeded—in raising expectations which the corporate system cannot fulfill.

They are also attacking education for a second reason: Blaming public education is a way of blaming ordinary people for the increasing inequality in society. It is a way of blaming ordinary people for the terrible things that are happening to them. The corporate leaders and their politician friends are saying that, if our society is becoming more unequal, if millions don't have adequate work or housing or health care, if we are imprisoning more of our population than any other country on earth, it is not because of our brutal and exploitative economic system and our atomized society and our disenfranchised population. No, they say, it is not our leaders or our system who are at fault. The fault lies with the people themselves, who could not make the grade, could not meet the standards. According to the corporate elite, the American people have been weighed in the balance, and they have been found wanting.

Where does the education reform movement fit in this picture?

My first experience with education reform came in September 1977, when I became Washington Director of the National PTA. It so happened that I began my job on the same day that Senators Daniel Moynihan and Robert Packwood and 51 co-sponsors filed the Tuition Tax Credit Act of 1977. The Tuition Tax Credit Act proposed giving the parents of children attending private schools a tax credit of up to $500 to cover tuition costs. The sponsors cited the SAT report as proof that the public schools were failing and that private schools needed support.

Like many others in the public school community, I saw tuition tax credits as a real threat. I met with representatives of the NEA, the AFT, AASA, and others, and we formed the National Coalition for Public Education to oppose tuition tax credits. Over the next several months we organized a coalition comprising over 80 organizations with some 70 million members.

The Tuition Tax Credit bill was a serious threat to public education. The entire federal budget for public elementary and secondary education at the time was about $13 billion. The Packwood-Moynihan bill would have taken about $6 billion from the public treasury. At the time, nearly 90% of our young people attended public schools. The Tuition Tax Credit Act proposed to give an amount equal to nearly half of all the federal moneys spent on the 90% of children in public school to the parents of the 10% of children attending private school.

Aside from its budgetary impact, the bill would have meant a reversal of the federal role in education. The historic role of the federal government has been to equalize educational opportunity. Tuition tax credits, since they are a credit against income and go chiefly to upper-income parents, would disequalize educational opportunity. Federal funding of private education would have established and given official sanction to a two-class system of education, separate and unequal.

The Tuition Tax Credit Act had enormous media and political support. It passed the House in May, 1978. We were able to stop it in the Senate only in August, 1978 with tremendous effort, and then by only one vote. Like the Tuition Tax Credit Act that started it all, the official education reforms such as school vouchers, charter schools, school choice, school-based management, raising "standards," the increased use of standardized testing, the focus on "School to Work," and other reforms, are calculated to make education more sharply stratified, more intensely competitive, and more unequal, and to lower the educational attainment of the great majority of young people. They are calculated also to fragment communities and undermine the web of social relationships which sustains society, and so to weaken people's political power in every area of life. Just look at some of the reforms:

Privatization and Fragmentation

Public schools have historically been at the center of neighborhood and community life in the United States. In addition, the schools have been a public good which relies on the whole community for support and in which the whole community participates.

School vouchers, tuition tax credits, charter schools, and school choice attack community connections among people. They attack the idea of a public good and replace it with the competition of isolated individuals competing to achieve their own private interests. In this way, privatizing education or establishing separate charter schools will dramatically undermine the power of ordinary people to affect the direction of society.

Voucher and choice plans also legitimize greater inequality in America's schools, as students with better connections or more self-confidence choose better schools. Who can argue with tracking students into good schools or poor schools when the students themselves have apparently chosen their fate?

School-based management is part of this trend. Though school-based management is usually touted as a way of "empowering" parents and teachers at the local level and of cutting back on the costs of central administration, its real purpose—aside from undermining the power of organized teachers—is to fragment school districts and communities, and further to disempower them. School-based management makes every school an island. It encourages people to think only about their own school and their own place within it.

Raising Standards

There is a world of difference between raising our "expectations" for students and raising "standards." Raising our expectations means raising our belief in students' ability to succeed and insuring that all the resources are there to see that they do. Raising standards means erecting new hoops for them to jump through.

For years Massachusetts has ranked just after Mississippi as the state with the greatest inequality among its school districts. Vast inequalities still remain among Massachusetts schools. Sharply raising standards while not equalizing resources at a common high level, and using "high stakes" tests as the engine of reform, is setting many thousands of children and many school districts up for failure.

Establishing a statewide core curriculum and curriculum frameworks can be very useful steps toward educational quality and equity. My limited conversations with teachers who have seen these frameworks in various disciplines, however, lead me to think that they are being established at unrealistic levels that will assure massive student failure.

Increasing Standardized Testing

The massive increase in standardized testing is exactly the wrong thing to do in our schools. At the very time when educators are calling for more "critical thinking" and "higher-order thinking skills," teaching is increasingly being driven by standardized, norm-referenced, multiple-choice tests. The effect will be to narrow the curriculum and push teachers into teaching techniques geared toward memorization and rote learning. With more focus on norm-referenced testing, the content of education disappears, to become simply the "rank" of the individual student. The effect is to attack the relationships among students and force them into greater competition with one another. Education is more than ever reduced to a game of winners and losers.

Lowering the School Leaving Age

Another thrust of such plans has been to encourage young people to leave school at an earlier age. In 1985 I was employed by the Minnesota Education Association to help design a strategy to defeat the reform plan proposed by the Minnesota Business Partnership. The Minnesota Business Partnership Plan was probably the most sophisticated education reform plan proposed in any state at the time. It proposed, among other things, moving from a K–12 to a K–10 system, and giving a "Certificate of Completion" to all students who successfully completed the tenth grade. Only a select group of students—projected to be about 20%—would then be invited back to complete grades 11 and 12. The clear effect would have been that a great many students would end their education at age 16.

What was the sense of this proposal? The Business Partnership claimed that the plan was designed to allow students greater "personal flexibility" and "choice." In fact it had a quite different purpose. Minnesota at the time had the highest school retention rate in the country: fully 91% of Minnesota's young people were graduating from high school, and a high proportion of these were proceeding on to college. By encouraging tens of thousands of young people to leave school at age 16, the Business Partnership—comprising some of the largest Minnesota corporations, like 3M, ConAgra, and Honeywell—would have created huge new pools of cheap labor in Minnesota, to work in stock yards and assembly plants and flip hamburgers.

The Massachusetts Education Reform Act of 1993 does not have exactly the same proposal, but the Massachusetts law moves in a similar direction. In 1998 Massachusetts will require that all students pass a "high stakes" test in the tenth grade to be eligible to graduate. At the same time, the schools will begin offering students a "certificate of competence" upon successful completion of the tenth grade curriculum. What will be the effect of the "high stakes" test, especially if dramatic steps are not taken to insure that the educational programs offered young people in many poorer or urban districts are dramatically improved? I suspect that many thousands of young people who would otherwise be graduating with a high school diploma will leave school instead with a "certificate of competence" after the tenth grade. (Only 48% of Chicago's young people recently passed the new "high-stakes" test required for graduation.) I suggest to you that the effect of the high stakes 10th grade test will be to lower the school retention rate, and that it has the same purpose as the proposed Minnesota reform: to enlarge the pool of cheap labor, and to make it seem as if it is our young people and not our system that is failing.

You may be aware that in 1995 for the first time in our history the gap between black and white high school completion rates was closed: 87% of black and of white young people between the ages of 25 and 29 have completed high school. Also, in the years from 1978 to 1993, the average SAT scores of black students rose 55 points. Are we now prepared to abandon these young people and undo this great progress?

Focusing on "School to Work"

Beginning with *A Nation At Risk*, nearly all of the education reform plans have been couched in terms of one great national purpose: business competition. According to these plans, the great goal and measure of national and educational progress is how effectively U.S. corporations compete with Japanese and German corporations in the international marketplace.

I think that most educators—most people, in fact—are downright uncomfortable with the idea that the fulfillment of our human potential is best measured by the Gross National Product or the progress of Microsoft or General Motors stock on the Big Board.

In the 1950s Charles Wilson, the former president of General Motors whom Eisenhower had appointed Secretary of Defense, declared, "What's good for General Motors is good for the country." In the 1960s, however, millions of ordinary people became engaged in the civil rights and the anti-war movements and the rank-and-file labor movement. People began increasingly to question the role that the corporations play in American society and began to question the Gross National Product as the real goal and measure of democracy.

Now come the corporate education reformers to tell us that the goal of human development is the success of Big Business! The education reform movement is trying to reassert the moral authority of business as the guiding light of human society and corporate profit as the measure of human achievement.

On a more concrete level, the "School to Work" program aims to shape every child to meet the needs of the corporations. What kind of terrible power are we giving these corporations, what gods have they become, if now we should sacrifice our children to them?

Let me hasten to point out that there is much that is being done in the name of reform that is good, and I am sure that each of you has programs in his own district which you could point to as education reform in the best sense. Education reform has two faces. The goals of the official "reformers" are destructive. Public education in the U.S., however, is a huge enterprise, involving millions of students and teachers and administrators. There is no way that this huge undertaking can be changed without the active involvement of tens of thousands of educators and others. These people—people like you and me and your teaching staff and other educators—do not share the goals of the corporations. Far from it: we genuinely want children and schools to succeed. So the effect of the massive involvement of educators at the grassroots has been, to one extent or another, to push reform in a more positive direction. In fact, I believe that the appointment of John Silber as Chairman of the Board of Education was precisely to put a stop to popular involvement in education reform. Silber's role is to put the genie of democratic education reform back in the bottle, so that the goals of the corporate reformers can be achieved.

It is important to see that the attack on public education does not stem from a "right-wing fringe," as some writers have charged, but from the most powerful corporate and government interests in American society. Business groups at the national level and in most states have led the call for vouchers and charter schools and new standards. President Clinton himself has made Charter Schools the focus of his efforts in K–12 education, and has made tuition tax credits the focus of new aid for higher education.

The assault on public education is part of a wider strategy to strengthen corporate domination of American society.

In the '60s and early '70s, at the time education was being greatly expanded, we experienced a "revolution of rising expectations," as people's ideas of what their lives should be like greatly expanded. These rising expectations threatened the freedom of elites in the U.S. and around to the world to control their societies. Beginning around 1972, both capitalist and communist elites undertook a counteroffensive, to lower expectations and to tighten their control. This counteroffensive took many different forms, all designed to undermine the economic and psychological security of ordinary people.

For example, the export of jobs and restructuring of corporations which have left many millions of Americans unemployed or underemployed did not happen by chance. They are government policies. Corporations were given tax incentives to move their operations overseas. The huge debts incurred in corporate buyouts were made tax deductible. The safety net of social programs instituted during the New Deal and Great Society was dismantled.

The gutting of these social programs was not a matter of fiscal necessity, as we were told, but of social control. David Stockman, while Budget Director for President Reagan, boasted that the Administration, by slashing taxes on corporations and the rich while vastly increasing military expenditures, had created a "strategic deficit" precisely in order to dismantle social programs. Why? Because programs such as food stamps and Aid to Families with Dependent Children and unemployment insurance make people less vulnerable to the power of the corporations. A succession of presidents, Republican and Democrat, has continued to cut the social safety net, to make people more frightened and controllable.

The current supposed "crisis" in Social Security is a case in point. There is nothing wrong with the Social Security system that a few adjustments—such as removing the upper limit on salaries that are taxed—could not fix. Yet the government and corporations have mounted a scare campaign similar to the attack on public education to suggest that the Social Security system is near collapse and cannot survive without radical "reform," such as privatization. The goal is to make people feel insecure and vulnerable.

What changes are needed in public education? We know that public education has important problems. We do not claim that the schools are not in need of change. The problem, however, is that the changes being proposed move in the wrong direction. They exacerbate the worst thing about the public schools: their tendency to reinforce the inequality of American society.

At the heart of the public education system, there is a conflict over what goals it should pursue. On one side stand educators and parents and students, who wish to see students educated to the fullest of their ability. On the other side stand the corporate and government elite, the masters of great wealth and power.

Their goal is not that students be educated to their fullest potential, but that students be sorted out and persuaded to accept their lot in life, whether it be the executive suite or the unemployment line, as fitting and just. The goal of this powerful elite for the public schools is that inequality in society be legitimized and their hold on power reinforced. This conflict is never acknowledged openly, and yet it finds its way into every debate over school funding and educational policy and practice, and every debate over education reform.

A key question for us is, "What are we educating our students for?" The choices, I think, come down to two. We can prepare students for unrewarding jobs in an increasingly unequal society, or we can prepare our young people to understand their world and to change it. The first is education to meet the needs of the corporate economy. The second is education for democracy.

The goal of the schools must be education for democracy. With this goal we would substitute high expectations for low, cooperation and equality for competition and hierarchy, and real commitment to our children for cynical manipulation. With the goal of education for democracy I believe we could build a reform movement that would truly answer the needs of our children and truly fulfill the goals that led us to become educators.

There is no time for me here to outline a program of positive education reforms, although I have listed ten possible principles of reform on a separate sheet.

Let me say in general, however, that the process of formulating positive reforms should begin with a far-reaching dialogue at the local and state levels, involving administrators, teachers, parents, and students, about the goals of education. This dialogue should examine present educational policy and practice to find what things contribute to self-confidence and growth and healthy connections among young people, and strengthen the relationships of schools to communities, and what things attack this self-confidence and growth and undermine these relationships. A similar dialogue should be organized in every community and at every school. It might include public hearings, at which parents and teachers and others are encouraged to state their views on appropriate goals for education, and to identify those things in their local school which support or retard these goals. Superintendents would have to be both leaders and careful listeners at such hearings.

What conclusions can we draw from this analysis? I suggest several. One is that you as educators are under attack not because you have failed, but because you have succeeded. A second is that you did not make a mistake, five or ten or twenty-five years ago, when you became an educator. The work you have been doing for all these years has made a tremendous contribution to our society, and you should be proud of it. A third is that your job now is more important than ever, because you have a mission. Your mission is to play a leading role defending public education and forthrightly leading change for the better. Your role is to help lead the fight for education for democracy.

The theme of your Summer Institute is "Building Stable Institutions in an Unstable World." The key to building stability in our public schools is threefold: understanding why they are under attack, understanding what is of value in them, and forging a direction for change. What can we do, as superintendents and educators? I have a few suggestions:

1. M.A.S.S. should prepare superintendents to play a leading role in reversing the attack on public education, by establishing a standing committee responsible for planning a long-term, serious campaign; preparing a range of literature and other materials for use at the local level; and holding training and strategy sessions. The literature should explain the attack on public education: why it is happening, the role that the official education reforms play in this attack, and call for positive reforms. M.A.S.S. should organize discussions, perhaps using the Superintendents' Round-tables or some other vehicle, for superintendents to compare their own experiences dealing with these issues.

2. The most important thing to do is to reach out to the community with information explaining the attack on public education. We should remember that the community begins with us—that is, with all the many people involved in public education: teachers, administrators, parents and students. If we can educate and mobilize this great community force, we can achieve a great deal.

3. We should, through dialogue with other educators and with parents and students, develop positive education reforms consistent with achieving education for democracy.

4. We should create local and statewide coalitions to expose the attack on public education and to change the direction of reform toward education for democracy. We should use Massachusetts as the base for a national movement for education for democracy.

We are called to a great purpose. We are called to build a movement capable of defending our institutions from corporate attack and capable too of transforming them, to lead them in a more democratic direction. We must build a movement to take back America from the corporate powers and the masters of great wealth, to place our country truly in the hands of the people.

We will not be alone in this battle. The great majority of people in our schools and in our communities share the same fundamental beliefs about what our schools should be like and what our society should be like. We can build upon shared values of commitment to each other and to future generations, and shared belief in democracy.

For most of the twentieth century, the people of the world have been trapped between capitalism and communism. Neither of these systems is democratic. Neither has held much promise for most people. Now communism has collapsed. I believe our task as we approach the end of the twentieth century is to create human society anew on a truly democratic basis, in which human beings are not re-shaped and restructured to fit the needs of the economy, but rather social and economic structures are reshaped to allow the fulfillment of our full potential as human beings. Thank you.

Note

1. The following speech was delivered as the keynote Address to the Massachusetts Association of School Superintendents Summer Institute, 1997. The audience included about 275 school superintendents and assistant superintendents.

II.   YOU'LL NEVER BE GOOD ENOUGH: SCHOOLING AND SOCIAL CONTROL

A COUPLE MONTHS AGO THESE SAMPLE questions from the new MCAS (Massachusetts Comprehensive Assessment System), given to all Massachusetts students in grades 4, 8, and 10, appeared in the *Boston Globe*:

> MUSIC: Write a piano concerto. Orchestrate and perform it with a flute and drum. You will find a piano under your seat. BIOLOGY: Create life. Estimate the difference in subsequent human culture if this form of life had developed 500 million years earlier, with special attention to its probable effect on the English parliamentary system. Prove your thesis. HEALTH: You have been provided with a razor blade, a piece of gauze, and a bottle of Scotch. Remove your appendix. Do not suture until your work has been inspected. You have 15 minutes.

The "sample" was a parody, of course, but it made an important point: the test was impossible. Students were subjected to from 11 to 13 hours of tests in 17 days— longer than the entrance tests required for college, graduate school, and law school combined. Some school systems, concerned that young people would not have the stamina to get them through day after day of test-taking, supplied high-energy snacks and drinks to the kids. Parents were encouraged to get their children to bed early. Teachers were told not to assign homework during the weeks of testing.

These are "high-stakes" tests. When they are fully operational, students in grades 4 and 8 will need to pass the state tests to be promoted; students in grade 10 will have to pass to be eligible to graduate. Teachers will be "held accountable" for their students' grades. (Forty percent are expected to fail.) Schools in which students perform poorly on the tests can be placed in receivership by the state and their faculties dismissed.

The contents of the MCAS are secret:[1] no educators in Massachusetts except certain officials of the Department of Education and the Board of Education have been allowed to examine the tests for their age-appropriateness or their relationship to what is actually taught. The tests were devised by a company which had recently been fired by the state of Kentucky for major errors in the design and marking of tests it had administered there.

In literature circulated to parents and students before the tests, corporate backers of "higher standards" boasted that "These are very, very tough tests—the toughest that most Massachusetts students have ever taken" and that "good attendance and passing grades" no longer entitle a student to a high school diploma. To prepare our students "to compete with children from all over the world," said the corporations, much more is required.

Tests similar to MCAS are being required of young people in state after state. President Clinton is fighting for national assessments along the same lines.

What's behind this rush to testing and "higher standards?"

Making Schools "Lean and Mean"

As is often the case, these developments inside the schools reflect events in the wider society.

In the past two decades, corporations have adopted new management techniques designed to undermine worker solidarity and integrate workers more thoroughly into the company machine. Known variously as "continuous improvement" or "management by stress," or "kaizen," the Japanese term for it, the technique consists essentially of dividing the workforce into competing "teams" and "stressing" the production system by imposing higher and higher production quotas. As workers work faster and faster to meet the quotas, the company achieves several key goals: production is increased, jobs are eliminated, "weak links" in the system break down and are replaced.

Most important, "continuous improvement" creates great anxiety in workers about their ability to meet the ever-increasing goals, and encourages workers to replace solidarity among themselves with loyalty to the Company Team. It forces workers into constant speed-up. Workers are kept running so fast to meet company goals that they don't have time to think or talk about their own goals or work together to pursue them.

Corporate-led education reforms use similar strategies. They use "School-Based Management" to isolate teachers in each school from their colleagues around the system. Teachers are then encouraged to join with management as a "team" to compete for students and survival with other schools.

The reforms use testing to keep raising the standards which students and teachers must meet, far beyond what their parents were expected to achieve and beyond anything that would be of value. The purpose is the same as "continuous improvement" in a factory: raise the anxiety level and keep students and teachers running so fast to meet the goals set by the system that they have no time to think about their own goals for education or for their lives.

These reforms will have terrible effects. Many students who would otherwise graduate from high school will drop out. (In Texas and Florida, where "high-stakes" testing is in place, high school drop-out rates which had been dropping have already begun to rise.) Young people who fail to meet the new standards will be condemned to marginal jobs and told to blame themselves.

The reforms redefine education as a process whereby young people constantly "remake" and sell themselves to the corporations. The reforms attack the self-knowledge and understanding of unsuccessful and successful students alike, as young people are encouraged to redefine themselves—their own goals, their own thoughts and hopes and desires—out of existence, to make themselves acceptable to our corporate masters.

Our children have qualities more important than those desired by corporate Human Resource directors. Education conceived in this way makes economic productivity the goal and measure of human of society and makes the corporations the judges of human worth. It undermines the notion that human beings individually and collectively possess goals which transcend capitalism.

Conflict over Educational Goals

There is no more vital issue to understand in education than this: The corporate and political elite who dominate education policy have goals for education which contradict the goals of the people who populate the schools: teachers and students and their families.

Public schools were supported by the industrial elite in America with the explicit intention of strengthening elite control over the working population. In the middle of the nineteenth century Horace Mann, the founder of the "common school," explained the rationale for public schools: "...common schooling would discipline the common people to the point where they would not threaten the sanctity of private property or practice disobedience to their employer." Public schools have been used ever since to instill in young people a respectful attitude toward those in power. William Bennett, while Secretary of Education in the Reagan Administration, explained, "The primordial task of the schools is the transmission of social and political values." In a class society, the values which the schools are designed to transmit are the values of the dominant class—competition, inequality, the sanctity of private property, and the belief that the good things in society trickle down from the elite.

At the heart of the education system, there is a conflict over its goals. On one side stand educators and parents and students, most of whom share democratic values and want to see students educated to the fullest of their ability. On the other side stand the corporate and government elite, the masters of great wealth and power. Their goal is that students be sorted out and persuaded to accept their lot in life, whether that be the executive suite or the unemployment line, as fitting and just, and that social inequality be legitimized and their hold on power reinforced.

This conflict over the goals of schooling is never acknowledged openly, yet it finds its way into every debate over school funding and educational policy and practice, and every debate over education reform.

What's Wrong with the Schools?

The corporate critique of the schools has served to cover up what's really wrong with them: the schools promote inequality, competition, and unquestioning acceptance of the social order.

The elite pursue these educational goals in many ways. Shortages in school funding undermine the work of students and teachers and tell them that they are not valued. School-business partnerships promote business values in the schools. Textbooks teach that history is made by presidents and kings; ordinary people are dismissed as passive victims or a dangerous problem. But many of the means of achieving elite goals for education are far more subtle:

- The schools assume that there are big differences in people's intelligence and that most people are not very smart, and are designed to "prove" these low expectations. Teachers are trained to find supposed differences in children's abilities; standardized, "norm-referenced" tests are designed to sort kids out and produce a range of test scores which match the social hierarchy—in other words, which show that richer people are smarter. Shortages of teachers and textbooks, lack of support for their work, and countless other devices are means by which students and teachers are set up to fail.

- The schools use competition and ranking to legitimize the social hierarchy. Students reluctant to compete for approval get low marks: what is really a conflict over values is seen as a failure of students' intelligence. For teachers, school life consists more often of an isolated struggle to survive than being encouraged to join with other teachers to nurture students.

- Course content often has no value except as a measure of students' willingness to master it. Much of the content consists of "facts" torn out of their social context, with all the life sucked out of them, because their life is rooted in the class war the elite seek to obscure.

These and other means are used by schools to prepare most students for working lives spent performing boring tasks with unquestioning obedience in a "democracy" in which the goals of society are not up for discussion and in which the idea of people acting collectively for their own goals is considered subversive.

What's Right with the Schools?

Teachers and students and their families share goals which contradict the goals of the elite, and they work to achieve these goals in every way they know how in spite of elite domination. The gigantic effort by corporate and political leaders to impose education reform is necessary precisely because the people in the schools have worked for their goals with enough success to threaten elite control.

When teachers stimulate and challenge; when they encourage all their students to learn and inspire them to think about the world as it really is; when they create a nurturing environment; when they fight for smaller class sizes; when they offer each other words of support: when they do any number of things they do every day, they are opposing elite goals for education and working for the shared goals of ordinary people.

When students help each other, or raise critical questions, or refuse to join in the race for grades and approval; when they exercise their curiosity and intelligence; even when they hang on the phone for hours, talking about "life," they are resisting elite goals and working for a better concept of life.

When parents listen sympathetically to their children, or talk with their friends or each other about the school or raising kids: when people do these things that they do every day, they are resisting elite goals and working for the opposite values of solidarity and equality and democracy.

To the extent that students succeed in real learning and teachers in teaching and parents in raising their children to be thoughtful and considerate, they succeed in spite of the education system, not because of it.

The remarkable thing about the public schools isn't that some teachers become demoralized and "burned out," or that some students drop out or do poorly, but that so many teachers and students achieve so much in the face of a system designed to fail.

Education and Revolution

Capitalist society is based on slavery: the enslavement of workers to the wage system and the enslavement of human beings to things. Education worthy of the name must help set us free, not further bind us in chains. The conflict over the goals of education is part of the class war over the goals of society. Only a movement which challenges the goals and values and power of the elite can change education.

There are a thousand questions about society which elite institutions will never raise but which are critical to our future. The revolutionary movement must consider anew the goals of human society and the measures of human achievement. It must re-examine our relationship to technology and to Nature. It must enable people to transform work and play into sources of creativity and fulfillment.

We do not have the power at this point to change education, but we can begin to pose these questions. The most liberating and humanly fulfilling education for all of us will come as we take part in the struggle to overthrow elite rule and recreate human society.

Note
1. This has since changed. Now 80% of test items are open for public viewing after the tests have been administered.

by John Spritzler

I. FALSIFYING HISTORY AND OURSELVES: ANTI-DEMOCRATIC PROPAGANDA IN THE CLASSROOM

A POPULAR COURSE IN THE UNITED STATES for middle and high school students about the Holocaust gives a false account of anti-Semitism and related events in Nazi-era Germany carefully designed to drive home the lesson that most people are prone to bigotry and are a dangerous force. The course, called "Facing History and Ourselves" (FHAO), is funded by liberal foundations and corporations (and in the past, grants from the U.S. Department of Education) and wealthy individuals. It reaches one million students a year in schools across the country. Foundations and corporate leaders support "Facing History and Ourselves" because it helps discredit the central idea of democracy—that ordinary people are fit to rule society.

FHAO's main resource book, *Facing History and Ourselves: Holocaust and Human Behavior*, is a 576-page collection of short readings and questions carefully selected to convey a negative view of people by lying about the facts. Contrary to the views promoted by FHAO, the true facts about Germany during the Holocaust show: 1) working class Germans fought the Nazis; 2) anti-Semitism did not come from ordinary people; and 3) anti-Semitism was a weapon used by Germany's industrial and aristocratic elite to attack not only the Jewish minority but the entire working class.

German Opposition to The Nazis Was Widespread

Facing History's discussion of resistance in Germany to the Nazis begins with an Einstein quote: "The world is too dangerous to live in—not because of the people who do evil, but because of the people who sit and let it happen." The "Facing History" account claims that only a few isolated individuals resisted Nazism. The truth is quite different.

When the President of Germany appointed Hitler Chancellor on Jan 30, 1933, the Nazis had just suffered a major defeat in the national election. It had become clear that the Nazis could not out-poll their main opponents, the working class Marxist parties. Additionally, Nazi storm troopers were being physically attacked by workers in industrial centers and small towns across Germany. The elite installed Hitler as Chancellor because they feared that working class power was getting out of hand, and they were desperate to find a political leader who could lead the upper classes in a ruthless war against the working classes. Standard histories of this period, such as William Shirer's classic *The Rise and Fall of the Third Reich*, describe how this happened.

Every time Germans had a chance to vote for or against Hitler, the great majority voted against him. Hitler ran for President in March, 1932 and got only 30% of the vote; in the run-off election the next month he got only 37%, versus 53% for the incumbent Field Marshal von Hindenburg. Nazi electoral strength peaked on July 31, 1932 when Nazi rhetoric about representing all Germans and not special interest groups lured some voters away from the numerous small, special-interest conservative parties. The Nazis won 230 out of 608 total seats in the Reichstag (parliament). But their main foes, the Social Democratic Party (SDP) and the Communist Party—both of which were led by Marxists and received mainly working class votes—jointly captured 222 seats in the same election. Voting records show that the richer the precinct, the higher the Nazi vote.

Working class Germans not only voted against the Nazis, they fought them in the streets. In the German province of Prussia alone, between June 1 and June 20, 1932, there were 461 pitched street battles between workers and Nazis, in which eighty-two people died and four hundred were wounded.

In his classic account, *The Nazi Seizure of Power: The Experience of a Single German Town*, William Allen gives a detailed account of events from 1930 to 1935 in a small German rural town with a population of 10,000 mainly middle-class Lutherans.

Allen describes a typical incident. Three weeks before the July 31, 1932 Reichstag elections, twenty-five men in the Reichsbanner (a Social Democratic Party militia organization) got into a fight with sixty Nazi SA (militia) men while crossing a bridge in opposite directions. Homeless people in a nearby Army compound rushed to help the Reichsbanner, and when police arrived there was a surging crowd of about eighty persons pelting the Nazis with stones.

In the next Reichstag election on Nov 6, 1932 the Nazis lost 34 seats, reducing them to only 196 deputies, while the Social Democratic Party and the Communist Party won a total of 221 seats—25 more than the Nazis. This was the last free election before Hitler came to power.

This last free election suggests how little support anti-Semitism had in the German electorate. The Social Democratic Party condemned anti-Semitism as "reactionary" and was known for its history of refusing to combine with anti-Semitic parties in election runoffs even when it would have gained from doing so. The Communist Party also rejected anti-Semitism. (In fact the Nazis lumped Communists together with Jews as being all part of the same evil conspiracy.) Votes for these two parties were votes against anti-Semitism.

After this election the Nazis were in steep decline. The party was literally bankrupt and unable to make the payroll of its functionaries or pay its printers. In provincial elections in Thuringia on December 3, the Nazi's vote dropped by 40 percent. Gregor Strasser, a top Nazi who had led the party during Hitler's time in prison, concluded that the Nazis would never obtain office through the ballot. In his diary in December, Hitler's right-hand man, Joseph Goebbels, wrote: "[T]he future looks dark and gloomy; all prospects and hope have quite disappeared."

And yet, only one month later, President Hindenburg appointed Hitler Chancellor. Industrialists, bankers, large landowners and the military had pressured Hindenburg to appoint Hitler. They feared the growing strength of the working class and were convinced that only Hitler would do whatever was necessary decisively to defeat workers' power.

The elite feared not only working class votes, but a general strike that could lead to civil war. Two months before Hitler's appointment, General Kurt von Schleicher told the current Chancellor, Franz von Papen, "The police and armed services could not guarantee to maintain transport and supply services in the event of a general strike, nor would they be able to ensure law and order in the event of a civil war." When Hindenburg subsequently dismissed Papen and appointed Schleicher as Chancellor, he told Papen: "I am too old and have been through too much to accept the responsibility for a civil war. Our only hope is to let Schleicher try his luck." Schleicher, responding to the same Great Depression and the same kind of working class militancy that forced FDR to offer Americans a New Deal, tried to pacify the German working class with similar promises, but workers didn't trust him. After just fifty-seven days in office the elite decided that only Hitler could do what had to be done.

Twenty-six days before Hitler's appointment as Chancellor, Baron Kurt von Schroeder, a Cologne banker, had a private meeting with Hitler, three other Nazi leaders, and Papen. During this meeting Papen and Hitler agreed that Social Democrats, Communists, and Jews had to be eliminated from leading positions in Germany, and Schroeder promised that German business interests would take over the debts of the Nazi Party. Twelve days later, Goebbels reported that the financial position of the (previously bankrupt) Nazi party had "fundamentally improved overnight."

FHAO explains Hitler's appointment as Chancellor by telling students that Schleicher, Papen, and Hindenburg represented powerful people with little popular support who made a deal with Hitler: "He had the popularity they lacked and they had the power he needed."

This sophisticated-sounding analysis is wrong. The election results alone showed that Hitler's popularity was quite limited and in decline. Millions of Germans were actively, many even violently, opposing the Nazis. What Hitler offered the elite was not popularity, but the determination to lead an all-out attack on the working class.

Within two months of being appointed Chancellor, Hitler arrested four thousand leaders of the Communist Party along with others in the Social Democratic and liberal parties and carted them off to be tortured and beaten. On May 2, 1933 Nazis occupied all trade union headquarters, confiscated their funds, dissolved the unions, and sent the leaders to concentration camps; any known working class radicals were put in prison camps or went into hiding. By 1938 tens of thousands of working class leaders were in the concentration camps or prison and hundreds had been killed. Eventually the Nazis rounded up three million political prisoners.

Even after the Nazis took over the government, destroyed the unions, and imprisoned opposition leaders, the German working class fought them. This resistance is described by John Weiss in his book, *Ideology of Death: Why the Holocaust Happened in Germany*. Weiss explains that resistance took many forms. No worker loyal to the Nazis was ever elected to workers' councils by his mates. When the Nazi government escalated its attack on Jews by destroying their property, killing ninety, and sending thirty thousand to concentration camps during the infamous "Kristallnacht" on November 9-10, 1938, workers distributed tens of thousands of leaflets protesting Kristallnacht and millions of other anti-Nazi leaflets. Red flags flew defiantly over factories and posters attacked the regime. In working class districts, youth gangs painted anti-Nazi graffiti and regularly beat up members of the Hitler Youth.

Later, even with three million political prisoners in the camps, workers still refused to make peace with the regime. Industrialists reported thousands of examples of slowdowns, stoppages, and sabotage, as well as some strikes and mass protest meetings. During the war, the Krupp corporation alone reported to the Gestapo some five thousand examples of such "treason." Most work stoppages, the Nazis believed, were used as a safe way to protest their rule. In the first and only elections for factory delegates to the Labor Front, Nazi candidates were over-whelmingly defeated, and Nazi-appointed workers' "representatives" were scorned. Propaganda meetings were sparsely attended and the Hitler greeting ig-nored. Workers harassed or beat up workers who supported the regime, and they distributed antiwar slogans and songs. Even as late as 1944 workers fought pitched battles against Nazis in the bombed-out rubble, forcing the SS to seal off the workers districts and capture thousands. The Nazi Security Service itself re-ported that most workers remained opposed to the Nazis.

Like workers in the cities, many rural Germans rejected anti-Semitism, sometimes to the point of risking their lives to help Jews. For example, near the war's end, SS guards marched starving Jewish prisoners to death in zig-zag paths across the German countryside. Despite twelve years of Nazi propaganda declar-ing Jews to be sub-human enemies of the German nation, and despite threats from the guards to shoot anyone who offered the Jewish prisoners aid, German civilians in the towns of Ahornberg, Sangerberg, Althutten, and Volary offered food and water to the Jews. In Allen's book detailing events in a single town, he reports that, despite the Nazi drive to enroll every school child in the Hitler Youth or the League of German Girls, and the abolition of all other school clubs, none-theless: "In fact, even pupils sympathetic to Nazism felt enough of a sense of soli-darity with fellow-students of the Jewish faith so that they refused to sing the 'Horst Wessel Song' [a Nazi marching song] in their presence."

In FHAO's book there is no inkling of the mass working class resistance to the Nazis, no hint that Holocaust-era Germany was in a state of extreme class war—a virtual civil war. Instead, FHAO writes, "Although the [Nazi] storm troopers operated outside the law, they encountered very little opposition. Indeed many openly supported their efforts." The accounts in the FHAO text all deny the widespread nature of resistance. A typical one is from Primo Levi who claims, "[T]he German people as a whole did not even try to resist." To suggest how self-centered and morally weak people are—even opponents of the authorities—FHAO points to a professor "of Nobel-Prize caliber and impeccable liberal creden-tials" who replied to a Nazi commissar's banning of Jews from Frankfurt Univer-sity by asking the Nazi, "Will there be more money for research in physiology?"

In the fantasy world of FHAO, the only resistance to the Nazis came from rare individuals. For example, fourteen students led by Hans and Sophie Scholl and calling themselves "White Rose" distributed thousands of anti-Nazi leaflets before being caught and beheaded. They in fact were part of a massive working class resistance. But this is how FHAO describes them: "Among the few Germans to act on what they knew were Hans Scholl and his younger sister Sophie." Ignoring working class battles against the Nazis, FHAO suggests that what little resistance there was came from the upper classes. They write, "Although the Nazis were able to destroy the White Rose, they could not stop their message from being heard. Helmuth von Moltke, a German aristocrat, smuggled copies to friends in neutral countries."

Similarly, FHAO lies about the massive resistance to the Nazis when they ordered doctors and nurses to kill patients with mental or physical impairments that rendered them "unfit Aryans." The outcry against the Nazi euthanasia program spread from relatives of the murdered people to the entire country, and included public demonstrations and press editorials. But FHAO singles out a minister who "worked behind the scenes" against the euthanasia, writes that his fellow pastors "gave him little support," and asks the student, "How do you account for the fact that few Germans protested 'euthanasia' even though it was directed against 'Aryan' Germans as well as Jews and other minorities?"

Anti-Semitism: An Elite Weapon

Facing History and Ourselves identifies human nature as the source of anti-Semitism and other prejudices. Its resource book begins with chapters devoted to this theme. One unit on stereotypes and prejudice cites a psychologist who writes: "[W]e tend to see others as representatives of groups. It's a natural tendency ...But [it] has unfortunate consequences." The resource book's introduction quotes a former student: "This course made me look inside myself. I for one know that I have felt prejudice toward someone of some other group. These things are all a part of being a human being, but cooperation, peace and love are ingredients also."

Facing History's central theme is that bigotry stems from people's nature as human beings, but that people also have the potential to resist this impulse and to act morally and courageously. This central point, however, is wrong. Bigotry does not stem from human nature; it is fomented by elites who use it as a method of social control. Facing History's description of Nazi anti-Semitic propaganda divorces it completely from its role as an elite weapon against the German working classes. Facing History in this way deflects attention from the real source of the problem of bigotry and blames ordinary people instead.

The key fact that makes it possible to understand anti-Semitism in Nazi Germany is that Nazi anti-Semitic propaganda was designed to shift the focus of people's anger away from capitalists. This was a time when capitalists all over the world were in mortal fear of losing power to a revolutionary working class. The enormous unemployment and economic hardship caused by the Depression were leading millions of people to question the capitalist system. Taking advantage of the fact that the Bolshevik (Communist) government in the Soviet Union was notoriously anti-democratic, capitalists everywhere used the "Bolshevik menace" to rally followers against the working class in their own countries, whose revolutionary potential is what truly frightened them.

The Nazis used anti-Semitism to strengthen the forces opposed to working class revolution, or "Bolshevism." Nazis lumped Jews and "Bolsheviks" together, accusing them of being a single diabolical conspiracy against the German people. When people got angry at capitalists, the Nazis singled out Jewish capitalists and in the next breath blamed "Bolshevik" workers.

In the years leading up to Hitler's appointment as Chancellor, Germany was in the throes of the Depression and the world seemed to be falling apart. Record numbers of small merchants and artisans were driven into bankruptcy by banks and big business depriving them of cheap credit and large department stores underpricing them. When small businessmen and artisan associations denounced big business, the Nazis countered that blaming fellow Germans was a "Jewish-Marxist" sham. They said the real problem was that department stores could sell cheap Russian goods because Jewish Bolsheviks exploited Christian workers to benefit German Jews.

The peasants also were being driven into bankruptcy. Demanding "free trade," big business backed government policies that forced the peasants to dump their produce for low prices, and charged them exorbitantly for loans and supplies. Police seized the possessions of bankrupted peasants. As Weiss recounts, unlike all the other parties, the Nazis organized demonstrations and violent blockades against the police and authorities auctioning off peasant property. The Nazis railed against the "fertilizer Jews," the "grain Jews," the "bank Jews," the "stock exchange Jews" and the "commodity trading Jews," but also against "Jewish Bolsheviks" to blame city workers. A famous Nazi poster attacked the working class anti-Nazi street fighters by portraying one of them protecting a Jewish financier sitting on a bag of gold labeled "War, revolution, inflation—profits of eastern Jews." The poster asks, "Is this your battle against capitalism, Marxist?"

The conservative upper classes of Germany were the backbone of anti-Semitism. The newspapers and institutions they controlled spewed anti-Semitic propaganda, and their children disproportionately joined Hitler's SS troops from the beginning. Anti-Semitism was used to recruit and ideologically motivate elements of the population who could be used to carry out violence against opponents of the Nazi regime.

Anti-Semitism, however, was not the basis on which Nazis sought support among the general public. In fact, when it came to winning middle class votes, the Nazis actually had to downplay anti-Semitism. In *Germans Into Nazis*, Peter Fritzsche writes: "Germans do not appear to have voted for the Nazis because they blamed the Jews for their troubles...[A]nti-Semitism played only a secondary role in National Socialist [Nazi] election campaigns. It was not the main feature in electoral propaganda or in the pages of the leading Nazi newspaper, *Volkischer Beobachter*." William F. Allen reports the same thing in the town of "Thalburg" just prior to the Nazi takeover: "Social discrimination against Jews was practically non-existent in the town...If Nazi anti-Semitism held any appeal for the townspeople, it was in a highly abstract form, as a remote theory unconnected with daily encounters with real Jews in Thalburg. Thalburg's [Nazi] leaders sensed this, and in consequence anti-Semitism was not pushed in propaganda except in a ritualistic way."

In the hundreds of pages which Facing History devotes to the subject of anti-Semitism in Germany, all discussion of the role of anti-Semitism as a weapon in the ferocious class war raging in Germany is conspicuously missing. Helping students understand the real origin and role of anti-Semitism is not Facing History's intent; its intent is to use the horror of the Holocaust to convince students that bigotry comes from human nature. The implicit message, and the reason Facing History gets support from wealthy and powerful people, is that the way to fight bigotry is not to help ordinary people succeed in their struggles against elite power, but rather to admonish people to rise above their innate prejudices.

The Myth That Most Germans Wanted to Kill the Jews

The Facing History and Ourselves text contends that the Holocaust is proof of the latent bigotry of most people. Supposedly the Holocaust could not have happened unless most Germans wanted it to happen. But, as we have seen, Germans were sharply divided over support or opposition to the Nazis, and even among the middle class attracted to the Nazis, anti-Semitism was not the basis for that attraction. The wealthiest Germans, on the other hand, bankrolled the Nazis, used anti-Semitism to deflect popular anger away from themselves and against working people, and used terrorism against Jews to intimidate opposition to elite rule. To carry out the Holocaust, the upper class needed only to cow most Germans into obedience; they neither required nor obtained the agreement of most Germans with their genocidal goal.

Hitler was aware of the widespread opposition to his rule and knew he had to abolish elections altogether. He suppressed his opponents with his new governmental power and then held one last election on March 5, 1933.

On February 27 the Reichstag [Parliament] building erupted in flames. Hitler declared it a Communist crime. The next day, civil liberties for all Germans were suspended—for the duration of the Third Reich. Only the Nazis and their Nationalist allies were permitted to campaign for the election unmolested, while thousands of Communist, Social Democrat and liberal leaders were arrested and beaten.

In the midst of this Nazi terror, with Hitler already Chancellor and the working class parties effectively suppressed, the Nazis still captured only 44 percent of the total vote.

After the Nazis were handed the reigns of government by the German elite, they used that power ruthlessly not only against anyone opposing them politically, but also against anyone expressing solidarity with Jews. In *The Gestapo and German Society*, Robert Gellately writes, "When it came to enforcing racial policies destined to isolate Jews, there can be no doubt that the wrath of the Gestapo knew no bounds, often dispensing with even the semblance of legal procedures. It is important to be reminded of the 'legal' and 'extra-legal' terror brought down on the heads of those who would not otherwise comply...Sometimes they [those who wanted to aid Jews] were driven to suicide."

The Nazi "Final Solution," the plan to kill all European Jews, did not begin until 1941, well into the war period. The Nazis, and the German elite that put them in power, launched World War II intending to crush any possibility of working class revolution in Europe by enslaving virtually the entire European working class. They thought they could legitimize the slavery with racist ideology.

War is the most powerful weapon that ruling classes have for commanding obedience. In peacetime the Nazis would not have been able to convince sufficient numbers of people to kill innocent people just because they were Jewish. As "leaders of the nation at war," the Nazis declared Jews to be the nation's enemy, and made opposition to the genocide tantamount to treason. Germans were drafted into military and police units and given their genocidal orders.

Most of the drafted men who obeyed their commands did so for reasons that had nothing to do with wanting to kill Jews. These men were stationed as occupying forces in Poland, Russia, and other foreign countries, surrounded by hostile populations. Breaking ranks by refusing orders meant, at the very least, implicitly denouncing the only people who provided material support and social contact far from home. Outright disagreement with the German government's war aims meant declaring oneself a traitor. Few men, in such circumstances, could imagine refusing orders from their legal government in time of war to kill those declared to be the enemy.

Because the Gestapo terror and mass arrests had eliminated organized and visible opposition to the Nazi regime and its killing of Jews, individuals opposed to the killing felt more alone than they really were, and hence lacked the confidence to challenge the authorities. At the same time, Hitler knew how little support there was for the genocide, which is why he shrouded the Final Solution in secrecy and banned public discussion of it.

The notion that the Holocaust could only have happened because most ordinary Germans wanted to kill the Jews is not supported by the weight of scholarly evidence. Yet Daniel Goldhagen, the author of *Hitler's Willing Executioners: Ordinary Germans and the Holocaust*, advances this notion, and has received acclaim for it in the *New York Times*, *Time*, and other corporate media. Goldhagen makes fraudulent use of historical evidence to argue for his thesis. For example, Goldhagen cites "ritual murder" accusations leveled against Jews as evidence for rampant anti-Semitism in Germany before the First World War. He writes, "...in Germany and the Austrian Empire, twelve such trials [for ritual murder] took place between 1867 and 1914." Goldhagen, however, omitted the remainder of the sentence which appears in his source; it reads "eleven of which collapsed although the trials were by jury." As Norman Finkelstein and Ruth Bettina Birn point out, honest use of the evidence by Goldhagen would have contradicted his thesis.

If Facing History approached the Holocaust from the perspective of asking why the working classes of Germany failed to defeat the upper classes, despite the fact that they outvoted the Nazis and fought them in the streets, then it would be a valuable course in our schools. Instead Facing History misleads students into thinking that there was no substantial fight against the Nazis, or even disagreement with them, and then cynically asks students to ponder what this means about the moral character of average people.

Why Did the Nazis Succeed in Seizing Power?

What, then, does explain the Nazi victory over working people in Germany? The answer is that Nazism could only have been defeated by a popular armed revolution, and there was no democratic model of revolution appealing to the majority of Germans and no revolutionary leadership committed to such a model. The Social Democratic Party had long since abandoned the goal of revolution and committed its considerable power to protecting the Weimar republic against Communist revolution. The German Communist Party offered only an anti-democratic idea of revolution which had already proved itself a disaster in the Soviet Union.

The problem was not that the Nazis reflected the real values and goals of most Germans. The problem was that the Marxist leaders of the working class parties, the Social Democratic and Communist parties, failed to champion the revolutionary aspirations of the majority of Germans.

If the Marxists had provided leadership for ordinary people's revolutionary goals, history might have been very different. The Social Democratic Party (SDP), however, which controlled the major trade unions, acted like a special interest group and only bargained for trade-union concessions, rather than mobilizing the working class for social transformation.

In these years (that is, 1929-33) the German Communist Party did espouse workers' revolution (this changed in 1935), but the anti-democratic model of Soviet-style revolution could hardly have been expected to gain majority support. In the USSR at the time, having crushed the Workers' Opposition within the Communist Party, the Stalin leadership was consolidating its power, destroying any lingering illusions that the Bolshevik Revolution could lead to a promising new world.

The Lessons of the Holocaust

The real lessons of the Holocaust are that bigotry is generated by elites as a means of social control and that there is no limit to the horrors the ruling class will impose to stay in power. Until people overthrow elite rule and create real democracy, elites can and will commit mass murder.

Facing History talks about applying the lessons of history to our own lives. But the process should go in the opposite direction. We should use the experiences of our own lives, about which we have real knowledge, to try to understand historical events about which we have only the words of others.

The lesson of our everyday experience and the lesson of real history truthfully told is that ordinary people are the source of what is best in our world—caring relations of commitment to each other, trust, equality and solidarity. Left to themselves, regular people try to make the world better—without racial, ethnic or religious bigotry and without elite domination. This is exactly why the elite work so hard to make people mistrustful of each other. To Germany's elite in the

1930s and '40s, anti-Semitism seemed like a good way to create this mistrust. Anti-Semitism had a long history and a sophisticated, "scientific" aura based on new racial theories of "eugenics." Germans in respectable universities were taught that these were progressive ideas that would lead to a better society. Without this progressive facade, anti-Semitism would have remained a relic from the past.

Today crude forms of anti-Semitism and racism are largely discredited, so new kinds of propaganda are used. The goal of the propaganda is always the same—to blame ordinary people for problems that are in fact caused by the elite. The difference is that now the progressive facade is not about protecting society from people of this or that race or religion, but protecting it from the majority of people who supposedly have an instinctive tendency towards bigotry, and who supposedly lack the moral fortitude to do what is right.

Facing History And Ourselves is simply the newest, most sophisticated form of propaganda designed to do exactly what anti-Semitism was meant to do—convince us that ordinary people are the problem and elite rule the solution in creating a humane and just society.

II. Distorting Science to Attack the Idea of Democracy

THE CENTRAL IDEA OF DEMOCRACY IS THAT ordinary people are fit to rule. Throughout history the privileged few who rule over the many have sought to undermine this idea one way or another. The latest method that corporate leaders have adopted involves using liberal rhetoric with its catch words and phrases —"tolerance," "diversity," and opposition to "hate" and "racism"—to undermine the idea of democracy.

The new corporate approach is to convince people that genuine democracy might not be such a good idea because so many ordinary people are prone to bigotry and ready to follow demagogues, the way Germans supposedly eagerly followed Hitler. To spread this view, corporate leaders are posing as champions of "tolerance" and exhorting the public to be less "hateful." They do this in a manner designed to make it seem as if ordinary people are dangerous—the very source of bigotry and hate. The goal is to undermine the idea of majority rule.

A case in point is Facing History And Ourselves. The popularity of the Facing History Holocaust course is due to the fact that it purports to be against bigotry and prejudice. Facing History frames its discussion of prejudice, however, in the context of a profoundly negative view of ordinary people. If people are really the way Facing History says they are, then they certainly should not rule society.

Distorting a Famous Experiment

Facing History and Ourselves argues that the Nazis succeeded in carrying out the Holocaust because most people are not only prone to bigotry, but are also morally weak: they obey authority instead of their conscience. To make sure students draw this conclusion, Facing History precedes its discussion of the Holocaust (in its Resource Book, *Facing History And Ourselves: Holocaust and Human Behavior*) with a distorted account of a series of famous experiments on the psychology of obedience to authority, conducted by Yale psychologist Stanley Milgram in the 1960s.

Facing History distorts the account of the famous Milgram experiments to convince students that only extraordinary people can be relied on to stand up for what is right. As Facing History relates, in these experiments subjects were falsely told that they were part of an experiment to study the effect of punishment on learning and that the experiment required them to give short but very painful electrical shocks to other subjects who had agreed to be the "learner." Facing History tells students that when the authority figure in the experiment asked the subjects to administer the shocks, "the majority of normal, average subjects behave[d] in evil (felonious) ways" and that even those subjects who refused to give the shocks still didn't "denounce the researcher." Quoting Hannah Arendt, Facing History wonders: "How do average even admirable people become dehumanized by the critical circumstances pressing in on them?" "What," Facing History asks, "is blind obedience?" The effect on students of this account would be quite different, however, if Facing History informed students of two crucial facts which their Resource Book does not mention. First, the reason subjects didn't "denounce the researcher" was because they were told right after participating that the electrical shocks were fake and that the "learner" who cried out in pain was an actor.

Second, and more importantly, the conclusion drawn from the experiments by Stanley Milgram is quite different from the conclusion drawn by Facing History. The key distinction Milgram makes is that people obey and believe in what they perceive to be legitimate authority that serves a "desirable end," not just any authority. In his book, *Obedience to Authority*, Milgram concludes that "A substantial proportion of people do what they are told to do, irrespective of the content of the act and without limitations of conscience, so long as they perceive that the command comes from a legitimate authority." He adds, "Ideological justification is vital in obtaining *willing* [his emphasis] obedience, for it permits the person to see his behavior as serving a desirable end...The experiment is presented to our subjects in a way that stresses its positive human values: increase of knowledge about learning and memory processes. These ends are consistent with generally held cultural values. Obedience is merely instrumental to the attainment of these ends."

But Facing History wants students to view ordinary people as a dangerous element who just obey authority "blindly," no matter how evil it may be, and so they conclude the unit on this experiment by asking students: "What encourages obedience? Is it fear of punishment? A desire to please? A need to go along with the group? A belief in authority?" Facing History doesn't tell students that Milgram's own book suggests that the answer should be none of the above, but rather "a belief that the authority embodies positive human values."

Facing History describes a second experiment, conducted by Philip Zimbardo, also a psychologist, to reinforce its point that people are innately prone to hatefulness. In this experiment volunteer men were made to assume roles of guards and prisoners. Facing History quotes Zimbardo as saying that the mock prison had to be shut down because "the ugliest, most base, pathological side of human nature surfaced." (This quotation is supposedly from a journal called *Societies*, but librarians at Harvard University could find no trace of such a journal.)

Zimbardo's prison experiment in fact shows, if anything, that people are not innately hateful. In his web page discussion of the experiment, Zimbardo indicates that only one third of the guards exhibited cruel behavior, and this was prompted by their being ordered to subject the prisoners to very real physical and emotional abuse and then to suppress a very real rebellion. The cause of the cruel behavior in the experiment was not "human nature"; the cause was the experimenter creating circumstances that fomented cruelty.

As for the origin of prejudice, Zimbardo wrote a book on this subject which expresses views quite different from the ones Facing History attributes to him. In his *The Psychology of Attitude Change and Social Influence*, in a section called "Some Origins of Prejudiced Attitudes," Zimbardo says there are two major types of explanation for prejudice: "dispositional," meaning due to the personality of individuals, and "historical sociocultural." Zimbardo illustrates the latter approach by noting that "The economic advantage accruing to those in power over those they discriminate against is obvious in the institutions of slavery and apartheid...and in the unequal pay and limits on advancement of women and minorities. Prejudice and discrimination pay off for some people; they did so for the founding fathers of America who were slaveholders, and they still do for those

who exploit unskilled and blue-collar laborers in mines and farms and factories."
Regarding the "dispositional" explanation of prejudice, the idea that it comes from
something wrong with people's personality, Zimbardo writes, "However, this
view is not accepted by social psychologists as the full explanation of prejudice because it is too narrowly intrapsychic without acknowledging all of the social
causes of prejudice." Thus both Zimbardo and Milgram reject the conclusions
from their own experiments that Facing History draws from them.

Corporate Propaganda

Facing History's negative view of people is not an isolated fluke. Corporate leaders
of the most powerful institutions in society are attacking the idea of democracy in
novel ways. On November 16, 1999 FleetBoston Financial Corporation ran a full
page advertisement in the *Boston Globe*, promoting its sponsorship of Team Harmony. The ad's text makes it clear that when it comes to bigotry, FleetBoston believes that the problem is not people with wealth and power, but average
teenagers. Hence the ad describes Team Harmony as "a program developed to help
teens overcome bigotry and learn to respect people of all races and backgrounds."
It is especially audacious for Boston bankers to preach "tolerance" to teenagers
since it is well known that it was Boston's bankers who used discriminatory
mortgage policies (the notorious "redlining" of neighborhoods) in the 1960s to
create black residential ghettos.

Another example reveals the utter contempt that the elite have for regular
people. The *Boston Globe*, one of the nation's most liberal newspapers, now owned
by the *New York Times* and for decades the leading mouthpiece for New England's
corporate leadership, used the occasion of Dr. Martin Luther King, Jr.'s birthday
to accuse most people of having values and dreams the opposite of MLK's. On
January 17, 2000 the *Globe* itself ran a full page advertisement. Under the heading "Most People" the ad listed three dreams: Winning the lottery, Owning a big
house and car, and Being a movie star. Under the heading "Martin Luther King,
Jr." they printed his famous "I have a dream" speech. Message: regular people are
self-centered and petty whereas elite leaders like the *Globe's* owners share MLK
Jr's idealism and vision.

Turn The Attack Around

We should not let their use of liberal and progressive rhetoric disguise the fact that
corporate leaders are trying to undermine all of the truly progressive efforts of
people to make our society more equal and democratic. The very fact that corporations feel obliged to pose as champions of "tolerance" in order to gain public ap-

proval is itself evidence that the public is by and large opposed to prejudice and bigotry. The corporate portrayal of ordinary people as hateful, bigoted and selfish is meant to make people feel so alone and hopeless about the prospect of building a revolutionary movement for a better world that they will not even try.

Let's turn this corporate attack around, by having conversations with friends and neighbors and co-workers about the real elitist message behind the liberal rhetoric. My son took the *Boston Globe's* MLK ad to his high school and pointed out to his teachers and friends how disgustingly anti-people it was. They all agreed. Now the *Globe* has far less influence among those people, despite its liberal reputation. The more we expose how corporations lie about ordinary people to portray them as the source of the problems in society, the more confidence people will have in each other that they are indeed fit to rule society and create a real democracy.

by David Stratman

I. SHOULD TEACHERS HAVE SENIORITY RIGHTS?

TEACHERS' SENIORITY RIGHTS ARE UNDER ATTACK across the country. Under the banner of education reform, teacher seniority protections have been lost or seriously weakened in Chicago, Milwaukee, St. Paul, and Seattle, and are targeted in Los Angeles and Kansas City. In Boston, where the Boston Teachers Union and the Boston School Committee are negotiating a new contract as we go to press, the mayor has called for weakening seniority rights and a business-backed organization called The Boston Plan for Excellence has called for their elimination. A coalition of "community groups" and "parent organizations" calling themselves the "Voices for Children Coalition" is trying to intervene in the negotiations "on the side of the children"—against seniority rights.

How should parents react to this issue? Should we defend seniority rights for teachers? Or do these teachers' rights stand in the way of the best education for our children?

Hiring The "Best" Teachers
Voices for Children argues that seniority preferences in hiring must be eliminated so that "All schools should be able to hire the best person for the job." Common sense? Not really.

Who is "the best person for the job" for principals constantly pushed to cut costs? It's the youngest teacher, the teacher who is cheapest, least experienced, most compliant, most easily intimidated, least savvy, least experienced in unionism, least likely to speak out or fight back—or it's the principal's brother-in-law: some crony in need of a job, or the friend of some pol he owes a favor to.

This isn't just a problem of individual principals; it's how the system works. In important ways, corporate and government officials want the schools serving working class and poor children to fail, to justify their place in an unequal society. This is why they starve the schools for funds. This is why they keep classes large. This is why they make life in urban schools so difficult for teachers, while they deprive children in urban districts of books and supplies and sometimes even of desks. This is why they impose high stakes tests designed to push students out of school without a diploma.

What about the argument that principals need to be able to hire their own staff to make education reform work, especially that part of education reform that involves creating a special "team" unique to each school?

The real obstacle to better schools is not technical but political. The problem isn't that we don't know how to make urban schools better. Teachers already know many ways to help our children learn more effectively. The problem is that teachers and parents don't have the resources, the political support, the power to make better schools happen. The "every school is unique" approach is another management scam, designed to put schools in competition with each other, break down collegial relationships across school districts, and prevent us from building a movement for fundamental educational change.

Eliminating seniority will worsen the climate of fear and demoralization that years of budget cuts and attacks on teachers have already created in our schools. It will put creativity and courage ever more at risk. Teachers fought for seniority protection in the first place because without it they were defenseless against School Committees and principals who wanted to eliminate more expensive, experienced teachers or to intimidate teachers who resisted favoritism and corruption.

Eliminating seniority rights is also designed to destroy the institutional memory of unionism in the schools. Younger teachers have no real experience of union organizing and struggle; by getting rid of experienced teachers, school officials aim to keep it that way.

Seniority rights are critical to protect our children. Which teachers are most likely to be let go in the current climate of corporate-backed education reform? Exactly those teachers our children need the most: experienced teachers capable of handling the challenge of teaching in under-funded, understaffed schools and who are most willing to speak out against such atrocities as high stakes testing and other abuses. Without seniority rights, schools will become the personal fiefdoms of principals beholden to corporate forces hostile to good education for all children.

The Meaning of Seniority

Seniority is a time-honored means of eliminating favoritism in the workplace. It goes much deeper than union contracts. Seniority represents a fundamental human value, the solidarity between generations, where older workers share their experience with the next generation and younger workers protect older workers as they begin to slow down.

Education of course is not the only area where seniority is under attack. Seniority and other worker protections have been under attack for the last 25 years throughout American industry, to be replaced by favoritism and fear. The only difference is that, in industry, the attack on seniority is justified in the name of efficiency and competitiveness; in schools it's justified in the name of the children.

The Need For a United Movement

Many parents have had experiences where they were unhappy with a particular teacher. But the great majority of teachers are talented people dedicated to the well-being of children. Often the same conditions that undermine our children's school performance are the things that discourage teachers as well. We must see that teachers in trouble get help, just as we must get help for students in trouble.

The schools are rigged to fail. School officials are only too happy to see parents and teachers at each other's throats, leaving us powerless to affect schools for the better. Teachers and parents share the goal of success for all children. We can only succeed if we stand united.

The forces arrayed against seniority in Boston are the same powers which have given our children an inferior education for so long: the mayor, the Boston School Committee, the leaders of big business. The *Boston Globe* is the biggest opponent of seniority for teachers and the biggest promoter of high stakes tests for students. These are the last people parents should support.

Beneath its pro-child rhetoric, "Voices for Children" is setting parents and teachers against each other at exactly the time when parent-teacher unity is most needed to stop high stakes testing and other corporate-backed reforms. A real parent movement would unite parents and teachers to defend our children.

by John Spritzler

I.   HIGHER EDUCATION FREE FOR ALL?

JIM HIGHTOWER IS A TEXAN FAMOUS FOR HIS left-of-center activism and writings, including his book, *If The Gods Had Meant Us To Vote They Would Have Given Us Candidates*, and a just-started newsletter called *The Hightower Lowdown*. The last issue of the *Lowdown* had a good exposé of Wal-Mart's anti-working class policies. The current issue (May 2002) is headlined, "Let's make higher ed. free for all Americans" and consists almost entirely of reasons why that would be a good idea.

Having read the previous *Lowdown's* Wal-Mart feature I was prepared to enjoy the next issue's article on higher education, but as I read the article I realized that there was something very disturbing about it. That feeling was confirmed when I got to the passage that read:

> Free higher education also is a natural fit for our new global order, a fast-spinning world in which employees can forget about such old-fashioned niceties as corporate loyalty and job security, no matter how much of yourself you've dedicated to the company. Washington and Wall Street tell us that we must expect to get dumped frequently and scramble for new work, usually requiring higher skills. Okay, so in a wealthy nation like ours, which has become the world model for this new chaotic economy, let's lead the way in providing secure footing for our people by making sure that an infrastructure of free education and training is always in place. If this is the way the new world is going to be, let's adjust for that world.

In this passage Hightower explicitly declares that he accepts Washington's and Wall Street's "new global order" and only wishes to make it easier for people to "adjust for that world." When a man like Hightower—famous for lashing out at the likes of George W. Bush and Wal-Mart, author of a book critical of all mainstream politicians, and highly regarded on the left—repudiates the very idea of overthrowing the Washington and Wall Street elite and creating a very different world than their "new global order," one has to wonder: What's up with Hightower's *Lowdown*?

Hightower's apparent unwillingness to consider democratic revolution—the obvious commonsense goal for Americans fed up with the domination of our lives by corporate elites and politicians working on their behalf—prevents him from talking about the benefits of free higher education truthfully. What do I mean by that?

Why Really Did They Pass the GI Bill?

Hightower claims that the GI Bill, which made higher education nearly free for GIs returning home from World War Two, was passed because "such politically diverse forces as progressive labor unions and the American Legion" backed it enthusiastically, and "business and political leaders...simply didn't know what else to do." And he claims that the Bill had only positive results ("The GI Bill worked and it's now recognized as one of the most useful acts Congress ever passed...every dollar invested produced a $7 increase in our nation's output.") A more truthful discussion of the GI Bill would have examined its role in the actual context of the class struggle going on during those post-war years. Keep in mind that during the war, despite the fact that virtually all of the "progressive labor unions'" national leaders tried to enforce a No-Strike Pledge in obedience to President Roosevelt and the corporate class he represented, rank-and-file workers went on strike anyway, even though the only way they could do so was with wildcat (unauthorized by the union) strikes. As labor historian Martin Glaberman wrote in *Labor's Giant Step*, "When the war came to a close on August 14, 1945, the American workers had chalked up more strikes and strikers during the period from December 7, 1941, to the day of Japanese surrender three years and eight months later, than in any similar period of time in American labor history." Historian Jeremy Brecher notes that during the war, "Workers virtually made extra holidays for themselves around Christmas and New Year's, holding illicit plant parties and cutting production to a trickle. Workers often created free time for themselves on the job by other means. On one occasion, workers in an aircraft plant staged a necktie-cutting party in the middle of working hours, roaming through the plant snipping off ties of fellow workers, supervisors, and managers. The wildcat tradition and organization gave workers a direct counter-power over such management decisions as the speed of work, number of workers per task, assignment of foremen, and organization of work...Industry representatives claimed a decrease of labor efficiency of 20 to 50 percent during the war period." After the war ended, a huge strike wave began. "The first six months of 1946 marked what the U.S. Bureau of Labor Statistics called 'the most concentrated period of labor-management strife in the country's history,' with 2,970,000 workers involved in strikes starting in this period" including not only industrial workers but teachers, municipal workers and others. "By the end of 1948, 4.6 million workers had been involved in strikes; their average length was four times that of the war period."

Contrary to Hightower's assertion that big business leaders just "didn't know what else to do," the GI Bill's purpose, from their point of view, was two-fold. It was an attempt to replace the working class outlook for improving one's life—"Make the world better for everybody by acting in solidarity against the 'necktie-wearing' class of employers"—with the elitist view promoted in colleges and universities—"Make the world better for yourself by getting a degree and rising above others in a 'career.'" The GI Bill helped to distance many working class people from their parents' culture of solidarity and integrate them into the corporate culture of individualism. The effect of this transformation, to the extent that it succeeded, has been to enable corporate leaders to control people more effectively than during the "necktie-cutting" days before the GI Bill. Additionally, the GI Bill was an attempt to convince working people that if they accepted corporate control of society they would enjoy benefits (like college education) that workers had never had before.

Do College Degrees Really Raise People's Salaries?

Hightower promotes free higher education by arguing that it will raise everybody's income. "Today a basic bachelor's degree is an all-around money maker, typically providing 75% more earning power than a high-school diploma and often adding more than a million bucks in additional income over a lifetime of work." In truth, the supposed economic benefits to workers from being able to go to college are questionable. The transformation of our society from one in which few working class people went to college into one in which a larger proportion do so has been accompanied by the growth of "lower tier" colleges, junior colleges and professional schools designed to prepare their students for "careers" in the new global economy that do not pay as much as people with only a high school degree used to make in jobs with a history of solidarity. This is why fewer married couples today than in previous decades can raise children on the income of one parent. And it is why people are working far more than the 40 hours per week that union solidarity once won. Hightower talks about the relation between higher education and earning power as if there were no class struggle going on over these things. But the truth cannot be told without taking the class struggle into account. Despite more people going to college now than before, our society is growing more and more unequal because the corporate elite want it to and, for the moment, they have the power to make it so. They will use their power this way no matter how many people have college degrees. When more people go to college, it just means that more jobs get defined as requiring a college degree; it doesn't mean the job pays more. (Some jobs in day care centers require a college degree but pay only $10.50 per hour.) It may be true that people with college degrees earn, on average, more than those without them; but it is a fallacy to suppose, as Hightower suggests, that if everybody had a college degree they would automatically earn, on average, what the smaller number with degrees earn today. It doesn't work like that. College degrees don't determine what jobs pay. The employers determine what they will pay. And they make this decision in such a manner as to maximize their control over the working class, one method of which is to have very unequal pay for different categories of workers. When few workers have college degrees, employers pay those with degrees more. But if all workers had college degrees, employers would find some other excuse to pay most less and only a few more; unless, of course, worker solidarity actions like strikes made this impractical. Furthermore, insofar as people learn in college to rely on their individual "merit" to rise in the world rather than to rely on solidarity to make the world better for everybody, the "college-degreeing" of the working class will only help corporate leaders control and exploit it more easily.

Is "Equal Opportunity" Equality?

Hightower argues for free higher education by promoting the illusion that America is a "land of opportunity." He writes, "Fundamentally, education is opportunity, which is what America is all about." Let's stop for a moment and consider what this really means. What is the "opportunity" that capitalist America is all about? All of the inequality imposed by capitalism, and all of the dog-eat-dog competition it relies on to control people, is justified by people at the top of society with appeals to an individualistic and fundamentally selfish value expressed by the notion that "as long as I have an opportunity to rise to the top it doesn't matter how unequal our society is or how much I have to screw other people to succeed." Working class culture rejects this "opportunity to succeed" nonsense. When the company says it will give raises to the "most deserving" employees, the ones who "merit" it, workers see what's really going on. It's a way to divide and control. Teachers, for example, have consistently opposed "merit" pay for this reason. Yet here is Hightower, espousing this anti-working class value as an opportunistic way of defending his call for free higher education. Once again, he is trying to deny the reality of class struggle and make it seem as if the benefits he ascribes to free higher education can be obtained by adopting the values and accepting the power of the corporate elite rather than by challenging them and aiming to defeat them.

What Do We Really Want?

The only argument for free higher education that Hightower makes that seems truthful to me is his point that people should be able to learn things they are interested in. I could not agree more. But how can this happen in a way that leads to a more equal and democratic world? Hightower himself answers this question without realizing it. He begins his article on higher education by observing that whenever a politician announces a "bold" new plan you can be sure "that there's really nothing bold about it at all," since it's been vetted by all the "big-money contributors." He adds that "People are yearning for a politics that, as we say in Texas, has hair on it. A politics that sweats, growls, brawls...that's worth the prize, that produces results for ordinary folks and the common good of our society." Again, I could not agree more. But if Hightower took his own advice here he would reject the big money-vetted language of "equal opportunity" and "adjusting" to the "new global order."

The bold new plan we need is to aim for what we really want: a society in which education enables people to develop their talents and pursue their interests to help each other, not compete against each other to "get ahead" by serving the goals of big business; a society in which people share in the work as best they can and have equal access to what society has to offer, from material goods and services to higher education. Elite power and privilege do not fit into this kind of society.

So let's be honest about this goal of a good world where higher education is available to everybody. This is a revolutionary goal. To win it we will have to build a movement based on working class values of solidarity, not corporate values of individualism, and we will have to defeat the corporate elite, not "adjust" to it. You don't need a college education to understand this.

Part Six

CULTURE *and* VALUES

by John Spritzler

I.   WHY ARE FAMILIES UNDER ATTACK?

THE COVER OF THE MARCH 1997 *Fortune* magazine asks, "Is Your Family Wrecking Your Career?" Inside is an article headed "Oh, Quit Whining and Get Back to Work! It's heresy to say so, but let's say it anyway: Sometimes your job is more important than your kid's Kodak moment." The article describes the demands that top-ranked corporations place on working couples trying to raise children and make time for their families. The culture of the most successful corporations, according to the article, is one in which devotion to the company comes first, before family. The message to *Fortune's* CEO readers seems to be that successful corporations must be anti-family.

The anti-family culture reflected in this pro-business magazine is something that millions of people must buck everyday as they work to make their families healthy and keep them intact. In spite of politicians' talk about "family values," the pressures on working families have grown more intense in the last decade in many different ways.

Capitalists would have us believe that the pressures on families result from economic necessity. This is not true. From 1947 to 2000 the productivity of American workers has almost quadrupled.[1] We could produce more now than we did then if our families sent only one parent to work for twenty hours a week or each parent to work for ten hours. The "Leisure Society" that was foreseen in the '60s is just as feasible economically as the massive "downsizing" and overtime work that capitalists prefer. The necessity driving the attacks on the family is not economic but political. It results from capital's need to control working people by attacking the most fundamental bonds of solidarity among human beings.

Why Is Capitalism Hostile to Families?

Families are a social institution within which the values of selfishness and competition—the bedrock values of capitalism—are not viewed as appropriate. In healthy families, the important things like emotional support, shelter, medical care and food are shared according to need: not sold, but given freely. People work hard in families, not for pay but out of love and solidarity. The self-serving values and behavior that are viewed as normal when engaged in by corporations, if practiced inside a family are seen as sick. Corporations are built on greed and competition: buy low and sell dear, move the factory to where labor is cheaper, bring in scabs to break strikes, pit people against each other, sell tobacco to kids. To capitalists, anything is okay as long as it makes money. The corporate leaders who engage in the most vicious practices are frequently rewarded with the highest salaries. Healthy families are a challenge to capitalism. The countless things we do as family members, caring and providing for one another, making family events from an evening meal to a large family reunion, helping each other in an emergency, giving advice and hugs, listening sympathetically, enjoying each other's company, and even squabbling and arguing to resolve conflicts or giving valuable negative feedback—all these things we do everyday in our families have a significance which often goes unnoticed. They are efforts to make our little corner of the world the opposite of the world of buying and selling. Capital's hostility to families is part of a broader hostility to the values of working people generally. Working class culture values solidarity and equality over selfishness and greed. It's a culture that says you shouldn't cross a picket line and if you do you're a scab. Working class struggles have always drawn much of their strength from family ties. Working class family values are an active force against capitalist power. The great sit-down strikes of the '30s, the valiant struggles of Hormel meatpackers and Staley workers and Detroit newspaper strikers in the '80s and '90s, and the strikes by janitors and grocery store workers in more recent times, have all depended on family ties and values of solidarity and equality forged in the families of working people.

How Capitalism Attacks Families

One key form of capitalist attack on the family lies in a process called "commodification," in which capital seeks to undermine the natural forms of human interaction in all spheres of life and replace them with commercial relations. In particular, capital strives to turn loving family relations into mere "commodities" —services bought and sold in the marketplace. By reducing important aspects of our humanity to commodities, capital creates an image of human "freedom" in which people are "freed" of all social commitments and all social norms and morality. The ruling elite hope in this way to undermine bonds of solidarity and reduce people to solitary individuals, isolated and powerless. The owning class is trying to do more thoroughly to the family what it has long done to people at work. Corporate owners don't want labor to be a social activity that people engage in collectively for shared goals—a process which makes people very conscious of their power—but rather a commodity the owners can purchase by the hour. By purchasing our labor, capital seeks to take control of the labor process and product out of our hands. Capital tries to chop working people up into pieces of "usefulness"—our ability to turn a screw or punch a number or fry a hamburger—so that we ourselves can be treated like commodities: cheap and easy to replace. In recent years the impact of this process on specifically family-related aspects of our lives has been accelerating.

"Outsourcing" Mom

Corporations used to hire only men for jobs that paid enough to support a family. This demeaned women and undermined family solidarity by making it impossible for husbands and wives meaningfully to share outside work, child-raising, and housework. But capital's "reform" of the unequal roles of men and women in the family is a further attack. In the last 30 years, capital has outsourced or automated millions of "family wage" industrial jobs and cut the pay of others, thereby forcing working class wives into the labor market to compete for the remaining low-paid jobs, all in the name of "freedom for women." Now families are stressed even more, since both parents typically have to work at least one job, and sometimes two or three, leaving little time to devote to children or relaxation, to community service, or to anything else. Additionally, capital is attacking mothers by trying to commodify everything about them that makes them valuable members of a family.

- Having driven mothers of infants and toddlers to take jobs, capital now forces them to purchase mothering as "day care" from a growing industry whose employees are often themselves mothers of small children. (This is particularly ironic in the case of mothers on welfare forced into day-care jobs.)

- After forcing people to work such long hours that they don't have time to prepare their own meals, capital is using restaurant chains, like "Boston Market" specializing in "home-cooked, family-style" meals, to move hard-pressed moms (and dads) from their own homes, where cooking was an act of love, to corporate kitchens where it's wage labor.

- Capital is moving women out of their own homes to be maids in wealthier homes working for a growing housekeeping industry.

- Corporations are making Grandmother's wisdom a "wholly owned subsidiary" by hiring women to give advice on child-rearing and other domestic questions to their employees. The more corporations undermine families, relocating people away from family and friends, the more "Corporate Grandma" is needed.

- Capital even puts a mother's womb on the market with the growing phenomenon of paid "surrogate mothers," whose motherhood and humanity is commodified as a womb put out for hire.

Downsizing Dad

Capital is challenging the simple truth that a child's relation with his or her biological father is valuable. The image of fathers has come under increasing attack, as more TV sit-coms feature fathers as incompetents (*The Simpsons* and *King of Queens* are current examples) and movie plots involve abusive fathers (*The Breakfast Club*, *Affliction*, and *Daredevil* to name only a few.) Many courageous women have long been forced by circumstances to raise their children alone. Now, however, as celebrities like Camryn Manheim (Ellenor of TV's hit lawyer show, *The Practice*) choose to have and raise babies without a father (both in real life and as her fictional character, in the case of Manheim), Hollywood sends the message, "Who needs a father?" Academics deride fatherhood in books like *Feminism, Children, and The New Families*, in which Susan E. Krantz dismisses the notion that "two parents are necessary for the well-being of a child" and argues that "the role of the father is overemphasized." Academic "experts" are trying to split off Dad's "male presence" from the rest of him and make it just another commodity. Writing in the *Journal of Marriage and the Family*, Alan J. Hawkins and David J. Eggenbeen state, "Men may be important to children's healthy development, but biological fathers can readily be replaced by other adult men" (Cited in David Blankenhorn, *Fatherless America*, p. 80). Stepfathers may be nice people, but the claim that children have no need for a close relation with their biological father cannot bear the weight of common sense or scientific scrutiny. (For example, a study of 17,000 British children born in 1958 showed that children in step-families "experienced far worse outcomes than did children who grew up with their two biological parents." Blankenhorn, p. 191.) The "any male will do" notion is ideologically driven by capital's desire to commodify men. This commodification of men is quite apparent in states like Massachusetts, where the "progressive" agenda is well advanced, and divorce courts aggressively separate fathers from their children. (The author has personal experience with Massachusetts' family courts.) Courts routinely restrain fathers from seeing their children, sometimes for years, without due process, evidentiary hearings, or the rules of evidence that are accorded accused criminals. The courts' attitude is that a father's only important relationship to his children is financial, so there's no real loss if a loving father is barred from seeing his children.

Splitting up Mom And Dad

Liberal politicians and advocacy organizations have increased the rate of divorce in the United States enormously by enacting policies based on the premise that fatherhood is not important. The result has been a host of social, psychological and economic problems suffered by children and caused by their fatherlessness.[2] A major cause of the increased divorce rate has been the introduction of "no-fault" divorce coupled with the policy of family courts of awarding the mother solely, instead of both parents jointly, exclusive physical custody of the children (unless the mother is grossly unfit) and requiring the father to pay child support sufficient for the mother and children to maintain their former standard of living, even though it impoverishes him (courts often garnish the man's paycheck directly.) Once rare, divorce is now common and two thirds of divorces in the U.S. are initiated by women.[3] The state has essentially told women, "Feel free to leave your husband whenever you feel like it, no matter how trivial the reason, because the state will make sure you keep your children and your husband's income." The result is that in millions of broken families the state has moved in to assume the role of head of the family and "parent" to both the mother and father. All concerned—the mother, the children and the father—have become more directly controlled by and, in the case of the mother and children, more dependent upon the state, and therefore less able to stand up against the capitalist class. It would be difficult to imagine a policy better suited to covertly undermine marriages and families.

The liberal attack on marriages would not be able to succeed, however, were it not for the helpful role of the right-wing "pro-family" and pro-capitalist religious leaders and their ilk. Together these groups play a "damned if you do and damned if you don't" routine that makes people feel hopeless about improving the situation. The right-wing religious leaders point to the evils of the liberal agenda on families but they insist that the only alternative is a patriarchal society where women must submit to men. Some women and some men may support this view but most men and women want relationships based on equality. But no mainstream leadership articulates what most people want in this regard. Although it is economically perfectly feasible, what leader today calls for all wages to be raised enough, and corporate practices to be changed, so that a mother and father can each work a half-time job (or only one parent work outside the home full time, if they prefer) and raise their children comfortably on the income? With no opposition except from the right wing, which calls for a patriarchal nightmare for women, the elite get a free pass to carry out their liberal attack on our families.

Making Childhood "Lean and Mean"

In healthy families, parents love and protect their children as special people. They value them for themselves, not as a means to an end. Capitalism, in contrast, uses children as little workers and consumers, and tries to replace relations of love with marketplace transactions. Corporations flood Saturday morning TV with shows designed to manipulate children to measure their parents' love by the toys and "Happy Meals" they buy. For capitalism, parental love is a cash transaction that passes through the Toys'R'Us cash register. Millions of children overseas work in factories preparing goods for the U.S. market. In the U.S., children are increasingly told that childhood is a time to prepare themselves to meet the needs of corporations. Corporate leaders call for increased standardized testing in public schools, so that we can "better compete with Germany and Japan." Capital insists that children be graded from "A" through "F"—to teach them to compete against each other, and to sort them like cuts of beef so that corporations in the market for labor will know what "grade" of employee they're hiring. Corporate "education reformers" view our children not as people who should receive a well-rounded education, but rather as commodities to be sorted, graded, and prepared for sale to corporations.

Homosexual Families and the New World Order

In recent years the capitalist class has aggressively promoted the idea that homosexuality is as good and natural and moral a basis for a family as heterosexuality, and that anyone who disagrees with this view is a bigoted "homophobe." Television promotes homosexual families with lesbian characters like Carol and Susan on *Friends*, Melanie and Lindsay on *Queer as Folk*, and the characters on Showtime's lesbian series *The L Word*. Judges in Massachusetts have legalized homosexual marriage. While they attack traditional families, corporations increasingly treat homosexual couples as if they were married. The Massachusetts Department of Education encourages students to form "Gay-Straight Alliances"[4] to eliminate any stigma associated with homosexuality, despite the fact that the current Republican governor, Mitt Romney, purports to be a solid "conservative" on the issue.

Marriage and sexuality are not just about procreation, and to the extent that children are not involved there would be no reason for legislation to meddle in these private affairs between individuals. But since marriage and sexuality do often lead to procreation, society has a responsibility to decide what to promote and what to discourage in this otherwise private sphere of life. The concerns that people have about laws regarding marriage and society's attitude towards homosexuality are largely related to the impact of these things on children. Most people believe that the best thing for children is to be raised by their real mother and father in a strong and loving family. An important reason people disapprove of homosexuality is because it is impossible for a gay couple to make this kind of family. This is why parents don't want the schools teaching their children that it makes no difference if they marry someone of the same sex or the opposite sex. Most people rightly believe in tolerance when it comes to civil rights for homosexuals, but they don't believe that society should endorse the idea that a homosexual relationship is just as good or healthy a basis for a family as a heterosexual one.

Capital attacks people for feeling this way, and calls them bigots, because it likes the direction in which homosexuality moves society. In capital's ideal world where everyone is an isolated individual, sexuality is not a social relationship connecting parents with children, but just a way people use each other, and children are just something you buy. If two men want a child, then they can rent a womb and buy an egg from a surrogate mother. Why not? It's just a business transaction the way all human relationships ought to be. Or if two women want a baby, just buy some sperm. Why not? Fatherhood is just a commodity like toothpaste or clothing. A professor of law testifying before Congress described sperm donors as "providers of gametes," and offered the legal opinion that "A consumer's right 'to make contracts with providers of gametes' cannot be prohibited or limited except to assure that such contracts 'are knowingly and freely entered into' " (Blankenhorn, p. 179). This is the capitalist idea of Paradise, in which people are no more than their constituent parts: a womb, a source of sperm, a "male presence," a child support check, a "day care provider." No longer will children's mothers and fathers be unique and beyond price.

How Can We Defend Our Families?

The media are full of very sophisticated anti-family messages, which can come from both the right and the left. Liberals denigrate the value of families in which children are raised by their real mother and father, and they sometimes suggest that such families are often patriarchies with abusive fathers. Conservatives often call for "family values" in which women are subordinate to men and inequality prevails. Neither liberal nor conservative views reflect true family values of equality and commitment to each other. There are immediate steps we can take to defend families. One step is to reject anti-family propaganda for what it is. Another is to recognize the attack families are under and to see that it is part of capital's attempt to control ordinary people. Fully to defeat the attack on our families, and to create a truly pro-family society, we need to build a revolutionary movement that challenges capitalism, its values, and its right to rule society. The revolution we need is one which aims to extend to all of society the kind of relationships we work so hard to build within our families.

Notes

1. See: http://www.bls.gov/opub/rtaw/pdf/table24.pdf.
2. See: http://www.childrensjustice.org/fatherlessness1.htm.
3. See: http://health.discovery.com/centers/loverelationships/articles/divorce.html.
4. See: http://www.doe.mass.edu/hssss/GSA/Intro.html.

II. POLL SHOWS AMERICANS WANT GLOBAL SOLIDARITY, NOT COMPETITION

AN OPINION POLL CONDUCTED BY THE University of Maryland Program on International Policy Attitudes, and reported in the *Chicago Tribune* February 6, 2001, showed that 83% of Americans polled favored the United States joining an international program to cut world hunger in half and 75% said they would be willing to pay extra taxes to achieve this. Americans favor foreign aid for humanitarian reasons: 81% wanted either to maintain or increase aid to Africa, 77% wanted to reduce hunger and disease in poor countries, 76% to pay for child survival programs, 65% to fund the Peace Corps, and 61% to help women and girls in poor countries. In contrast, only 27% backed aid to Israel and Egypt and only 27% backed military aid in general. (Israel and Egypt each currently receive more U.S. aid than any other countries.)

One striking fact about these numbers is that, when asked how much of the federal budget actually did go to foreign aid, half of those polled guessed it was more than 10%, when if fact it is only 1%. Also, 81% favored channeling aid through private charitable organizations or other direct means rather than through governments, apparently, according to the *Tribune*, "because they believe corrupt officials steal most of the money." We who want a world based on solidarity, not competition, should never forget that we are the vast majority.

III. WORSHIPING A STRANGE GOD

IN CONTRAST TO THEOCRACIES LIKE IRAN, "secular" nations like the United States claim to have a separation of church and state. People can belong to whatever religion they wish, and there is no official state religion. Insofar as "church" refers only to specific organizations and to beliefs about the supernatural, the claim is justified. But religions also codify moral beliefs about what kind of behavior is right and wrong in the everyday "secular" world of life lived on earth. When separation of church and state purports to exist, a religion that does not call itself a religion—that is, a morality or code of conduct—may sneak in through the back door and claim the "secular" realm as its domain, all in the name of "separation of church and state." My point is not that we should have a state religion, but that we already have one.

In the United States, where capitalism asserts its power in a particularly unrestrained way, powerful people use the logic of separation of church and state to enforce a capitalist morality of self-interest and competition on the entire society. Most people, however, hold to a very different morality, one which all the major religions of the world are based on, the Golden Rule—not the capitalist version ("He who owns the gold makes the rules"), but the one we all learned as children.

The Golden Rule,[1] both its positive version—"Do unto others…,"—as well as its negative version—"Do not do unto others…,"—expresses a universal human standard of morality and appears universally in the world's religions.[2]

Two thousand years before Jesus was born, an ancient Babylonian sacred teaching said, "Do not return evil to your adversary; Requite with kindness the one who does evil to you, Maintain justice for your enemy, Be friendly to your enemy" (Akkadian Councils of Wisdom, as cited in Pritchard's *Ancient Near Eastern Texts*).

A Buddhist holy teaching written centuries before Jesus was born said: "Shame on him who strikes, greater shame on him who strikes back. Let us live happily, not hating those who hate us. Let us therefore overcome anger by kindness, evil by good, falsehood by truth."

Hillel, a great Jewish rabbi who lived just before Jesus' day, taught, "What is hateful to thee, do not to another. That is the whole law and all else is explanation." (b Shabbatt 31a; cf. Avot de R. Natan ii.26) The Positive Golden Rule is also found in Jewish literature. (Mishneh Torah ii: Hilekot Abel xiv.I)

Jesus said, "All things therefore that you want people to do to you, do thus to them." (Matthew 7:12)

Islam teaches: "That which you want for yourself, seek for mankind." (Sukhanan-i-Muhammad, 63)

A Buddhist holy teaching is: "In this world hate never yet dispelled hate. Only love dispels hate. This is the law, ancient and inexhaustible." (*The Dhammapada*)

In ancient China, Confucius taught, "Do not impose on others what you do not desire others to impose upon you." (Confucius, *The Analects*. Roughly 500 BCE)

According to Hindu sacred literature: "Let no man do to another that which would be repugnant to himself." (*Mahabharata*, bk. 5, ch. 49, v. 57)

Buddhist sacred literature teaches: "Hurt not others in ways that you yourself would find hurtful." (Udanavargu, 5:18, *Tibetan Dhammapada*, 1983)

Historically human beings the world over have tried to shape social relations with fundamental codes of conduct such as the Golden Rule,[3] and they sanctified these codes as an authority standing above the state or ruling regime by means of religion. In secular capitalist states, however, the practical effect of separation of church and state is to exclude the universal morality enshrined in the Golden Rule from having any authoritative influence on any of the vital matters that the state asserts to be "secular." Churches must restrict their criticism of capitalism to ineffectual platitudes and "the people" must keep their criticism within the framework of capitalist morality—that is, self-interest.

The Origin of Our Separation of Church and State

The medieval Catholic Church was notoriously ruthless in suppressing heretics, women suspected of being "witches," free-thinkers, and anyone who it feared might threaten its absolute power in the religious realm. At the same time, the Church defended a feudal world view and morality that had positive as well as negative aspects. These positive aspects are important reasons why the Church still has so many followers today.

In the Middle Ages the Catholic Church proclaimed that feudal relations were the way that all people, though holding very different stations in life—as lords, peasants, priests or soldiers—nonetheless acted together as an organic whole to serve the will of God. Lords and peasants and priests were certainly different, not equal. But they all served a common purpose and merited the dignity that this implied. The privileges of any group were only a means for that group to play its role in the larger common good. With privilege came obligations, and with obligations came certain rights. People were meant to serve the greater whole, not their individualistic desires. In keeping with this view, the Church defined greed and avarice as a sin. Ecclesiastical law applied this concept to the practical issues of the day. It specifically declared usury (which today refers narrowly to a "loan shark" charging excessive interest on a loan, but which in the Middle Ages referred not only to demanding any interest for a loan,[4] but generally to one person taking advantage of another's misfortune to extort an oppressive bargain of any kind) to be sinful and punished it. The Church, for the same reason, said it was a sin to "buy low and sell dear."[5] And while Jesus said to render unto Caesar what was Caesar's, by the Middle Ages the Catholic Church was a power in Caesar's as much as in the spiritual realm. A sense of the Church's determination to enforce its morality on everyday social relations can be seen from this passage from R.H. Tawney's *Religion and the Rise of Capitalism*:

The high-water mark of the ecclesiastical attack on usury was probably reached in the legislation of the Councils of Lyons (1274) and of Vienne (1312)…No individual or society, under pain of excommunication or interdict, was to let houses to usurers, but was to expel them (had they been admitted) within three months. They were to be refused confession, absolution and Christian burial until they made restitution, and their wills were to be invalid. The legislation of the Council of Vienne was even more sweeping. Declaring that it has learned with dismay that there are communities which, contrary to human and divine law, sanction usury and compel debtors to observe usurious contracts, it declares that all rulers and magistrates knowingly maintaining such laws are to incur excommunication, and requires the legislation in question to be revoked within three months. Since the true nature of usurious transactions is often concealed beneath various specious devices, money-lenders are to be compelled by the ecclesiastical authorities to submit their accounts to examination. Any person obstinately declaring usury is not a sin is to be punished as a heretic and inquisitors are to proceed against him. (pp 46-7)

In the twelfth century the Church's intellectual leaders—the Schoolmen—were able to apply lessons from the Bible to everyday life so that the Church could say with confidence and authority what was sinful and what was not. The moral outlook of what we now refer to as Capitalism, the Church defined as sinful.[6] People were supposed to serve the will of God and only worry about economic production and accumulating personal wealth secondarily and only insofar as it was necessary to carry out their appointed tasks for the larger society. While achieving wealth was not in and of itself sinful, it was sinful to have that as one's chief goal in life. Saints eschewed wealth and material possessions. A poor man could enter heaven more easily than a rich one. (Hypocrisy of course was not unknown among many Church leaders, but in spite of it the Church set the standard for what was right and what was wrong, and it was a very different standard from what prevails today.)

The Catholic Church tried to adapt ecclesiastical law to the changing times that saw the rise of merchants and world trade and complex commercial financial and credit arrangements. But the theory behind the ecclesiastical law was rooted in the premise of a simpler feudal society of lords and peasants, masters and servants, each feeling bonds of personal loyalty and obligation. The new world at the close of the Medieval period was one in which peasants were becoming rural wage workers on the land, hired when needed and let go when not. Land was becoming capital for investment. The new lords of the realm lived in towns and preoccupied themselves with business matters never mentioned in the Bible and undreamed of by the Schoolmen. As late as the seventeenth century the Church was still trying to rein in behavior that now is considered legitimate. The Church condemned feudal lords in England who stopped acting like stewards of the land and instead viewed their land primarily as a source of wealth accumulation. These large landlords, motivated by the profits that could be made by turning the land over to sheep grazing and selling the wool at a high price, were "enclosing" their land to stop peasants from cultivating it, and thereby driving peasants off the land.

But now the Church was on the defensive. Men of business came to view the Church's "interference" with their business as illegitimate. How could the Church deny the need for charging interest on a loan to a world-trading merchant as if it were the same thing as taking advantage of one's peasant during a poor harvest? Not only men of business, but new religious leaders as well, men like Martin Luther and John Calvin in the sixteenth century, undermined the stature of the Catholic Church, espousing ideas that led to the formation of the rival Protestant churches.

The Protestant Reformation introduced new ways of thinking that were seized upon by the rising capitalist class. The institutions of the Church (including its ecclesiastical courts with their claim to rule on matters of everyday life and business) were dismissed as not necessary, since according to Protestantism each individual had a direct relationship with God. Because each person's destiny was determined by his or her personal relation to God, there was little need for concern about the collective welfare. The Church taught that man was saved through faith and good works; the reformers taught that man was saved through faith alone. The realm of the spiritual became private to each person. The individual was paramount. Individual rights and liberty and character were the new themes, replacing the older vision of society as an organic whole in which individuals served a common spiritual end by carrying out their respective social obligations. The world of Caesar, now dismissed as "not spiritual," became no longer a legitimate arena for religion to judge. Quite the reverse. Caesar now became the judge. Wealth was a sign of Godliness; poverty a sign of un-Godliness. Godliness was defined as having personal character traits that happened to be those admired by the rising capitalist class—prudence, thrift, energy, self-control. The pursuit of wealth, once secondary to doing the will of God and posing temptations to sinfulness at every turn, was elevated to be the primary occupation of the most Godly people. The poor served God by being good workers and not engaging in the sin of idleness.

In the twenty-first century we still have many Christian churches and many church-goers, but the priests and the ministers know that this is no longer an era when it matters much what they say or do. They either keep quiet about their opinions concerning the behavior of the wealthy and powerful, or they state them in deliberately vague and ambiguous terms. Their pronouncements never have teeth in them. (These are the best church leaders. The worst, like the Reverend Jerry Falwell, are outright cheerleaders for capitalism.) The Catholic Church, with its historical link to feudalism and feudal morality based on viewing society as an organic whole, and its history of being the Establishment Church defending the old world view against the new capitalist class with its individualism and Protestantism, still asserts its anti-individualism in the form of opposition to abortion and homosexuality. But this is merely the Catholic Church's last hurrah.

During the first Gulf War a Catholic friend of mine in Walpole, Massachusetts, went to every priest and minister in town and asked them simply to give a sermon applying their own religion's doctrine of a just war to the ongoing war, no matter whether their doctrine approved or disapproved of the war. None of the ministers or priests would do it. The General Conference of the United Methodist Church, the church George W. Bush has been a member of since 1989, opposed his war in Iraq in 2003 as immoral. What greater sin could there be than waging an immoral war? But the church did not tell the President that (in the words of *The Book of Discipline of The United Methodist Church* which defines the conditions for membership and the steps to be taken when members do not meet them) "he hath no more place among us."[7] Similarly, the Pope issued statements opposed to the war, but he never declared it a sin to wage the war, although he could have. Had the Pope declared that it was a sin for leaders to support the war and for soldiers to fight in it, the warmongers would have faced a serious crisis of legitimacy. But they were spared this predicament.

The half-hearted measures of the churches to stand up to Caesar today are a far cry from the days of the thirteenth century when the Church compelled money lenders to submit their accounts for examination to see if they were taking advantage of debtors; or the days of the sixteenth century when the Pope excommunicated King Henry VIII of England for divorcing Catherine of Aragon, forcing the King, a devout Catholic, to leave the Catholic Church and found the independent Anglican Church.

Our current separation of church and state rests upon the agreement by the churches to restrict the sphere of religious concerns to the realm of personal and private behavior. Corporate leaders and politicians like President Bush in the United States are mounting ferocious attacks on "the weakest among us" and on working class people right and left with acts of material self-interest that would have made the medieval money-lenders fear for their souls. In earlier centuries the Church would have condemned these acts as sinful and punished the offenders in ecclesiastical courts with punishments that hurt in their lifetimes, not just their afterlives. These same corporate leaders are launching wars based on lies and killing thousands of innocent civilians simply to strengthen their wealth and power. Most of these leaders are members of a Christian church and attend services with some regularity. Yet their churches do not condemn them, do not declare their acts to be sinful, and certainly do not excommunicate them. Insofar as they still stand for anti-capitalist values of concern for and commitment to one another rather than selfish materialism, the major Christian churches have caved in to Caesar and accepted defeat.

What Is Our "Secular Democracy?"

Religion is conventionally equated with beliefs about God or the supernatural. What makes religion a powerful force in the world, however, is that it codifies beliefs about transcendental values that determine what kinds of behavior are right and wrong. Therefore it makes sense to generalize the meaning of religion to include such beliefs, regardless of whether or not they are arrived at by reference to God or the supernatural. With this definition of religion, the dominant religion today in U.S. society is not Christianity but Capitalism. Although the vocabulary of religion is not used by Capitalism in reference to itself, we can see how remarkably well it fits.

Capitalism's one God is economic productivity. It has no other gods besides this—neither in heaven nor on earth. It sacrifices everything to this God. Catastrophically for the human race, Capitalism sacrifices to its all-powerful god that which is most valued by the majority of the world's people—caring and trusting relations between people. When greater economic productivity and profits can be achieved by trampling people's dignity, or by condemning people's concern for one another, or by attacking solidarity among working people, or by undermining relations of love or mutual aid, or by poisoning trust among diverse races and nationalities, or by subverting good will towards man, or by instigating war to destroy peace on earth, then Capitalism does not hesitate to crush these incarnations of the "false god" of human solidarity. Economic productivity today is what the "Will of God" was in the past. Whatever serves it is good; whatever does not is bad. In the religion of Capitalism, one worships God by selfishly pursuing material wealth and by beating the competition no matter what the cost to other human beings. In the religion of Capitalism, all human beings are created in the image of a capitalist—selfish and in competition with each other. This is the natural order of the universe, and, say the priests of Capitalism, it is good because God's Invisible Hand, working in mysterious ways, ensures that a world based on selfishness is the best of all possible worlds.

All of our major public and private institutions have been taken over by the new religion of Capitalism. The religion of Capitalism is the Official Establishment Religion. The pulpits from which it is preached are our television and radio stations and newspapers. The cathedrals that glorify it make up the skylines of our cities' financial centers. The altars where it is worshiped by the faithful are our stock exchanges. Its Commandments are enshrined in contract law. Its high priests are CEOs and its saints are billionaires. Its church bureaucracy is the government, sanctified by rituals called elections. Its Deacons are mayors and governors whose greatest wish is to offer sacrifices like tax breaks to entice capitalists to worship economic productivity in the local diocese. Its parochial school system is the entire public school system; instead of rapping knuckles with rulers to enforce obedience, it administers standardized tests (which are designed to ensure a certain number of failures so that children will learn they are all in competition with each other to see who will be a winner and who a loser) for the same purpose—to instill fear. Its Crusader soldiers are in the 82nd Airborne Division. Its theologians lead our universities (least importantly the divinity schools.) Its Heaven is where Bill Gates and Mega-Bucks lottery winners luxuriate. Its purgatory is a homeless shelter. It's fire and brimstone is shock and awe. And its Satan? Anybody who dares to say out loud that there can be a better world.

The Official Establishment Religion denies our most important freedom—the freedom to create relations of trust and concern for one another, solidarity and dignity. Its "fiduciary responsibility" law makes it illegal for corporate management to give first priority to anything other than the self-interest of the investors. Labor laws against "sympathy strikes" make it illegal for workers to strike in solidarity with other striking workers. Laws prohibit public school teachers from bargaining over demands to make the schools better for their students; they can only bargain for their own interests—"wages and working conditions." The mass media tells whites that blacks are dangerous criminals or recipients of jobs they don't deserve, and tells blacks that whites are racist oppressors. By threatening job layoffs companies make people fear that their co-worker might be doing something secretly to save his or her job at the expense of one's own. By imposing "two-tier" wage schemes that pay younger workers less for the same work as older workers companies pit young against old. Everywhere that people try to help and support each other and develop relations of trust and understanding, the religion of Capitalism attacks such efforts with laws or management schemes or simply by ensuring that the law of the marketplace—pure self-interest—trumps all other social relationships.

The religion of Capitalism even turns people against each other on a global scale. It spreads lies about foreign peoples to justify raining shock and awe upon them, and by doing this in the name of ordinary Americans it foments hatred between Americans and other peoples. Permanent war is its strategy. It does all of these things and more to destroy positive relations among people and to crush their dignity in order to make them more controllable. It has to do this because the high priests of the Capitalist Religion understand that most people, in their hearts, are heretics—their God is not Economic Production but relations of trust and caring. The high priests of Capitalism know that if real democracy prevailed the Capitalist Church and their exalted position in it would not survive.

Notes

1. Different religions at different times have varied with respect to whether "others" referred to people of different religions or not. But regardless of whether society was conceived as universal or tribal, the Golden Rule was understood as the proper basis of behavior within it.

2. Another code of conduct found in many religions is the principle of "an eye for an eye, a tooth for a tooth" which, to many a modern ear, seems barbaric. But this principle actually was formulated as an attempt to reduce violence among people, as the following account of its origin demonstrates.

"The law of 'an eye for an eye' is usually called the law of retribution, or 'lex talionis' (Latin, lex [law] and talio [like]; the punishment is like the injury), or the law of equivalency.

1. History of the legislation. The lex talionis is found in three passages in the Old Testament (Ex. 21:23, 24; Lev. 24:19, 20; and Deut. 19:21). A similar law is found in the ancient Mesopotamian code of Hammurabi. Earlier codes legislated financial compensation for bodily injuries, but Hammurabi seems to have been the first to require physical injury for physical injury. This has led some historians to conclude that there was a time when monetary compensation redressed personal injuries because the state did not consider them to be crimes against society.

The law of equivalency was a significant development in the history of jurisprudence in the sense that what used to be a private matter between two families was now taken over by the state and considered to be criminal behavior. This fits very well with the Old Testament understanding of offenses against others as offenses against the covenant community and against the God of the covenant.

2. The principle involved. The law of equivalency was an attempt to limit the extent of a punishment and to discourage cruelty. The principle of this legislation is one of equivalency;

that is to say, the punishment should correspond to the crime and should be limited to the one involved in the injury (Deut. 19:18-21).

This law was a rejection of family feuds and the spirit of revenge that led the injured party to uncontrolled attacks against the culprit and the members of his or her family (cf. Gen. 4:23). The punishment was required to fit the crime, a principle still used in modern jurisprudence." [Bible Research Institute: http://biblicalresearch.gc.adventist.org/bible questions/eyeforeye.html]

3. The Golden Rule quotations and sources presented here are taken from *"The Golden Rule" and Christian Apologetics* by Edward T. Babinski

4. "Nevertheless, the 12th canon of the First Council of Carthage (345) and the 36th canon of the Council of Aix (789) have declared it to be reprehensible even for laymen to make money by lending at interest. The canonical laws of the Middle Ages absolutely forbade the practice. This prohibition is contained in the Decree of Gratian, q. 3, C. IV, at the beginning, and c. 4, q. 4, C. IV; and in 1. 5, t. 19 of the Decretals, for example in chapters 2, 5, 7, 9, 10, and 13. These chapters order the profit so obtained to be restored; and Alexander III (c. 4, *"Super eo"*, *eodem*) declares that he has no power to dispense from the obligation. Chapters 1, 2, and 6, *eodem*, condemns the strategems to which even clerics resorted to evade the law of the general councils, and the Third of the Lateran (1179) and the Second of Lyons (1274) condemn usurers. In the Council of Vienne (1311) it was declared that if any person obstinately maintained that there was no sin in the practice of demanding interest, he should be punished as a heretic (see c. *"Ex gravi"*, *unic.* Clem., *"De usuris"*, V, 5). [New Advent: http://www.newadvent.org/cathen/15235c.htm]

5. The twelfth century Church writer, Gratian, wrote in his Decretum, "Whosoever buys a thing, not that he may sell it whole and unchanged, but that it may be a material for fashioning something, he is no merchant. But the man who buys it in order that he may gain by selling it again unchanged and as he bought it, that man is of the buyers and sellers who are cast forth from God's temple" [pt. 1, dist. 1xxxviii, cap. xi]. St. Thomas Aquinas, in *The Summa Theologica*, writes that a man "who buys in order that he may sell dearer...is justly condemned, since, regarded in itself, it serves the lust of gain" [2a, 2ae, Q. 1xxvii, art. iv]. (Both quotations cited by R. H. Tawney in *Religion and the Rise of Capitalism*, pg. 35.)

6. "The assumption on which all this body of [medieval Church] doctrine rested was simple. It was that the danger of economic interests increased in direct proportion to the prominence of the pecuniary motives associated with them. Labor—the common lot of mankind—is necessary and honorable; trade is necessary, but perilous to the soul; finance, if not immoral, is at best sordid and at worst disreputable. This curious inversion of the social values of more enlightened ages is best revealed in medieval discussions of the ethics of commerce" [R. H. Tawney in *Religion and the Rise of Capitalism*, pg. 33].

7. *The General Rules of the Methodist Church* [page 2 and 3] state: "There is only one condition previously required of those who desire admission into these societies: 'a desire to flee from the wrath to come, and to be saved from their sins.' But wherever this is really fixed in the soul it will be shown by its fruits. It is therefore expected of all who continue therein that they should continue to evidence their desire of salvation, First: By doing no harm, by avoiding evil of every kind, especially that which is most generally practiced, such as...Fighting, quarreling, brawling, brother going to law with brother; returning evil for evil, or railing for railing; the using many words in buying or selling...Doing to others as we would not they should do unto us...These are the General Rules of our societies; all of which we are taught of God to observe, even in his written Word, which is the only rule, and the sufficient rule, both of our faith and practice...If there be any among us who observe them not, who habitually break any of them, let it be known unto them who watch over that soul as they who must give an account. We will admonish him of the error of his ways. We will bear with him for a season. But then, if he repent not, he hath no more place among us. We have delivered our own souls." (From *The Book of Discipline of The United Methodist Church*, 2000. Copyright 2000 by The United Methodist Publishing House)

Part Seven

HOPE *and* REVOLUTION

by John Spritzler

I.   REVOLUTION: AS AMERICAN AS APPLE PIE

A COMMON STEREOTYPE OF AMERICANS IS THAT we believe in rugged individualism and competition, and want nothing to do with radical notions of social change. And the most rugged individualist and conservative Americans were supposedly farmers from places like Nebraska and Kansas back before the turn of the century.

An excellent book, *The Populist Response to Industrial America*, by Norman Pollack (Harvard University Press, 1962) puts quite a different light on this topic. Pollack dug into libraries in Kansas, Nebraska, Minnesota, and Wisconsin to see what the newspapers serving farm communities were saying during the 1890's. He found that people in these communities saw capitalism as an attack on their values.

The *Farmers Alliance* of Lincoln, Nebraska wrote,

> The plutocracy of today is the logical result of the individual freedom which we have always considered the pride of our system...The tendency of the competitive system is to antagonize and disassociate men...The survival of the fittest is a satanic creed...A stage must be reached in which each will be for all and all for each. The welfare of the individual must be the object and end of all effort...Competition is only another name for war...[W]ithout a complete eradication of this system the people cannot for once hope for relief of a permanent character.

Three years later, under its new name, *Alliance-Independent*, it wrote, "A reigning plutocracy with the masses enslaved, is the natural development and end of individualism...The only possible permanent democracy is the democracy of unselfish socialism."

A Walnut Grove, Minnesota paper wrote, "The calamities that have heretofore and that now are upon us—as a nation—are but the measure or indicator of the extent that the standard of political and economic equality has been departed from in the practice of the competitive system."

The *Platte County Argus* described the "so-called great men" who rose to the top in the competition for the survival of the fittest as "moral cowards and public plunderers [who have] reversed the code of morals and stand up like hypocrites of olden times and thank god they are not like other men are..."

The *Topeka Advocate* wrote,

> Look at the multitudes who have been but recently thrown out of employment, and whose families have been destitute in consequence...It is cruel, it is inhuman, to attribute these conditions to laziness, drunkenness and incompetency. They are the natural product of a false and vicious system by which the few grow rich beyond all human need, and the many are doomed to eternal poverty and want...Remember that tramps are men, and that they are a natural product of our social system. There must be discovered some way to deal with them consistently with these facts. Can it be done without a revolution of our system? We think not.

In calling for revolution against the plutocrats, we in New Democracy are not turning our backs on the historic values of ordinary Americans. We are rediscovering them.

by David Stratman

I. JOHN ADAMS AND NEW DEMOCRACY ON REVOLUTION

I SAW THIS INTERESTING QUOTE FROM John Adams on the American Revolution the other day that I think pertains to the role of New Democracy in building the current revolutionary movement. John Adams wrote:

> What do we mean by revolution? The war? That was no part of the revolution. It was only the effect and consequence of it. The revolution was in the minds of the people, and this was effected from 1760 to 1775. In the course of 15 years this happened before a single drop of blood was shed at Lexington.

In "the course of human events"—the 15 years before Lexington and Concord—the colonists came to see the necessity and the possibility of "dissolving the bands" that held them to England and creating society on a new basis, reflecting the current of new ideas and possibilities which were exciting people's minds at the time in the Colonies and Europe.

Revolution was made possible by the new theories of human society that had gained currency. "Man is born free but is everywhere in chains," wrote Rousseau, speaking not only to the oppressive nature of aristocratic society, but of the natural goodness of human beings. It was only because Man is naturally good that society's institutions could be seen as oppressive, and only because Man is naturally good that a better world is possible.

The ideas which created the Revolution in people's minds did so because they convinced people that human beings were better than the institutions in which they were trapped. Rebelling against authority was justified. Overturning the institutions was the way to a better world.

Our goal from the first in New Democracy has not been so much to show that revolution is necessary but that it is possible. It is possible because most people reject the savage, greedy, competitive, anti-human values of capitalism and try to live their lives based on a different vision of human life than from the vision of the elites who dominate our society.

The Second American Revolution will occur when the American people come to see the idea of a truly democratic society—rule "of the people, by the people, and for the people"—not as a cant phrase but as an explosive formula for shattering the iron grip of warmongering, earth-devouring, anti-human elites on our lives and transforming the world with the best that we share with each other now. The key is to see ourselves and each other in a new light—to see that the people are not the problem in society, but the solution.

by John Spritzler

I.   THE *COMMUNIST MANIFESTO* IS WRONG

NINETEEN NINETY-EIGHT WAS THE 150TH anniversary of the first publication of the *Communist Manifesto* by Karl Marx and Friedreich Engels. Reading the *Manifesto* is a good way to decide what you think of Marxism for two reasons. First, it's only 46 pages long. Second, though written early in Marx's life, it was repeatedly reissued by the authors. It is fair to say the *Manifesto* represents beliefs Marx and Engels held throughout their lives. The great appeal of the *Manifesto* lies in the famous ending of the first section:

> What the bourgeoisie [the capitalist or owner class] therefore produces, above all, are its own grave-diggers. Its fall and the victory of the proletariat are equally inevitable.

The *Manifesto* offers hope. It purports to be a scientific basis for hope that capitalism can be defeated. It describes economic laws that supposedly operate independent of human will and make proletarian (working class) victory inevitable. Despite the fact that Communism has been discredited, Marxism still has profound influence in the world because it seems to offer hope for change. The problem with the *Manifesto* is that it points to a false hope, which has been the downfall of all social movements guided by Marxism.

The Marxist source of hope in economic laws is attractive mainly to those who do not see the revolutionary significance of ordinary peoples' lives and struggles. The *Manifesto* says nothing of the values of working people, either peasants or industrial workers. Instead Marx and Engels, with their "materialist" view of history, see economic development as the basis of progress, and capitalism as a historically progressive force. They judge various classes not in terms of human relationships or values but by whether they represent further economic development. The *Manifesto* believes peasants to be a backward class and declares that the bourgeoisie, by driving peasants off the land and increasing the urban population as compared with the rural, has "rescued a considerable part of the population from the idiocy of rural life." Similarly, the *Manifesto* sees the ruling elites, not the working class, as the source of enlightened ideas:

> Entire sections of the ruling classes are, by the advance of industry, precipitated into the proletariat...These also supply the proletariat with fresh elements of enlightenment and progress.

The *Manifesto* finds the source of revolution in these "economic laws." Revolution against capitalism to create a new, more humane social order will come when the capitalist system breaks down and it becomes clear that the bourgeoisie is "unfit to rule because it is incompetent to assure an existence to its slave within his slavery, because it cannot help letting him sink into such a state, that it has to feed him, instead of being fed by him." The problem with the capitalist class, in this view, is simply that it has outgrown its usefulness. Capitalist relations of ownership have become "fetters" on the productive forces which capitalism has itself created.

The *Manifesto* is blind to the conflict of values in society—solidarity versus competition, equality versus inequality—or to the fact that working people have values opposed to the values of capitalism. The *Manifesto* sees workers merely in terms of their material interests: "The proletarian movement is the self-conscious, independent movement of the immense majority, in the interest of the immense majority."

The reasons that the *Manifesto* places its hope on the industrial working class have nothing to do with the values of working people. The first reason given is simply that "the proletariat alone is a really revolutionary class. The other classes decay and finally disappear in the face of modern industry; the proletariat is its special and essential product." Industrial workers are important because their numbers increase under capitalism. The second reason is that "The proletariat, the lowest stratum of our present society, cannot stir, cannot raise itself up, without the whole superincumbent strata of official society being sprung into the air." Workers do not liberate human society as a conscious goal but as an inevitable by-product of their own uprising.

The real basis for hope lies not in some forces beyond human control, but in the fact that the working people of the world as individuals and as a class do not have only material interests which contradict capitalism; they also have goals and values which embody a different morality and a different view of human life from the capitalists, and they struggle to shape society with these values. Revolution is possible because the values of equality and solidarity and democracy by which ordinary people try to shape the world are revolutionary; the real force driving history is not technological or economic development but the struggle of ordinary people to create human society as they believe it should be. This was true before the rise of capitalism and the growth of an industrial working class and it is true now. The struggles of slaves against slave owners, peasants against feudal lords, workers against capitalists, and even workers against Communist governments are essentially the same. Success is possible, but not inevitable. Peoples' confidence in each other and in their values is what chiefly determines the outcome, not any laws of history that stand above flesh-and-blood human beings. There is progress in history, but that progress comes not from economic development but from the increasing self-knowledge and self-confidence of the working people who create human society.

Is it any wonder many workers feel insulted by the Marxist attitude towards them? Marxists think they have to "educate" workers to see that solidarity "is in their interest," assuming that working people place no more particular value on solidarity than as a useful way to get some material benefit. Marxist governments are dictatorial because they believe they have to mold workers to be more humane—and also make them work harder.

Marxism has failed because the hope it offered was false. We need to rebuild the revolutionary movement on a completely different footing, one that derives hope from understanding what people really care about and strive for in their lives.

by David Stratman

I.   DOES REVOLUTION MAKE SENSE?

AS REGULAR READERS OF NEW DEMOCRACY know, our purpose is to "establish a beachhead for the idea of revolution" in a world that desperately needs a fresh start.

I was recently in an email exchange with a thoughtful new reader. He liked our flyers, but said:

> My main disagreement comes from a belief that people do not make revolutions until they have no other choice. I expect conditions to come to that in this country, but I do not see conditions being anything near that point now...I don't think revolution is anywhere near being a winning plan at this time in history in the U.S.

There are two important questions here. One, is it true that people only make revolutions "when they have no other choice?" Two, does revolution make sense as the goal and strategy of a movement?

Revolutions Are Built on Hope

There is abundant evidence to show that revolutions are not based on despair. Just look at recent history. The world revolutionary upsurge of the 1960s did not come at a time when people "had no other choice." Far from it. Most of the dozens of countries that witnessed outbreaks of mass revolutionary activity were at the height of their post-WWII prosperity in 1968 and in the early 1970s. In the United States rank-and-file working people were in far better shape economically in those years, and yet in 1970 they executed the largest wildcat strike wave in U.S. history, and engaged in more strikes of any sort, authorized and unauthorized, in 1970–71 than any other year in the U.S. except 1946.

Perhaps the best refutation of the idea that people only revolt when they have no other choice is the May '68 revolt in France. French working people in 1968 were enjoying unprecedented prosperity. Consumer items long available to Americans had just become plentiful for the French. Yet 10 million French workers occupied their factories and offices for ten days. They took over local government with neighborhood committees in cities and towns around France. They came nearer than anyone before or since to making a revolution in modern industrial society.

There is no direct relationship between economic conditions and revolution. Working people make revolutions when enough people see that the values of our class are the salvation of the world.

A Strategy That Makes Sense

Building a revolutionary movement means deciding that we are going to win the class war. Only a revolutionary movement can inspire people with hope of real change. Fighting for anything less than victory just doesn't make sense. A movement that is not revolutionary can never solve our problems because it can never get at their roots. Even if such a movement could win major reforms—say, free health care for all—it could never get at the basic problem.

Humans are social beings. We need each other and want naturally to support each other from generation to generation. But we live in a society dominated by an elite which can only maintain its power by attacking those things about us which are most human: our understanding of ourselves and other people and our relationships with them. Nothing threatens the elite like working class solidarity. The attack on human relations is the fundamental problem in capitalist society, and it can only be solved by revolution and real democracy.

A revolutionary movement will unleash the energy and creativity and power that lie trapped within millions of ordinary people who have seen no other cause that could truly engage them. As the movement grows, people's sense of their abilities and what society could be like will grow with it. In a society which seeks to divide us from each other and kill our spirit, people building the revolution will find their moral and intellectual and emotional sides fully supported and engaged with other human beings.

Fighting for revolution means we can finally take the offensive. Instead of trying to stop another budget cut or another war, or fighting for a "lesser evil" candidate or a few fewer hours a week at a boring job or a little less environmental destruction, we can fight to overthrow the elite and create what we really want: a new world, without rank and privilege, without rich and poor, where wealth and work and leisure are shared by all. In such a world, there would not be millions working themselves to exhaustion while others go jobless, or a few with unimaginable wealth while millions have nothing. We would not be forced to choose between "Saving Jobs" or "Saving Trees." We would not despoil the earth in the name of Progress.

Any movement that does not have revolution as its goal is saying in effect that capitalism is the best possible world. It must accept capitalism as permanent and legitimate. Any such movement will sooner or later be making deals with the devil. It has no other choice.

A movement that is not fighting the system very quickly becomes its enforcer. Isn't this what happened to the labor movement? The AFL and CIO unions went very quickly from fighting on behalf of their members within a capitalist system to managing their members on behalf of the system.

Only a revolutionary movement can be truly democratic and truly rely on working people. Non-revolutionary movements always mimic the top-down relationships of the elite to other people, and they always suppress the revolutionary aspirations of their members; the leaders manage people's expectations so that people never expect more than the movement's leaders can deliver.

Fighting for a new world cuts through artificial divisions of gender and race and nationality, and allows us to unite around our deepest shared values and aspirations for a world based on commitment to each other.

Fighting for a new world gives us workable measures of success for building a long-term movement, and gives us the perspective that makes a long-term movement sustainable. Our measure of success is not victory or defeat on this or that issue, but how well we have built the size and solidarity and consciousness of the revolutionary movement along every step of the way. Our perspective comes from understanding the place of our movement in time and space—in the history of human aspirations shared by ordinary people in every part of the globe.

Fighting for revolution allows and demands that we abandon petty concerns and narrow issues and think big. Revolution forces us to try to understand the whole world and to imagine a new one. As we explore the inter-relatedness of the problems which we face, we can begin to understand all the many human inter-connections which will provide the solution.

A truly revolutionary movement will touch people's deepest desires and encompass their highest dreams. It will be an unstoppable force.

II. COUNTERREVOLUTION: THE ROLE OF COMMUNISM IN THE 20TH CENTURY

MOST AMERICANS HAVE RIGHTLY REJECTED Communism as a response to capitalism. Nevertheless Communism was presented by both its supporters and detractors as the revolutionary alternative to capitalism, and now Communism is dead. Where does that leave us?

Think about Communism as a kind of global company union. Given the actual role Communism played, I believe its collapse leaves us in a stronger position to change the world. Capitalism has survived the twentieth century only because the opposition to it has been dominated by a system with as great a stake in suppressing democratic revolution as capitalism itself. Once we understand Communism's role, we can better see that democracy will win. Here are some illustrations of that role.

The Russian Revolution

In February, 1917 a popular uprising of working people and peasants toppled the Czar. Workers took over factories and established Workers Committees to run them. Peasants took over large estates and ran them communally. Ordinary people of all backgrounds set up "soviets"—democratically-elected councils—as organs of popular democracy. The Czar was replaced by a government of industrialists, big landowners, and liberal aristocrats, which tried to restore elite power. In October this government was overthrown by workers and soldiers led by the Bolshevik (Communist) Party. Working people around the world took hope. Capitalists and kings trembled. The age of modern revolution had begun.

At the time of the February Revolution, the Bolsheviks were just one of several small revolutionary parties in Russia. From February to October, however, the Bolshevik Party won the contest for leadership of the revolutionary masses. Almost alone among the Social Democratic parties of Europe, the Bolsheviks refused to support the great slaughter of World War I, instead calling on workers of all countries to turn their guns on their masters. Alone among the Marxist parties, the Bolsheviks came to believe that working class revolution was necessary and possible in Russia at that time. After the fall of the Czar, they relentlessly attacked the new government and called for workers' revolution against capitalism. They had a disciplined organization of tremendous energy, which, in the words of an anti-Bolshevik commentator, "seemed to be everywhere" with posters, literature, meetings, speeches, rallies, all expressing the demands of the people: "The land to the peasants! The factories to the workers! All power to the Soviets!"

The orthodox Marxist parties of the time believed that economic developments determine historical events. The great contribution by Lenin, leader of the Bolsheviks, to Marxism was to show that human actors need not wait on blind economic forces. Organized as a disciplined, politically conscious party, they can create the conditions for revolutionary change.

But Lenin's theory had a fatal flaw which turned Communism into an anti-democratic nightmare. Lenin was right about the central role played by consciousness in human affairs. He was wrong about what political consciousness is and where it comes from.

Revolutionary goals and values in fact come from ordinary working people. Revolutionary consciousness consists of working people's consciousness of themselves as the source of the values and vision to create a new world. Lenin, however, believed that workers have no goals or vision but their own self-interest. With other prominent Marxists, he believed that revolutionary ideas come not from workers but from intellectuals.

Lenin's idea of revolutionary consciousness led him to a concept of revolution totally controlled from the top down. While the Communists helped to lead the revolutionary struggle forward, they simultaneously sucked the vital democratic element from it and turned it into its opposite: a device for a new elite to control working people.

The Communists expected their revolution to spread throughout Western Europe. Voline, a Russian anarchist active in the revolution, commented that Lenin was correct in expecting that successful revolution in one country would "set fire to the world." His mistake was in believing that Communist revolution would spread in this way. Lenin could not see that Communist revolution was sterile:

> ...it could set fire to nothing, for it had ceased to `burn' itself...it had lost the power of spreading, a character of great causes, because it had ceased to be a great cause...[Lenin] believed that the ultimate fate of the Russian Revolution depended upon its extension to other countries. Exactly the opposite was true: extension of the Revolution depended upon the results of the revolution in Russia.

Joining the Club

After their original hostility, the capitalist powers began to see the Soviet government as one with which they might usefully deal. The United States recognized the Soviets in 1933. In 1935, the Soviets signed trade agreements with France and Great Britain and a military pact with France. The Soviets were becoming members of the elite club. The Communist International called for Communists worldwide to join with "democratic capitalists" in a Popular Front Against Fascism. Stalin purged the Party of revolutionaries, executing them or sending them to the gulags.

With their revolutionary reputation largely intact, the Soviet Union began to play a key role in preventing working class revolution anywhere in the world.

A critical test for the Communists as allies of capital came with the civil war in Spain. In 1936 General Franco, leader of the Fascist movement, rebelled against the mildly reformist government. Workers armed themselves and beat back the Fascist armies, spreading social revolution as they went. Workers seized factories in Catalonia and other provinces and ran them themselves. Peasants took over large estates and farmed them collectively.

The Soviet Union agreed to sell arms to them, but only on condition that they abandon the revolution. Soviet agents sent to Spain for the purpose began to round up and execute revolutionary leaders. After a bitter three-year struggle and the abandonment of the revolution, the civil war was lost to the Fascist forces.

World War II and the "Grand Alliance"

World capital feared that World War II would bring revolution throughout Europe. As the war drew to a close, this great fear seemed about to be realized. In France, Italy, Greece, and Yugoslavia, Communist-led resistance forces liberated large sections of the country before the arrival of Allied troops.

The great concern of Allied leaders was that French Resistance forces would liberate areas before Allied troops arrived, indeed the greater part of France, including Paris, was liberated by the armed forces of the Communist-led resistance, with the active support of the population at large. Liberation committees were established everywhere as organs of popular control. At the direction of Moscow, when the Allies arrived, the resistance forces gave over their weapons and their political power to them.

By 1945, there were over 300,000 armed partisans in the north of Italy. (In the fall of 1944, the Allies halted their advance up the Italian peninsula, to allow the German and Italian Fascist troops freedom to smash the partisans. The Allies maintained this truce until mid-April, 1945 when, in fear of partisan victory throughout the north, they again went over to the offensive.) Ten days before the Allies arrived, the partisans liberated Bologna, Modena, Parma, Piacenza, Genoa, Turin, Milan, Verona, Padua and the whole region of Venice, and placed them under the control of national liberation committees. But at the direction of the Italian Communist Party, the partisans surrendered their arms to the Allies and returned confiscated lands and goods to the capitalists and big landowners.

The Greek resistance was "within a hair's breadth of victory" over the Nazis and the Greek monarchy, backed by the British. But the Greek Communist leadership acceded to Stalin's demands to give over power to the British-backed forces and the working class forces were destroyed.

Only the Yugoslav Communist Party resisted the pressure from Moscow and completed the revolution.

Fernando Claudin, a former Spanish Communist leader, wrote, "in 1944-45 only the Communist parties could halt the revolutionary movement of the proletariat, and in practice this is what they did."

Why did the Communist parties of the world save capitalism? For two reasons. One, Stalin had made a deal with the U.S. and UK that France, Italy, Greece, and Yugoslavia would remain in the Western bloc after the war. Two, the Soviets feared that revolution from below in Europe would lead to revolution from below in the Soviet Union.

The Cold War: 1947-1989

As the immediate post-war years drew to a close, the world divided into two apparently hostile camps, which, however, had an abiding common interest: the prevention of working class revolution anywhere in the world.

While it still declared itself the world center of socialist revolution, the Soviet Union had become a firmly counterrevolutionary power. The Communist parties of Western Europe became part of the "loyal opposition," ruthlessly opposing any efforts to create movements to their left. The Communist parties of Eastern Europe were ruling apparatuses closely tied to Soviet power.

The counterrevolutionary development of the Communist movement meant that world capital faced a world without revolution. (China is another but similar story.)

The Cold War between the United States and the Soviet Union was much like what Orwell describes in *1984*: a perpetual state of war which provided the ruling elites of both societies a much-needed enemy to justify internal control.

The Cold War also provided each superpower with a rationale to protect its interests abroad. The U.S. attacked foreign lands to "save them from Communism." Soviet tanks smashed into Hungary and Czechoslovakia "to save them from capitalism."

Why Did Communism Collapse?

There are two curious things about the "collapse of communism." One is that the policy changes—"perestroika" and "glasnost," for example—which resulted in the "velvet revolutions" in Eastern Europe were initiated by Communist leaders themselves. A second is that, in most cases, the same elites, even the same individuals, are still in charge. The Communists have become capitalists. What's going on here?

I traveled in Eastern Europe in February and March, 1990 to study the fall of Communism. Three months after the revolution in Romania, I asked a senator representing the Hungarian minority of Cluj-Napoca the cause of the economic crisis under Ceausescu. He said, "Workers in Romania have been on strike for five years. They show up for work, yes, but nobody works more than two hours a day. They smoke, drink, play cards, talk. Nobody works." I asked my guide and translator in Torun, Poland, the same question. We were in a hotel bar at the time, around 10 a.m. on a Thursday. He said, "You want to know the reason? Look around you!" The bar was full of people talking and drinking. "All these people here are at work. They check in and say, 'I have to run an errand.' Then they go out to drink."

Why did Communism not prevail? Because Communism did not have the same means to enforce its everyday rule as capitalism. In Communist countries, workers could not be laid off. Services like health care and education were free. The Communist system was a "command economy" in which nobody followed the commands anymore, and there was no practical way to make them work.

Capitalism is more efficient than Communism because it is better able to control people. Capitalism is based on an ideology of competition and market structures which force individuals to compete to sell their labor power. Capitalism is able to force people every day to face the possibility of failure and to face their fate alone. In capitalist society you're supposedly "the master of your fate." If you're rich, it's because you're smart. If you're working at a boring or dangerous or low-paying job, it's because you're stupid. If you're unemployed, you're a failure. Meanwhile the rent and food and medical bills pile up.

Restructuring these societies is meant to enable the Communist elite to pit workers against each other for jobs and factories against each other for markets. Introducing massive unemployment into these societies brings the massive insecurity that goes with it. Finally the Eastern elite will have at their disposal the whips of hunger and insecurity that have served Western capitalists so well.

Democracy Will Win

Communism worked only while people maintained some faith in its revolutionary promises. When its credibility eventually crumbled, so did its ability to function. We are told that the collapse of Communism represents the triumph of capitalism. But this would only be true if capitalism and Communism had truly been in a contest over conflicting social goals. In fact, despite certain differences, these systems share the same goal—elite control of workers. The collapse of Communism is a historic loss for the world elite.

The situation in the world is one of extreme danger for elites and great possibility for ordinary people. Millions, even billions of people worldwide are disgusted with capitalism and see no future in it. The people of Eastern Europe and China have tasted capitalist reforms and are spitting them out. The whole world is yearning for, struggling for real democracy.

Democracy will mean a world based on mutual support and equality. People will freely discuss and decide what their societies should be like in a world without presidents or Party bosses. People's real talents will be used and their capacity for good will flower. The wealth that people create will serve the shared needs of all rather than the gluttony and power of a few. Our work, our struggles will go to making the world a more caring and more beautiful place for the generation that is passing away and for the generations to come.

These ideals represent the deepest longings of human beings. They link together men and women of every race and nationality. We cannot be stopped. Democracy will win.

III. A DISCUSSION CONCERNING NONVIOLENCE

WE RECENTLY RECEIVED AN INQUIRY FROM the co-chair of a national anti-corporate organization who was interested in New Democracy. He wrote to ask us our principles. He then asked us our position on nonviolence, saying of his own organization, "We are committed to nonviolence in our efforts." I wrote him this reply:

Thanks for your note raising the issue of nonviolence.

I think it is a great mistake to make the question of means primary over goals, as it seems you are doing by insisting on the principle of nonviolence. To make all possible social change depend on a commitment to nonviolence means, I think, that the movement has decided from the start that it is determined to take only what the ruling elite are willing to give.

We need to first ask what kind of society we are trying to achieve, and then decide what will it take to get there. To achieve a society based on real equality and solidarity, we will have to destroy the power of the elite. Obviously the ruling elite will use any means at its disposal to maintain its power, and obviously too it has a huge capacity for violence, which it has shown itself to be only too eager to employ.

We are in a war which we need to win. Our weapons in that war are primarily moral power and political discussion and persuasion, and the capacity for millions, even billions, of ordinary people to resist elite rule in whatever ways they can devise, small or large.

Of course we and the great majority of human beings prefer peace and change by peaceful means. But that does not mean that peaceful change is possible or that nonviolence is appropriate as a principle.

In my view the principle of nonviolence is morally wrong and politically destructive. It is morally wrong because it suggests that people who violently resist oppression become morally equivalent to their oppressors—a view which, I believe, is extremely elitist. There have been countless times throughout history when ordinary people, in their struggle to defend themselves from the depredations of the elite, have been forced to resort to arms. According to the principle of nonviolence, the Spanish working class was wrong to take up arms against the Fascists, the Warsaw Jews wrong to revolt against the Nazis, the Vietnamese wrong to take up arms against a long succession of colonial powers, the Palestinian Intifadah wrong to revolt with sticks and stones against the Israeli occupiers. The "above-the-battle" attitude of nonviolence is anti-people and inappropriate to a democratic movement.

The principle of nonviolence has terrible effects on people: it disarms them morally and politically by encouraging them to become "passive resisters," beseeching some more humane elite forces to come to their aid. It undermines the view of people which I consider to be the most needful both morally and politically to create a democratic movement—that is, for people to see and rely on themselves collectively as the conscious agents of change and the creators of a new society.

However much we and other people desire a peaceful transformation of society, at some point there will come a contest of power. To win this contest, we will have to win a substantial part of the military forces to our side, or at least get them to be neutral.

To succeed in this we need to build a movement that is so broad and deep that the great majority of people become mobilized as an unstoppable force. What forms the battles will take which lead finally to the transformation of society into something more humanly satisfying and democratic it is impossible to foresee, but it is highly misleading to suggest that it can be done without force.

What we can see and do now is point out all the ways in which ordinary people are the force for what is good in this society and the source of the moral values of solidarity, equality, and democracy which should shape the next one. As the self-conscious movement for democracy grows, so too will people's vision of what society can be like and what it will take to get there. People will devise the means consistent with their goals.

Dave Stratman

by John Spritzler

I.   BILLIONAIRES, CRIME, AND CORRUPTION

WHAT DOES IT REALLY MEAN WHEN SOMEBODY claims to own hundreds of millions or even billions of dollars? What is a billionaire like David Rockefeller really telling us? He's saying that land he may never have set foot on, but which thousands of other people spend their lives farming, belongs to him alone. He's saying that buildings and machinery which he probably has never seen and certainly has never worked at, but which whole communities of people spend their lives working at to produce goods like clothing and automobiles, belong to him alone. He's saying that mansions and jets and yachts which were built by hundreds of other people who have none of these things belong only to him.

His claims are outrageous and disgusting. Modest differences among people are one thing; but when some individuals are not even in the same ball park as everybody else it is obscene. I don't care how "important" they claim to be, very rich people are hogs. They should be socially unacceptable.

Allowing people to be very rich has terrible consequences beyond just its unfairness. As the inequality between the richest and poorest people increases, the differences separating all the people in between also increase, the way marks on a rubber band get farther apart when you stretch it. This inevitably makes everybody more aware of differences in personal wealth. Who hasn't read with keen interest *Parade* magazine's annual "How much do people earn" issue? The effect on even the best people is to make them anxious about not being a "loser" relative to their peers. The effect on the most selfish people is the reason we have crime—both the illegal kind and the kind that is only legal because rich people make the laws.

Because we have a society in which being very rich is perfectly acceptable and the main way people are judged is by how rich they are, selfish people have a strong incentive to commit horrible crimes for money. Some sell drugs to children, kill their spouse to collect life insurance, scam elderly people out of their life savings, and much worse. Others stay within the law and sell pardons to fugitive crooks, make their employees work in unsafe conditions under the threat of being laid off if they resist, fire elderly workers just before they become vested for pension rights, and much worse.

Anti-social acts get committed every day for money. We need a world based on equality where we do not tolerate the kind of differences in personal wealth that motivate selfish people to hurt others. Only then will bad people have little or nothing to gain by their crimes.

Allowing people to be very rich guarantees a corrupt and undemocratic government. We can enact "Clean Election" reform laws or term limits until we're blue in the face, but as long as some individuals have enormous wealth they will figure out a way to buy power and influence, just as surely as the rivers flow to the ocean no matter how many dams are built. We can have very rich people, or we can have democracy. We cannot have both.

All the arguments about how we need the rich are wrong. They say rich people are important because they produce jobs. What does this mean—that people in an egalitarian society wouldn't be able to grow food and produce goods and provide services to each other? They say the "best and the brightest" people need great wealth to motivate them. But the people who genuinely contribute the most to society don't do it to get rich. Jonas Salk developed the polio vaccine knowing he would not make a penny off of it. If the rich all vanished from the face of the earth and their property became public property, and we the people decided that those doing useful and important work should receive compensation to enjoy an average standard of living, then people doing truly valuable and creative things in laboratories, factories, farms, schools and hospitals would continue working. And they would succeed in their efforts even more than today because they would be free to do what helps lots of people rather than what makes a few rich people richer.

They say rich people like Bill Gates deserve all their money because they make it by producing things people want. But Bill Gates didn't produce useful software. He acquired a monopoly ownership of software created by many other people, and fixed it so that part of the purchase price of every computer went into his pocket. Gates actually prevents better software from being produced.

They say it's important to have rich people because they give money to philanthropy. In fact, rich people prevent social resources from being used to solve the real problems in the world, like hunger. Their philanthropy projects are self-serving public relations gimmicks. Philip Morris Tobacco company, for example, is throwing some money at homes for battered women in Boston and advertising on the radio how "concerned" they are for women's health! Bill Gates made the news recently with his donations of money to fight diseases like AIDS in poor nations. His reason, however, is to avert social upheavals and revolution, not to make a more equal world. The CIA is so afraid of what people in Africa —who are dying because pharmaceutical companies won't provide AIDS drugs to poor people—may do, that they have declared AIDS a "national security threat."

The truth is that rich people are just hogs and they don't solve problems, they create them. They need people in the third world to be desperately poor and insecure because otherwise who would work in all their sweatshops? They need people in the U.S. to be economically insecure because otherwise who would put up with the long hours and stress and dictatorial control that the corporations impose on employees? And they need to pit people against each other to control them because otherwise people would make the world very different than what rich people want it to be. Our biggest problems are caused by the things rich people do to get rich and the things they do to prevent regular people from making this a more equal and democratic world.

I think we have a situation today like the "Emperor's New Clothes." Most people think it's wrong to be a hog. But it's taboo to say so when the hog hasn't been caught breaking a law. It's time to break the taboo and say what we really think. We teach our children in kindergarten to share. We don't allow them to grab other children's toys and coats and lunches, and we don't allow them to boss other children around. Why should we let grownups get away with it?

II.   NO, VOTING WON'T WORK

MILLIONS OF AMERICANS WELCOMED THE Ralph Nader 2000 electoral campaign as a breath of fresh air in the stale atmosphere of corporate-controlled parties and politicians. The more Nader lambasted the corporations and their

"Republicratic" party, the more popular he became, attracting larger crowds than Gore and Bush. Many people who didn't vote for Nader would have if they thought he could have won. The Nader campaign demonstrated, to those of us who blame corporate power for the problems in our society, that we are not alone.

But before deciding that an electoral strategy is a solution, we need to identify what exactly is the problem.

People increasingly realize that our seemingly unconnected problems—the stress and difficulty that working people face in trying to support a family, the insecurity of people with serious health care needs, the destructive education reforms faced by students and teachers, the pollution of our water and air—are all symptoms of the same problem. The majority of people, who want a more equal and cooperative and democratic world, are under attack by corporate and government leaders who dominate our society. The problem is that real democracy, in the sense of ordinary people shaping society by their values, doesn't exist—not on the job, not in our government, not in our major institutions.

Real democracy must mean that ordinary people exercise effective power at every level of society to shape it with their shared values and shared vision. It can't be reduced to pulling a lever every four years. Winning real democracy therefore can only be done by ordinary people, in every place of work and neighborhood, acting directly and collectively to take possession of the world from the elite who claim to own it. It means creating a new kind of society from the ground up, one based on equality and commitment to each other. It means people joining together to defeat all the efforts of the elite to impose capitalist relations of competition and inequality.

For people to gain the confidence to take matters into their own hands requires building a mass movement with exactly this goal—a revolutionary movement. Such a movement can succeed only by becoming a vast democratic force consciously determined to create a new society in its image. The movement must grow so large and popular that it can deprive the corporate rulers of the armed might of the state, by convincingly presenting itself, not the corporate-controlled government, as the legitimate authority. This is the solution to the problem of corporate power.

An electoral strategy actually undercuts this real solution. Urging people to vote is the opposite of urging them to join a revolutionary movement. The idea of voting is to elect other people to make changes for us. But the kind of changes we need can only be made by us. An electoral strategy keeps a movement passive, focused on what its candidates might do if elected, when it should be focused on what ordinary people themselves can do where they work and live. This is why the elite have historically used elections to contain anti-corporate movements.

An electoral strategy also prevents a movement from expressing the radical goals that most people want. Radical goals cannot be taken seriously in the absence of widespread confidence that there is a realistic way of achieving them. Only a mass revolutionary movement, in which ordinary people are the active force, can make radical changes in society. By making people place their hopes on some elected officials rather than on themselves, an electoral strategy eliminates any realistic basis for radical goals, and forces movements to trim and adapt their vision and message to what they believe is possible within the limitations of the established structures of power.

Nader's goal, for example, has never been to do away with corporate power but to regulate it so that it can operate in a more sustainable fashion. As he said in a recent *Harper's* interview, "a free democracy is a precondition for a free market." Nader is not opposed to capitalism but only to its excesses.

We believe that most Americans want not just a reduction in corporate power but a profoundly different kind of society based on different values. The top priority for the anti-corporate movement should be to make people see that they are not alone in this aspiration, so that they will have the confidence to take over control of society from the ground up, without waiting for politicians to do for them what politicians cannot and will not do.

III. AMERICA IS NOT A DEMOCRACY: WHAT ARE WE GOING TO DO ABOUT IT?

THE UNITED STATES IS NOT A DEMOCRACY. Sure, we have elections and all the trappings of a democracy. But if, by democracy, we mean a society shaped by the values of ordinary people rather than by the values of a wealthy and privileged elite, in which the popular vote actually determines the direction of the society, then no, we don't have a democracy. We have a plutocracy. Billionaires hold the real power because they own the media and the entire private sector and they use this leverage to control the politicians.

Billionaires ensure that every major public and private institution promotes their values of inequality, control from above and competition (for us, not for them). In many different ways they attack our efforts to create relations of solidarity and trust. They create resentment and mistrust between the generations by using two-tier wage scales that pay newly hired younger workers less for doing the same work for which older workers get paid more. They stress relations within working class families to the breaking point by paying so little that mothers and fathers between them have to work two or three jobs and have no time for their children or involvement in their communities. And they drill our children in public schools to compete with classmates (and others like themselves around the world) for grades and jobs in the grim "global economy."

On matters of huge importance to us, like whether we go to war, or have a decent job or receive health care when we need it most, the government makes decisions by consulting "important" people in the "business community," not working class Americans. Whenever the government decides to go to war, we're always kept in the dark about the true reasons why. All we get are the phony reasons and lies designed to make us go along with the war. LBJ used the lie about the Gulf of Tonkin to get support for the Vietnam war, and Bush, Jr. used the lie about WMD. These aren't exceptions. In every war it's the same story.

Likewise, the very rich, not "We, the People," determine the crucial domestic government policies that affect our lives. We—the great majority of Americans according to poll after poll over the decades—want universal health care, but government and corporate leaders refuse. We want better schools for all of our children with smaller class sizes in safe buildings with lots of books and an inspiring curriculum, and what do we get? Fancy private schools that teach the children of parents who can afford the steep tuition that they are smart and fit to be tomorrow's leaders. For working class children, boring standardized testing centers designed to make them feel insecure about whether they are good enough even to deserve a job that will pay a living wage. If there is not democracy in the public sector, forget about it in the private. We all know what it's like to work for any of the big or medium sized corporations that employ most of us. During work hours there is not even the pretense of a democracy—orders come from above, from "Them, the Owners" not "We, the People." No, this is not a democracy. It is a dictatorship of the rich.

Furthermore, most of us know that we do not live in a democracy. I know this is true because I have made a habit of asking strangers if we have a democracy (as opposed to the trappings of one) and they invariably say No. At the grocery store checkout counter the other day the magazines on display included *Boston Magazine* with a cover featuring a young woman with a T-shirt that said, "Got Democracy?" I asked the woman next to me in line what she thought the answer was to the question? She laughed and said, No. A couple of days earlier someone on the street collecting signatures for a ballot referendum asked me to sign. I said I wasn't a registered voter. She asked me why in the world wasn't I. When I told her I'd be the first in line to register to vote on the day we had a democracy, she smiled and said, "How true."

So what are we going to do about it?

If we want to live in a democracy we need to overthrow the plutocracy. But how? They have all of the power. They have the government, the military, the media, the money. How can we overthrow them?

We have what it takes, at least potentially. We have nearly three hundred million people who want to live in a democracy. How many people do they have who want to live in a plutocracy? Their money comes from us working for them. Their military power comes from our sons and daughters fighting for them. When we stand together and refuse to do their bidding, their power vanishes and ours becomes enormous. They understand this very well, even if we don't. Everything they do is designed to prevent us from standing together against them.

But to stand together and succeed, we must transform ourselves, from several hundred million people who each feel all alone in wanting to defeat the plutocracy into several hundred million people who know they are not alone. People who know they are not alone have the confidence to make concrete plans that can win. Until then, it seems foolish to even think about challenging the power of the plutocracy.

How do we do that? The first step, at least, is quite simple. We start talking to each other and saying out loud, "We don't have a democracy. What are we going to do about it?" We say it to our relatives. We say it to our friends. Our neighbors. People we work with. Strangers at the checkout counter. The person on the street who wants us to vote for some politician. We say what most people already believe, so they know they are not alone in thinking it. We stop pretending to believe we have a democracy.

A very specific thing we can do about it, in this election campaign season, is ask our friends and neighbors to join us in refusing to vote in the presidential election and in telling the world (or at least a friend or two) why. This is what the

MassRefusal/2004 (www.massrefusal.org) campaign is all about. Everybody from 18 to 100 years old can take this easy step together. It's safe and legal. Yet it not only strikes a blow at the ideological foundation of the plutocracy, it also enables all who do it to see themselves in a new light, as people who know that they are not alone and that it is no longer foolish to think about carrying out more ambitious kinds of mass actions to challenge the rule of the plutocracy.

Simple words, spoken by millions of friends and neighbors and people at work can completely change the "political reality" in our nation because the words are so true. They can undercut the sham of elections that make people think their only option is to "hold your nose and vote for the lesser evil." They can give people the confidence to rely on each other to fight little battles at work or elsewhere, while aiming to win the big battle against the plutocracy's stranglehold on our society.

Speaking the truth is more revolutionary in its effect than anything else we can do presently. It creates the basis for a powerful mass movement that can eventually take the kind of actions required to win a real democracy. And it answers the question posed by the fact of our current plutocracy: "What are we going to do about it?"

by David Stratman

I.   MAKING CONNECTIONS

A COLLECTION OF ESSAYS BY THE LATE British historian Tim Mason, *Nazism, Fascism, and the Working Class*, includes one entitled, "The Containment of the Working Class" (i.e., by the Nazis under the Third Reich). In it Mason writes:

> One of the great historic tasks of all labour movements has been to construct or reveal the connections between ostensibly distinct events or realms of working-class experience, to demonstrate these connections in day-to-day political practice, and to propagate them through newspapers, meetings, etc. In most capitalist states this has been an uphill task, even when it has been a legal activity. In the Third Reich the organizations of the working class could perform this task scarcely at all. Most workers faced management and the regime alone or in small groups, armed...only with the memory of the necessity of making these connections in their political judgements...

We don't face anything like the repression that working people did in Nazi Germany, of course, but still there is a good bit of fear in our society, especially on the job. People in many types of work are afraid that one cross word might get them in trouble, even fired. Teachers and nurses are threatened as never before if they object to any of the current educational atrocities being imposed on their students or to the treatment of their patients.

But even with our relative freedom, there are powerful forces that make it difficult to make connections among issues. For example, there are social taboos against placing developments in their context in the capitalist social order; you're hardly allowed even to speak the word "capitalism," unless it's to say, "God bless our capitalist system." In addition, our society is very atomized; with fewer strong social connections among people, the political connections among the issues that affect us are not as easy to perceive. Our jobs and training are often very specialized, encouraging a tunnel vision of reality. Social connections like those among workers in a factory are intentionally undermined by the company/union management team, and replaced by management-dominated "team-building" structures; when workers in a plant try to stand up to the company, they usually find themselves doing it alone or in small groups. In much the same way, relationships among teachers across a school district are broken by such management devices as School-Based Management. We are constantly pressed for time—time to think about bigger issues and the connections among them, time to interact with friends and draw a larger picture. When we drop exhausted in front of the TV at night, we are presented with atomized views of reality, in which nothing connects with anything.

The pressure to view things narrowly and out of context is a form of social control. Without seeing connections, we can't make sense of the world; and if we can't make sense of the world, we can't change it. "Making connections" among the many different issues and areas of our experience is a vital task of the revolutionary movement.

II.   WHY WE CAN CHANGE THE WORLD[1]

I'D LIKE TO THANK THE DIVERSITY COMMITTEE for the invitation to speak here today. I want to talk with you about why I think it is possible for us to make revolutionary change in the world.

I wanted to begin these remarks by talking with you about a series of experiences that changed my life. The experiences began in Dorchester, a white, blue-collar Irish Catholic section of Boston in 1974. Then it occurred to me that none of you was born in 1974, and maybe none of you had much idea of what had gone on in 1974 and 1975, the first years of busing in Boston. (Raise your hand if you were alive in 1974. Raise your hand if you think you know anything about the battle over busing in Boston.)

My wife and I and two small children moved into Dorchester in 1974, the first year of busing. Our neighborhood, called St. Mark's, had been the center of the anti-busing movement outside South Boston. The school year began with terrible conflict. School buses carrying black children were being stoned in South Boston, and there was racial conflict in many parts of the city. Our daughter was just beginning kindergarten at the Patrick O'Hearn School in Dorchester.

The principal of three small elementary schools called a meeting of parents to organize Home and School Associations—the equivalent of PTAs—at the schools. He set up the meeting at the Adams Street Library, deep in the heart of the white section of Dorchester. There were about 45 parents there, all of them white. As the meeting began, the principal made a snide comment clearly directed at the missing black parents, saying, "Well, I guess we can see which parents really care about their children." Immediately eight white parents—not me; I was new to the neighborhood and was keeping my head down—jumped up and told the principal, "Of course the black parents aren't here. They're afraid to come to this part of the city. You should have held the meeting in neutral territory where everyone could feel safe."

I admit I was pretty surprised by their reactions. I was an ex-college professor and was also a Marxist at the time. With my academic and leftist background, I had fully expected these Irish Catholic parents to be very anti-black.

What happened next was even more surprising to me. The principal then talked about conditions at the three schools. The Patrick O'Hearn, he said, was being ruined by the new kids—the black children. The school was built only to hold 280 students, but 80 more had been bussed in, so that the gym was converted to four "open-space classrooms." This time even more parents objected, saying that it wasn't the black children's fault that the school was overcrowded. It was the fault of the Federal Court and the political big shots who had designed the busing plan.

This meeting began my political education away from the stereotypes I had in my mind about white working people and toward something very different. It also began changing my understanding of what busing in Boston was all about.

In the next couple of months nine other white parents from that meeting and ten black parents got together and formed an organization which we called

Better Education Together (BET). We said that we felt as parents that we were trapped between two bad alternatives. On the one hand, the Boston School Committee had delivered an inferior and segregated education to all our children for years. On the other hand the Federal Court was making the situation worse. It closed down 34 schools in the black neighborhoods in the first year of busing, it was breaking up the relationships between parents and schools and parents and teachers that give ordinary people some degree of political power in the schools, and it was making the issue in the schools not education but race. We said that the issue in the schools was not race but education. We felt that we as parents had the same hopes and dreams for our children and the same fears, and that nobody was going to fight for our kids but us.

So we held coffees in each others' living rooms, where black and white parents had a chance to talk about their feelings about our children and find out how much we had in common. We wrote up literature with the pictures of four black and four white parents on it, explaining why they were part of Better Education Together, and we went to every neighborhood in the city—to white South Boston and black Roxbury, to different sections of Dorchester, to Brighton and Allston and Hyde Park. Everywhere we went, people would come up to us, some of them with tears in their eyes, and say, "Oh, I'm so glad to see this. I thought nobody felt this way but me."

Better Education Together continued for two years. We didn't win any great victories—for example, the Federal Court refused to let us become parties to the desegregation case—but we had a big impact on the debate over busing in the city. For years white and black politicians and the media had made the question, "Are you for or against forced busing?" and had successfully kept people completely divided. We were able to bring together black and white parents around our common goals and common values: our belief in our children and commitment to their success, and our belief that ordinary people can and must depend on each other, no matter what the color of our skin. In the summer of 1975, there were hundreds of parents from white South Boston and black Roxbury and elsewhere who went together to the Boston School Committee to demand smaller class sizes. On two occasions we ran the School Committee out of the room and took over their chambers to have a real parent discussion about education.

How did these experiences change my life? I had spent several years while a professor actively involved in opposing the Vietnam War; in fact my involvement in the anti-war movement had cost me my job. But when American participation in the war ended, the movement—which should have continued to try to make fundamental change in American society—collapsed. At about the same time I became disenchanted with Marxism. Communism, it was clear, was just as undemocratic as capitalism and not a desirable alternative. So, like a lot of other people at the time, I was in despair that it was possible to change the world. But my two years active experience with the black and white working people of Boston convinced me that ordinary people are much better than the institutions that affect them—the Church, the schools, the media, the politicians. My experiences of the working people of Boston gave me hope that we can change the world.

Now what does all this have to do with Diversity, and what does it have to do with you? Let's try to take a long view, for a minute, of the world that you will graduate into in a few years. As you know, it's a world that is becoming more and more unequal. For example, in 1980 the average executive's pay was about 19 times that of the average worker; by 1997 it was 419 times. In the last 20 years working people have produced fabulous amounts of wealth, but most of that wealth has gone to the top 1% of people in our society, who now own four times the wealth they had in 1977, while the bottom fifth of the population have actually gotten 10% poorer in these years. Average workers' wages are no better than they were in 1973. At the same time, people are much more insecure, many being forced to work two or even three temp jobs or low-pay jobs to keep their families afloat. We have rampant homelessness in the wealthiest country in history. The U.S. imprisons more of its population—now over 2 million—than any other society in the world. Governments in many states are imposing "high stakes tests" —such as MCAS in Massachusetts—tests which are designed to fail, as a way of legitimizing a two-tier society, in which most people are without money or power in a profoundly undemocratic society.

Now I'm sure that you've heard these statistics before. It's not a secret that the rich are getting richer and the poor poorer, even during this, the longest economic boom in U.S. history.

How do the wealthy elite at the top reinforce their hold on society? Well, they have a lot of different ways to do this, but two of the most fundamental elite strategies, I think, are competition and isolation. By competition, I mean that they set individuals or groups against each other by disguising what people have in common. For example, this is what they did during the Boston busing crisis: they pitted white and black parents against each other so that neither would get better schools and both could be controlled. Better Education Together was able to step into that fight though and focus on what we had in common. We said that the real fight was not white against black but ordinary people against the elite—the politicians and media and corporate leaders who were behind it all. In this way we built a united movement.

The other elite weapon, isolation, is related to competition. This is something we all experience. By isolation I mean the fact that all the messages we receive from the normal sources—the media, political and corporate leaders, the movies we watch, the books we read, the classes we take in school—these are dominated by the corporate outlook that tells you that fundamental change in our society is impossible because "Nobody really feels this way but you." They tell you that, if you are upset at the direction of our society, that's your problem. You're all alone, and you might as well give up. You might have very strong feelings that this society should be different. You might believe in real equality. You might wish that our society was truly democratic, and that instead of trying to beat out each other for the right job or the right grade or the right school placement, we should be working together to make this a better world for everyone. But you're encouraged to keep these feelings to yourself, because "Nobody feels this way but you." You begin to doubt yourself. You think, "Maybe I am crazy to think things could be different." So you keep your mouth shut. You have been isolated.

What does "Diversity" have to do with this? Many good people support the "diversity" concept, because they see it as a way of building unity and respect for each other across cultural divides. But diversity is about "celebrating and respect-ing our differences." Despite many people's best intentions, it's not really about finding what we have in common, but about focusing on differences as if these supposed differences are what define us as human beings. Diversity as a frame-work, as a way of thinking about each other, will always stand in the way of the goal that most of us share, of multi-racial, multi-ethnic unity.

Diversity in fact is no different from the basic capitalist view that society consists of various groups competing for their own interests. Such a view does not present any threat to capitalism or to inequality but reinforces it. It reinforces it in two ways. First, it makes us think that "the enemy" is not the elite at the top of society, but some other group—say, white people or black people or men or women; "social change" in this view consists just of making inequality more per-fectly unequal—I mean, not getting rid of inequality itself but insuring that every group gets a piece of the action. Second, it increases our sense of isolation and powerlessness. It makes us feel that we, or the members of our supposed group, are all alone, cut off in our struggle from the rest of humanity.

There is only one kind of movement capable of challenging elite power over our society and creating a truly democratic and caring society, and that is a movement which unites ordinary men and women of every race and nationality, black and white and brown and Asian: a movement based not on our differences but on the fundamental values of solidarity and equality which we share. Such a movement would cut through the surface differences to see each other not as the problem but as the solution to creating a better world.

You are all thoughtful young people, I am sure, and this means that each of you is on a quest. You are trying to figure out who you are and what your role is in the world. What should you do? Try to get rich? Keep your head down and try to get by? Try to change the world? Probably you're all thinking all these thoughts simultaneously, trying them out.

Is there any hope in the world? Is there any basis for you to have faith in other people, so that, when you do think thoughts about changing the world, you don't feel all alone? Let me leave you with the basic insight that was the outcome of my two years' involvement in the Boston busing battle.

We know that capitalism is the most dynamic social system in history. We know also that the fundamental dynamic of capitalism is the principle of competition, the idea of dog-eat-dog. The logic of capitalism is that this world should be a loveless and savage place: we should each be trying to screw each other all the time. But we can look around and see that this isn't true. We can see that most people, in the little piece of the world that we think we can control—which might just be with our friends or our classmates, or our wife or husband or students or colleagues—that in this little piece of the world most people try to create relationships the opposite of capitalism. We try to create relations based on love and trust and mutual respect and commitment. We may often not get very far in our efforts—capitalism is a very powerful culture hostile to equal and committed relationships—but to the extent that we have any committed and loving relationships in our lives, we have created them by a struggle against capitalist culture.

This means, I think, that most people are already engaged in a struggle to change the world. You are, your friends are, your parents are, your teachers are. Most people are already involved in a fight against capitalism. None of us are alone in our struggle, and we can succeed if we build on this great, shared human longing for a better world where we're all equal and all depend on each other.

Thank you.

Note

1. This is a speech to the Cambridge School of Weston delivered on March 16, 2000. I was invited to make the speech by the school's Diversity Committee. As I explain in my speech, however, I do not agree with "diversity" as a concept. The speech received a standing ovation.

III.   WHAT IS MISSING FROM THE WORLD?[1]

RETREATS LET US STEP BACK FROM THE PRESSURES of our everyday life and get an overall view of the situation. I would like to make a few comments on the historical situation we are in and what I believe we can do about it.

What's our situation? The ruling elite, the capitalist class—whatever you want to call them—have been on the attack against working people for the last 25 years in a brutal class war. But this attack has a specific history.

From the end of WWII until the early '70s, the world elite tried to control people through prosperity. Give people more money, steady jobs, two cars in the garage, a chance to send their kids to college, they thought, and people will buy into the system and be content. Well, it didn't work out that way. Instead of being more content, people became more rebellious. They demonstrated for Civil Rights. They fought against the Vietnam War. They went on strike. They fought against their union leaders and demanded democracy in their unions. 1970 saw more strikes than at any other time in U.S. history except 1946 and more wildcat strikes than any other year. In 1968 revolutionary movements swept the world: China and Poland and Vietnam and Czechoslovakia, Mexico and Italy—virtually everywhere on the globe. In May, 1968 ten million workers in France occupied their factories and offices for ten days and came near to making a revolution.

The global elite had to respond to this situation. To cope with the worldwide "revolution of rising expectations," capitalist and communist elites embarked on a strategy of lowering people's expectations. In every area of life they attacked people's sense of economic and psychological security. Beginning with the wage-price freeze in 1971, they put the brakes on economic growth and promoted unemployment. After a decade of intense efforts, they delivered a series of deadly blows to working people: the defeats we know as PATCO, Hormel, Staley, Caterpillar, Detroit News, and others too numerous to name.

They prepared the ground carefully. They slashed government programs and repealed the Great Society and the New Deal in the name of balancing the budget, creating millions of homeless and poor desperate for jobs. They told working people loud and clear, "Stay in line or you'll be on the streets with them." They waged tireless campaigns telling people that "We live in a global market," and we have to compete with foreign workers and even with each other. They told us in a million ways that we have to fear each other: whites are racists, blacks are criminals, men are brutes, women are mindless bimbos, your coworkers are fools.

The unions worked closely with their corporate masters in bringing about these defeats. The union leadership relentlessly repeated the corporate message, "Join the Company Team" to compete with other workers and attacked solidarity among working people. The major defeats suffered by workers were a result not of corporate power but of union betrayal: the Machinists forced to cross picket lines at airports to defeat PATCO; the entire Hormel chain continuing to work during the P-9 strike; the "selective strike" strategy imposed on the Cat workers by the International in 1991, and other examples that we're all aware of. In these and other situations, the problem was not that the union leadership did not know how to fight but that it was fighting for the other side.

The government and corporate war hasn't just been against workers in the workplace but against people in every area of our lives. The corporate-led campaign for education reform, for example, is really an attack on our children and grandchildren, to make the schools "lean and mean." Kids are told to run faster and faster, work harder and harder to make the grade set by the corporations. To get them to fit into a more unequal and undemocratic society, the aspirations and self-confidence of our children must be crushed.

There's one final point I want to make about the situation and that is the utter failure of communism and socialism as revolutionary alternatives to capitalism. This is crucially important for us. For one thing, the working class movement of the late nineteenth and twentieth centuries was profoundly influenced by Marxism; many of the activists in the CIO organizing drives of the '30s were communists or socialists, and many labor activists now still subscribe to these ideas. For another, the failure of communism has made it appear that there is no possible alternative to the capitalist system.

The lack of a revolutionary alternative to capitalism has had a very negative effect on people's ability to organize a new movement for change. If there is no alternative to capitalism, then it seems we will forever have to give in to the companies' demands for jointness or pay cuts or two-tier systems and all the other claims made in the name of "competitiveness." With no alternative to capitalism, we cannot oppose its logic. What strategy makes sense in the face of this situation? Well, an electoral strategy doesn't make sense, because the real powers pulling the strings are behind the scenes. The politicians are just front men, and changing them doesn't matter.

A reform strategy—like the reform of the unions, for example—doesn't work, because the unions are part of the corporate system and they can't be reformed. Other reforms—like, say, reforming the schools—can't work, because the schools reflect the relations of power in society. And it's the relations of power in society that are the real problem. If we haven't changed the relations of power, we haven't really changed anything.

So what strategy does make sense? To figure this out, let's look more closely at the nature of the class war.

What is class struggle and the class war all about? I was talking a few months ago with Larry Solomon, and he said something very important about the Cat workers. He said, "We knew we were fighting for everyone. That's why we held on for so long." The Staley workers were locked out for 27 months, but they fought on at great sacrifice to their families and themselves until their final betrayal by the AFL-CIO and the International Paperworkers Union, because they knew that their struggle was about more than just the families involved. There are many strikes and working class struggles where the sacrifice is all out of proportion to any possible gain. What does this show us?

Though strikes and lockouts and other class struggles almost always involve specific issues, these issues are just the occasions for class struggles. Under the surface the struggles are over two different sets of values, two different ideas of what society should be like, two different ideas of what it means to be a human being. On the one side stands the owning class. The corporate class values competition and inequality and top-down control. On the other side stands the working class, which values solidarity and equality and control from the bottom-up. The class war is only partially about economics. At its core it is about the goals and direction of society and the values that should shape it. Each class in this war is trying to impose its view of humanity, its values, its power over society. I made a speech in 1985 to Local P-9 at Hormel. At one point I said, "Your strike isn't just about safety and wages. Your strike is about what it means to be a human being." Everybody in the local stood and cheered.

Now, as you all know by now, New Democracy proposes that our strategy should be to win the class war. What makes me think that we can win? To explain this, let me explain our most basic insight.

Part of the problem with Marxism and the way we've all been trained to see class struggle is that we view it too narrowly. If people aren't out demonstrating or on strike, we think nothing's going on. But that's not true. Everywhere we look, and at every point in our lives and in other people's lives, people are engaged in a struggle against capitalism to assert their values against capitalist values. This is why we can win.

Think for a minute about the capitalist system. We know that capitalism is the most dynamic social system that has ever existed. It has penetrated every part of the globe, and it works its way into every area of our lives. We also know that the basic principal of capitalism is the principle of competition, the idea of dog-eat-dog. The logic of capitalist culture is that we should each of us be trying to screw each other all the time. The logic of capitalism, in other words, is that this world should be a savage and loveless place. But we can look around and see that this is not so. We look around and see that most people in their everyday lives—with their wife or husband or their co-workers or their students or their patients—most people in the little piece of the world they think they can control struggle against the logic of capitalist relations to create relationships based on love and trust and solidarity and mutual respect. I'm not saying any of us is perfect. But to the extent that any of us has mutual and loving relationships in our lives, we have created them by struggle against a capitalist culture that is profoundly hostile to them.

This means, I think, that most people are already engaged in a struggle against capitalism to create a new world. The smallest acts of kindness and solidarity on the shop floor or in our classrooms or in our neighborhoods or our homes and the most public and collective acts of class struggle are all part of a struggle to humanize the world and make it conform to our idea of what it should be. The moral values present in people's everyday lives—values of solidarity and commitment to each other—these are the real basis of every great movement for social change.

We don't have to invent the revolutionary movement. The movement already exists. It exists in the little things that people do for each other everyday; it exists in the help people give each other on the shop floor and their resistance to the company and the union; it exists in the love of husband and wife for each other and the support they give their children; it exists in the efforts of teachers to teach, and in the resistance of students to much of what they are taught. It exists in this room, in our efforts to figure out the world and how we can help change it.

Are all these relationships of human solidarity perfect? Does friendship and equality and resistance to capitalism shape everything in society or everything we do? Of course not. That's why we need a revolution—because everything that we value is under attack. But the revolutionary movement that we are part of is already a powerful force for change which the ruling class spends its every waking minute trying to control.

Our job as self-conscious revolutionaries is to make this already-existing movement aware of its earth-shaking significance, more confident of its power and more clear in the tasks that confront it, so that it can succeed.

By declaring revolution as our goal, we will not be isolated. Far from it. Instead we will be giving legitimacy to feelings and aspirations and values that millions of people share and know in their hearts to be right, but are constantly told are wrong. By declaring revolution our goal, we can build a movement that reaches into people's deepest feelings and expresses their strongest desires. By declaring revolution our goal, we can build a movement engaging the great majority of humanity.

How do we put this strategy into effect? This is one of the questions we will want to answer this weekend. But I think that certain things follow from this analysis. One is that spreading our message—this new understanding of working people and the possibilities of revolution and real democracy—is crucial. A second is that we cannot rely on politicians or union officials or structures to build this movement: we have to rely on the people. A third is that we have to think big. We have to reach out to the whole world. We have to think of the whole world, not just our little corner of it, when we are trying to figure out the connections among people and issues. We have to think not in terms of some crummy compromise or "lesser evil." We're for the world as it should be and as it can be.

Let me return to the historical significance of what we're doing. Marxism provided the underpinnings for the working class movement of the late 19th and 20th centuries, and Marxism has failed. It failed because it accepted the capitalist view of human motivation, which led it into an anti-democratic and anti-people nightmare in the Soviet Union and elsewhere. The effect of that failure has been to undermine the possibility of working class movements ever since. The revolutionary aspirations of the twentieth century have been trapped beneath the dead weight of Marxism. No new and successful revolutionary movement is possible except on the basis of a new way of seeing the world.

Great social movements are founded on great social visions. We in New Democracy are proposing a new social vision to replace capitalism and to replace the failed vision of Marxism. We are proposing a vision of ordinary people as the source not only of the material wealth that labor creates, but also of the positive values in this society and the values and social relations on which we can base a new one. We are proposing a democratic vision of a new society in which the goal is not mindless economic growth or greed or personal aggrandizement, but our shared fulfillment as human beings.

What is missing from the world now? Not the need for revolution: there are millions hungry in the midst of plenty; there are millions suffering from over-work and millions more without work; there is a planet being raped by an economic system run amok; there is a whole world of human beings whose relations of solidarity are under attack by a ruling elite that cannot survive without under-mining the human bonds between us.

What is missing from the world? Not the desire for revolution. There are millions of people in the U.S. and billions worldwide who yearn for, work for, struggle for a better world, who will gladly be part of a revolutionary movement. What's missing is a vision of ordinary human beings that can free us from the dead weight of the past and make democracy and revolution possible. This is the vision that I am proposing to you, and this is what we together can offer the world.

Note
1. New Democracy held a retreat in Madison, Wisconsin where 19 people discussed building a revolutionary movement. I addressed these remarks to the retreat.

by John Spritzler

I. WHAT KIND OF SOCIETY DO WE WANT?

IS THERE A REALISTIC ALTERNATIVE TO Capitalism and communism? For the last century these two systems have each claimed to be the only alternative to the other. The fact that both are terrible has made fundamental change seem hopeless.

But capitalism and communism are bad for a specific reason: they are both forms of elite rule based on the same profoundly wrong ideas about people. Both social systems view ordinary people as selfish and unfit to rule. Both assume that the highest goal of society is to increase economic production.

With different ideas about people, a different kind of world is possible.

Four Principles For a New World

- ONE: In a good society the value of any policy would be measured by its impact on human relations. The most important things that people produce are not commodities, but human relations of love, solidarity, mutual aid, and trust. These relations are what make security and happiness possible. When economic production helps fulfill these human relations, it is positive. But economic growth is by no means always beneficial and should not be the goal of human society.

- TWO: In a truly democratic society work would be voluntary. The reward or punishment for contributing more or less than one's fair share would be the better or worse quality of relations one has with others as a result. Most people seek to give their lives meaning through work, creativity, and acts that benefit others. People want to do the work that they believe is required to enable themselves and others to live, prosper, and be happy. When people are free to do this they don't need to be compelled. We see this today in all sorts of volunteer work, as well as the countless things people do for each other without even thinking of it as "work." Compulsion, in the form of no pay for no work or more pay for more work, is only required when people are not free and an elite is forcing ordinary people to work for them.

- THREE: In a society based on solidarity and trust, the economics of producing and distributing things would be like sharing within a family, rather than buying and selling for profit in a marketplace. The wealth of any society is the fruit of collective efforts. People are naturally inclined to share goods and services according to need with those they trust. We see this sharing today within families, despite the pressure from capitalism to make competition and self-interest the dominant motivation everywhere. The circles of trust within which people share according to need will greatly widen when society is no longer ruled by elites who view human solidarity as a threat to their power.

- FOUR: Democracy consists of ordinary people with shared fundamental values actually shaping all of society according to their values. Democracy means that everywhere people live and work, they decide what their own goals are and how they will cooperate to reach them. It means all concerned have an equal say. It means people are free to assemble to discuss anything and everything with full access to all information, and they are free to make and carry out any decision no matter how revolutionary.

What would a society based on these ideas look like? Probably it would look different in various places and change over time as people experimented with different ways of doing things. Whatever the details, it would be a world where people supported and trusted one another, where people felt safe among strangers, where people didn't feel alone in dealing with natural catastrophes, sickness or bad luck, where children were optimistic about their futures, and where people found real meaning in what they did all day.

INDEX of NAMES

THE PEOPLE AS ENEMY: The Leaders' Hidden Agenda in World War II
John Spritzler

The official view of WWII was that it was "the good war," but presented here is a very different, and disturbing view that argues that the aims of the national leaders were not democracy and self-determination, but were opportunities to suppress and intimidate working people from rising up against elite power. Understanding this is especially important today because the myths of WWII are the same myths that are being used in the "war against terrorism" by government and corporate leaders to control people and pursue ends that have nothing to do with protecting us from terrorism.

> The level of working class rebellion that he [Spritzler] uncovers and recounts is amazing and often inspiring. —*Socialist Review*

> The research is impressive. A strong argument, well-documented.
> —Howard Zinn, *A People's History of the United States*

> The arguments are compelling and extremely well documented. This book belongs in the libraries and classrooms of every educational institution in America. It's that important. —*Groundscore*

JOHN SPRITZLER holds a Doctor of Science degree (in Biostatistics) from the Harvard School of Public Health where he is employed as a Research Scientist engaged in AIDS clinical trials.

216 pages ✪ Paper 1-55164-216-6 $24.99 ✪ Cloth 1-55164-217-4 $53.99

THORSTEIN VEBLEN AND THE AMERICAN WAY OF LIFE
Louis Patsouras

Thorstein Veblen (1857-1929) was an unrelenting critic of the American way of life. In his first and best-known work, *The Theory of the Leisure Class*, Veblen defined the social attitudes and values that condoned the misuse of wealth and the variety of ways in which the resources of modern society were wasted. Though most famous for the term "conspicuous consumption"—a pattern of consumerism that more than survives to the present day—he also attacked other American institutions and traditions, but his ideas were often dismissed because of his reputation as an eccentric.

By setting Veblen's work in its social and intellectual context, and by considering Veblen not just as an economist or a sociologist—as has been the case up to now—Patsouras also examines Veblen's politics, in particular the early manifestations of American socialism and anarchism, as well as his support of labor unions. Veblen's views are then compared and contrasted with other well-known historical and contemporary thinkers.

LOUIS PATSOURAS is Professor of History at Kent State University. He is the author of *The Anarchism of Jean Grave* (Black Rose Books).

380 pages ✪ Paper 1-55164-228-X $24.99 ✪ Cloth 1-55164-229-8 $53.99

PARTICIPATORY DEMOCRACY: Prospects for Democratizing Democracy

Dimitrios Roussopoulos, C.George Benello, editors

With its emphasis on citizen participation, here, presented in one volume are the best arguments for participatory democracy written by some of the most relevant contributors to the debate, both in an historic, and in a contemporary, sense. This wide-ranging collection probes the historical roots of participatory democracy in our political culture, analyzes its application to the problems of modern society, and explores the possible forms it might take. Part II, "The Politics of Participatory Democracy," covers Porto Alegre, Montreal, the new Urban ecology, and direct democracy.

The book is the most encompassing one so far in revealing the practical actual subversions that the New Left wishes to visit upon us. —*Washington Post*

Contributors include: George Woodcock, Murray Bookchin, Don Calhoun, Stewart Perry, Rosabeth Moss Kanter, James Gillespie, Gerry Hunnius, John McEwan, Arthur Chickering, Christian Bay, Martin Oppenheimer, Colin Ward, Sergio Baierle, Anne Latendresse, Bartha Rodin, and C.L.R. James.

DIMITRIOS ROUSSOPOULOS, a political economist who has written widely on social and politico-economic issues, is the author *The Public Place* and *Dissidence: Essays Against the Mainstream*. C.GEORGE BENELLO (1927-1987) taught sociology at Goddard College in Vermont until his untimely death.

380 pages ✪ Paper 1-55164-224-7 $24.99 ✪ Cloth 1-55164-225-5 $53.99
